BIBLE & ETHICS
IN THE CHRISTIAN LIFE

Revised & Expanded Edition

Bruce C. Birch & Larry L. Rasmussen

AUGSBURG/Minneapolis

BIBLE & ETHICS IN THE CHRISTIAN LIFE
Revised & Expanded Edition

Library of Congress Cataloging-in-Publication Data

Birch, Bruce C.
    Bible and ethics in the Christian life / Bruce C. Birch, Larry L. Rasmussen.—Rev. and expanded ed.
        p.   cm.
    Bibliography: p.
    ISBN 0-8066-2397-7
    1. Ethics in the Bible. 2. Christian ethics. I. Rasmussen, Larry L. II. Title.
BS680.E84B57 1989
241—dc19   88-39769
                                                                           CIP

Manufactured in the U.S.A.   AF 10-0706

04   03   02   01   12   13   14   15   16

To the students, faculty, and staff
of Wesley Theological Seminary,
Washington, D.C.
and Union Theological Seminary,
New York City

CONTENTS

PREFACE TO THE REVISED EDITION

When the first edition of this volume was published, its purpose was to bridge the gap between biblical studies and Christian ethics. Few materials which systematically linked the two fields existed, and most were only article-length.

The scene has changed dramatically in only a decade. Numerous excellent studies have appeared.[1] The initial purpose of that first volume, to encourage interdisciplinary work, has been largely served.

What we did not anticipate, however, was the first edition's widespread use as a classroom text. That has been gratifying, even when it was not the volume's initial purpose. The response punctuates a circumstance long recognized by teachers of ethics, namely, that few scholarly but nontechnical works exist which treat both fundamental Christian moral concepts and the most important sources of the Christian moral life. This new edition is drafted as just such a basic text.

The changes and additions are many. We have enlarged especially the sections on the basic working concepts of Christian ethics. There are new chapters on the vocabulary of morality ("Charting the Moral Life"), on decision making, and on character and social structure. We have addressed anew and expanded the discussions of the authority and uses of Scripture in the moral life and the roles of the community

7

of faith. We have deleted dated materials and revised all those portions of the original volume affected by recent discussions and events. We have emphasized and developed community and community dynamics, as well as moral agency, as themes common to both biblical materials and Christian ethics. We have supplied endnotes which cite literature helpful to further study. We have included an index as well as a bibliography.

Our intention, then, is to provide a text appropriate for several settings—basic courses in Christian ethics in college, university, or seminary; courses and independent study which directly address the relationship of Scripture and ethics; and church study groups on the Christian moral life.

Many individuals, too numerous to list, have our thanks for this new edition. Most have contributed by their responses over 10 years to the first edition. Others have read and responded to the new materials. Carla Meier, Elizabeth Bounds, and David Hopkins offered helpful responses to selected chapters. David Gushee not only read the entire manuscript with a critical eye but did the other tasks of a research assistant as well. Martha Lindberg Mann put her sharp editing pencil to work on every page. Lucy Fullerton prepared the bibliography and index of Biblical references. We are indebted to all, and grateful.

INTRODUCTION

The meaning of a dance is in the dancing of it. The meaning of the Christian life is in the living of it. There is little reason to talk about dance or receive instruction in dance unless at some point we ourselves dance, or our understanding of dance lets us enjoy the dance of others. Likewise, there is little reason to discuss the Christian life unless that discussion enhances our living of it, or our understanding of those who do so.

This book is about the Christian moral life. It cannot substitute for it, nor perform it. The book's purpose is to enhance the understanding of it, and, for those who choose the Christian moral life for themselves, the "dancing" of it as well.

The moral life, from the beginning, has been at the heart of Jewish and Christian faiths. Faith communities have always struggled with questions of what sort of persons their members should be and how they should act. They have continually sought faithful response to God in day-to-day affairs. They have steadily tried to shape life in keeping with a vision of what it ought to be.

Amidst this, the Bible has been considered the charter document for the Christian moral life. Its contents have been enlisted again and again to fashion both character and conduct, and to provide guidance and authority. In quest of illumination, generation after generation has sought to relate their own moral deliberations to the struggles and tales of the biblical communities. Discussions about obligation, virtue, value, or vision in the Christian life are rarely carried far without reference to Scripture.

As fields of study, Christian ethics and biblical scholarship have a special charge within Christian reflection. They are called upon most directly to aid the faith community in traversing the distance between the primal documents of the faith—its Scriptures—and expressions of the faith in daily life. Students of both fields, whether lay or professional, rightly assert the importance of each to the other.

Yet it is not at all clear how Bible and ethics are properly related. What *is* clear is that it is not a simple matter. Our goal in this volume is to achieve clarity about the relationship while honoring the complexity.

Achieving this goal entails a core set of questions which invariably appear whenever the subject is Bible and ethics:

- What kind of authority for Christian morality is the Bible?

- At what points and for what purposes in the moral life might biblical materials play an appropriate and influential role?

- How should different kinds of biblical materials function in the moral life? How are they made available and properly used?

- What comprises "the moral life" and what are the basic categories, elements, and tasks of Christian ethics? At what critical points does Christian ethics draw upon biblical materials, for what purposes?

- What are the roles of the faith community in the moral life? Specifically, what are the manifold uses of Scripture in the church for fashioning moral character and conduct?

In short, we strive to address a set of recurring and crucial questions about the Bible's use and authority in Christian ethics. We hope to do so in ways which provide clarity about the moral life itself, its components and scope. This book is about the Christian moral life and the formative and normative place of Scripture in it.

1

CONSENSUS AND QUESTIONS

There exists an important two-part consensus, held by biblical scholars and ethicists alike.

The first can be stated most succinctly by saying that *Christian ethics is not synonymous with biblical ethics*. One obvious reason is that biblical communities did not confront some of the moral issues and historical forces which shape our lives today.

New Power, New Choices

In 1973 Stanley Cohen and Herbert Boyer first spliced genetic material from one microbe into another to create a bit of life that never existed before. James Watson and Francis Crick had, in 1953, determined the chemical arrangement of DNA (deoxyribonucleic acid), a double helix strand which carries the hereditary blueprint of all living things. In 1987 the United States Patent and Trademark Office decided that patents for new life forms can be extended from microbes to higher life forms, including (new) mammals.[1] In 1988 the Office determined that companies holding patents on new animal forms can require farmers to pay royalties on the animals and their offspring through the 17-year life of each patent.[2]

The ancient peoples of the biblical communities did not possess the knowledge and power to manipulate the very building blocks of life itself. It is we who have "cracked" the genetic code and positioned ourselves to create new life forms. "Cellular engineering," "gene-splicing," and "genetic counseling" are new entries in the dictionary of human responsibility, as are "biotechnology" and "bioethics." Barely in their infancy, they are new creations harboring awesome potential power. Like all increases of human power, they carry corollary moral responsibility.

Nor did those ancient peoples of the Book fondle nuclear triggers and enough destructive power to radically alter if not terminate life as we know it. "Nuclear fission" and "fusion" are recent additions to our vocabulary, as are "strategic missiles" and "strategic defense initiatives" in space. They name developments which would have baffled the biblical world, since as a stark historical fact such capacities did not exist until well into the 20th century. To bear the moral burden for the very *possibility* of future generations' existence is a new moral datum we have not yet fully assimilated.[3] Heretofore, human beings simply *assumed* that life would go on, however destructive their behavior. They—including the biblical communities—*could* not be cosmic un-Creators. Today, however, saving the future, any future, is a human choice. In the wide wash of mass destruction, borders are rendered meaningless, and no place is ultimately safe.

"Acid rain" is another new term which signals the increased human impact upon the natural environment. Our generation and those which follow can no longer assume, as countless generations before have, that "nature is never spent." (The phrase is from "God's Grandeur," a poem by Gerard Manley Hopkins, s.j.) Nature is wondrously fecund and resilient, to be sure. It is nonetheless true that the works of nature can be destroyed. A population now surpassing five billion people pushes very hard against the carrying capacity of the environment. "Carrying capacity" is itself a new phrase in our lexicon.

While there is much in human nature that binds all of us together across vast stretches of time and culture, and much moral wisdom and folly which makes its way from age to age, it is yet undeniable that Christian ethics today must find its way amidst moral questions which never appeared on the horizon of biblical ethics. Christian ethics cannot be a synonym of biblical ethics when ethics includes unprecedented moral issues.

There are other reasons the two cannot be equated.

A Different Face

Sometimes a moral issue remains much the same in its basic outline, yet the context is so altered that the biblical response no longer applies. Hunger and starvation are gruesome realities which make this simple point. People starved in the ancient world in exactly the same way they do now. Cells died in an excruciating process of physiological deterioration, then as now. But addressing the *causes* of hunger and starvation is far different in our time. The causes are due less to the eccentricities of weather than to poverty as a constructed human reality. Most hungry people are hungry because they are poor, not because food is unavailable. And pursuing poverty's causes leads into a set of local, regional, and international trade, finance, and other economic and political arrangements more complex and far-reaching than any the poor and hungry of the biblical world knew. The basic moral issue of responding to hunger remains. The context is considerably altered, however. The character of the response must be as well.

Historical Faith

Yet another reason Christian ethics and biblical ethics cannot be equated derives from the nature of the faith. Judaism and Christianity both insist they are *historical* religions. They do so with a vigor almost unparalleled among the world religions. The God they worship is a God of history, present in ways appropriate to our character as finite and historical beings who occupy a certain time and place. This is the force of the Christian teaching about incarnation and the Jewish claim that God is Immanuel (God-with-us). Furthermore, the Jewish and Christian Scriptures themselves are the records of varied faith communities in varied circumstances seeking to discern "a word from the Lord" for their specific and often unique moment. They are Scriptures not of timeless realities but of historical peoples, places, and events. The later creeds mirror this as well: "[He] suffered under Pontius Pilate, was crucified, died, and was buried. And on the third day. . . ." Moreover, the biblical and post-biblical communities saw themselves and their history "on the move." It was part of a grand drama stretched between the beginnings of creation and its eventual consummation, when justice and peace will "kiss" (Ps. 85:10) and embrace all things. These communities sustained themselves in the conviction that their

13

God was a God "of the living," capable of doing "a new thing" (Isa. 43:19 JB).

A biblical faith historical in character means many things, not least that Jewish and Christian morality is historically and culturally expressed and conditioned. Such morality cannot be rent from its moorings without violating its own integrity. It cannot be transported as changeless content across centuries and simply "applied" in an unqualified way to different circumstances and different modes of life and thought. The nature of Jewish and Christian faith militates against this. Every historical faith does; such faith is intrinsically dynamic. Radically incarnate, it is gladly tied to the details of time and place.

Altered Judgments

Even if we did approach biblical ethics ahistorically—it is often tried—in countless cases we would simply refuse the results. This is a further reason Christian ethics and biblical ethics cannot be equated. Christian ethics today does not find sound justification for accepted biblical codes on slavery, for example, or for the treatment of women as property. Nor do we exact capital punishment for all the crimes some biblical communities did. "Time," and much serious, painful moral struggle has rendered some "ancient good uncouth."

In a word, the ethics of the biblical communities are not and cannot be the same as Christian ethics for us. It is precisely *because* they are not the same that the issues arise which this book addresses. The distinction of Christian ethics from biblical ethics is the first part of the double consensus.

The second is this: *the Bible is somehow formative and normative for Christian ethics.* But in what ways formative and normative? The question has provoked an array of answers. Yet through them all runs a thread of agreement that the Scriptures are charter documents which bear an authority rarely granted any other single source.

Formative Knowledge and Power

The Bible is, after all, the major source of knowledge about the ultimate object of Christian moral allegiance, God in Jesus Christ, as experienced in the Spirit. Scripture is the major source of the story which is the very center of the faith community's identity.

14

Furthermore, the Bible has carried power to *create* moral problems which may not be problems for those who are not influenced by Scripture. The uninfluenced may be able to ignore certain moral issues which Christians cannot, precisely because of Scripture's strong role in Christian ethics. The earliest Christian attitudes toward Caesar are a classic example. Whether to fight in Caesar's army was not a wrenching moral problem for most males in the Roman Empire. But it was for Christians. Obedience to Rome, demonstrated with a pinch of incense offered to Caesar as Lord, was a religious and moral problem for Christians. By their own claim, "Jesus is our Caesar" (Acts 17:8) and the reign of God is accomplished by the victory of "the Lamb" (Revelation 5ff.), not by arms. Indeed, the fundamental loyalty of Jews and Christians to a *faith* community as the locus of the moral life, rather than to a *civic* community (as was the case for many Greeks and Romans) raised innumerable problems and tensions which have carried forward from biblical times into ours.[4] The outcome is a chronic church/state conflict that nicely illustrates the formative character of biblical materials for Christian ethics; in this case the power to create, rather than to resolve, moral issues. The same can be said with equal force about the central moral command to love neighbor as self, especially when the test case is the enemy![5]

The status of Scripture as a powerful authority will be discussed in detail later. Suffice for now to note this second area of consensus: The Bible is formative and normative for the Christian moral life. Christian ethics is not Christian ethics apart from Scripture.

Agenda

If biblical scholars and Christian ethicists are generally agreed on these two matters—Christian ethics is not a synonym for biblical ethics, yet the Bible is a shaping force for the Christian moral life—then the issue becomes this: What is the relationship of Scripture and ethics in the contemporary community of faith, in theory and in practice? That question generates a host of others which coalesce so as to compose the agenda for this book:

1. Any comprehensive and comprehensible method of relating Scripture and ethics must make clear its understanding of Christian ethics. What is the range of concern of ethics, its field of investigation? What categories and procedures carry on its work? What are the elements

15

of the moral life and the resources of Christian ethics for understanding and addressing them?

Once Christian ethics has clarified the varied dimensions of the moral life, how does Scripture address them? At what points in the Christian moral life do biblical materials have an appropriate impact? When and towards what ends do we employ Scripture? Do the kinds of biblical materials which are appropriate vary from one situation to another? What is the proper starting point? Do we begin with the biblical materials or with some issue demanding a moral decision? Or at some other point? What difference does the starting point make? Are there different starting points for different circumstances in the moral life?

2. What is the place of the faith community in the moral life and in the relating of Scripture and ethics? What are the roles of the faith community as a community of moral formation? At what points in the life of the community is the Bible brought to bear upon these roles? How does the church affect the practical relating of Bible and ethics, and how is it affected?

3. What is the authority of Scripture for moral decision making? How authoritative are nonbiblical sources of insight? Is the authority of Scripture somehow different from the authority of other sources? What is the relationship of these various sources? What controls might prevent people from simply choosing among biblical and nonbiblical sources in accord with convictions already held?

4. Any adequate method of relating Scripture and ethics must not only discuss the nature of the resources found in the Bible; it must also state how these can be properly employed by the faith community as it addresses contemporary issues. What kind of exegesis is appropriate to this task? How important is the original form, context, and meaning of biblical texts? Are all materials equally important? Are all appropriate? How do we choose among the bewildering variety of viewpoints in Scripture? Are there controls on our choosing? What is the relationship of one biblical reference to the whole of Scripture? Does the existence of an official set of selected biblical books—the canon—make a difference for how we use Scripture in moral matters? Does the nature of different biblical resources suggest different ways in which they might be linked with the moral life? What are these ways?

The remainder of the book pursues this agenda. We turn first to an understanding of Christian ethics.

16

2

CHRISTIAN ETHICS AS COMMUNITY ETHICS

"Community" and "moral agency" are the key themes of Christian ethics throughout this volume. Community is a synonym for social relatedness, moral agency an understanding of ourselves as moral creatures. This chapter begins the discussion of community for the moral life in general and Christian ethics in particular. The next chapter introduces the more technical term, "moral agency."

Community's Place

What we are able to discern and do results from our participation in various communities. A variety of social worlds have shaped us, determined our general bearing in life, even engendered our specific responses to particular issues. We cannot and do not muster moral insight for ourselves by ourselves apart from our communities, any more than we are or can be human beings apart from others. Everything we know about morality and the moral life, or anything else, for that matter, is finally a community enterprise and achievement. While it is true that individuals are not simply community clones, are unique, and may well rise above the moral level of their communities, it is true with equal force that even the most private decisions and achievements are the results of our social experience and could neither exist nor be understood apart from that experience. (The word "conscience" nicely illustrates this. While we often depict conscience as the individual's "still small voice" within, the etymological meaning betrays its true source. *Com* + *scire* means "knowing in relation," or "knowing together." Conscience is an expression of character, which is formed only in community.)

The central place of community in the moral life is a truism, a fact of life. But in societies whose communities emphasize individualism and nurture the illusion that individuals exist apart from or prior to communities and community influences, we must underscore community's place. Such societies frequently define "freedom" as independence, meaning freedom from all obligations except those chosen in accord with individual desires; and, indeed, freedom from the need for other human beings. North Americans especially seem to live without the working assumption that our lives are cast together in an inescapable social interrelatedness. Rather, the majority seems to contend that we are independent individuals who may choose to be, or not be, related to others. We perceive society in largely mechanistic ways, viewing it as an arena for balancing the needs, desires, and demands of various groups while focusing most intensely on our individual freedoms and rights.[1] Picturing society this way only reinforces the illusions of individualism. It is hardly a surprise that the more freedom we attain, the more we suffer from such social disorders as impersonal behaviors (some of them violent), isolation, alienation, emptiness, and loneliness; and the more we yearn for "genuine community" and are attracted to groups which promise it. (A guest of several weeks at Christ House, Washington, D.C., was heard to say: "I know the opposite of poverty. It's not riches. It's community.")[2]

The beginnings of an alternative arise in the recognition of the critical place of communities in our lives. In its most fundamental sense, community refers to any social grouping, any collection of people sharing something important. In this sense we all live in many communities, and in most modern societies we participate in several different communities in the course of a day. A neighborhood is a community, as are family and workplace, the professional organizations to which we belong, our group of friends, our church, schools, town, city, state, region, or nation, as well as any number of voluntary organizations in which we hold membership. We also claim community by socioeconomic class, racial, ethnic, gender, or creedal membership.

18

Our most intense communities invariably arise from common struggles and shared pain and joy. Our most meaningful ones are those in which we can "be ourselves," i.e., relationships in which we receive others and express ourselves without preconditions or qualifications—in a word, communities of love.

Our lives, then, are set within communities and are shaped by communities, all sorts of communities. We are not born into an undifferentiated schema of disconnected events and relations, but into corporate life already alive with communities which structure our social existence. The moral life cannot exist apart from these, and is only possible with a view to these communities. Whatever moral consciousness we possess does not exist prior to, apart from, or independent of social relatedness. Communities are the forms of our social relatedness and the material reality of the moral life.

If we accept this as a fact of human existence, we must recognize it as true with even greater force for the Christian moral life, and for Christian ethics. The reason is this: Community is at the very heart of Christian faith itself.

A Way of Life

A glance at the origins of both Judaism and Christianity is instructive. Whether we look at the formation of a people of God in the exodus/Sinai drama, or at the cross/resurrection/Pentecost account, the experience is *the experience of divine power as a power for "peoplehood."* And it is an experience together. The beginning experiences for both Jewish and Christian ethics are the experience of God as the One who generates community and the One who is experienced *in* community, as its deepest source and meaning.

Moreover, community was the commanding moral matrix for both Israel and the early church. When faith community members asked questions about character and conduct, they did not ask the imperious question later philosophers would sometimes pose as the guiding query: "What is the universal good, and what action on my part would be in accord with it?"[3] Instead they asked: "What character and conduct is in keeping with who we are *as a people of God*?" Identification with the faith community was central to the moral life; the community itself was the matrix.

In fact the moral life is not even its own subject in Jewish and

19

Christian origins. There was very little interest in "morality" per se, as a separate topic, or in some abstraction called "the moral life." Rather, morality and ethics were dimensions *of* community life in which the concern was how a people of God were to live with one another and with those outside the faith community. The broader interest was *faithfulness toward God as the way of life of a people.* Morality was an aspect of this; it was a dimension of community. "The moral life" existed for the sake of, and as part of, community faithfulness.

Paul's comments to the Thessalonica community illustrate this nicely. His first letter is the earliest complete Christian writing we possess. It is an epistle of moral exhortation.[4] He opens with thanks and gratitude for their life together, and the power of God among them. "You have shown your faith in action, worked for love and persevered through hope. . ." (1 Thess. 1:3 JB). He mentions that they observed "the sort of life we lived when we were with you, which was for your instruction" (1:5) and that they were moved to "become imitators of us, and of the Lord" (1:6). They have grown "in the kind of life you are meant to live: the life God wants. . ." (4:1). Paul uses the familial images of mother, nurse, father, and brother to express his, Silvanus's, and Timothy's emotional ties and moral responsibility to them. The trio's treatment of the Thessalonians has been, he says, "impeccably right and fair" (2:10) and the outcome is the upbuilding of the community in the Spirit. He emphasizes and encourages solidarity and intimacy among members of the community. This includes holding those who have died in memory and hope, and he points out that "in the Lord" the Thessalonians are as bound to faith communities elsewhere as they are to one another. Furthermore, as a community they should not "have to depend" upon those beyond the faith community; but because their lives are also lived there, their life-style should be seen "to be respectable by those outside the Church" (4:12). The *raison d'être* of all this is the "Good News" (3:2) of what God has done in Christ. The moral exhortation and encouragement which follows is "a life worthy of the God who is calling you. . ." (2:12).

Morality here, as in all Scripture, exists as part of and for the community's vocation as a community of faith in God. Morality's purpose is to aid and abet living "a life worthy of the God who is calling you." It is "theocentric" morality ("the God who calls you") whose form is community. God-community-person are the inseparable living elements of the moral life.

Community faithfulness to God and others is frequently portrayed in the simple terms of a "way of life." The followers of Jesus were called "People of the Way" even before they were called "Christians" (Acts 9:2) just as Jesus himself was presented as "the Way." The roots are deeply Jewish, since in Judaism much of the community's task was instruction in "the Way," using the written and oral *Torah*. What Wayne Meeks says of apostolic and other early Christian writings pertains equally to Hebrew Scriptures: "[They] had as their primary aim the shaping of the life of [the faith] communities."[5] This is a comprehensive process, to be discussed in later chapters. For now what is noteworthy is that the process shows itself in considerable part as a pattern, or way, of life. (Paul's frequently used phrase, usually rendered "to live a life worthy. . ." is, literally translated, "to walk a way worthy. . . .")

In sum, both Judaism and Christianity conceived of the moral life as the practical outcome of the community's faith, as shown in the sorts of lives members of the community, and the community as a whole, lived. The community's task was to socialize its members into forms of life which displayed the kind of conduct befitting the experience of God in community. To be a Jew was to learn the story of Israel and the rabbinic traditions well enough to experience the world from within these stories, and to act in accord with that experience as a member of an ongoing faith community. Similarly, to be a Christian was to learn the story of Israel and of Jesus and the ongoing church traditions well enough to experience the world from within those stories, and to act in keeping with that experience, as a member of that community.[6]

People of the Way

A more extended look at Christian ethics in its origins is necessary. Reference was made to "People of the Way," the name given members of the movement around Jesus in the earliest Christian communities. "The Way" denoted a particular pattern of living, the instruction and training required for this (called "discipleship," or a following in the Way), and the continuous remembering and retelling of the formative stories, above all the "Jesus story" itself (cf. Acts 18:24-26).

For some of the earliest communities this instruction took place in the synagogue as well as in homes, occurring as it did before the break of Christianity from Judaism. This transpired quite naturally, since such instruction had always been characteristic of the Jewish community. For Judaism, ethics was the crafting of a righteous, or just, life. It was a life which had to be learned, and it was learned as part of the ongoing life of the community.

"The Way" is a common metaphor in both Greek Scriptures (the Christian New Testament) and in Hebrew Scriptures (the Christian Old Testament). There is frequent reference to God's way, or "the way of the Lord." It commonly includes an ethical component which requires schooling, so that one might "walk in a way worthy" of the God who calls. Sometimes contrasting ways are presented as irreconcilable. Deuteronomy 30 closes with these words: "I set before you life or death, blessing or curse. Choose life, then, so that you and your descendants may live, in the love of Yahweh your God. . ." (30:19-20). Jesus' "Sermon on the Mount," especially in Luke's version, starkly contrasts blessing and curse (Luke 17:17-49). Jesus, in the tradition characteristic of sages, frequently speaks of the broad way that leads to destruction and the narrow way that leads to life, and the contrasting ways of either "serving God" or "serving *mammon*" (riches).[7] The *Didache,* a manual of church instruction from the second century, begins: "There are two paths to follow: one is life and the other is death. There is a profound difference between the two."[8]

Not all instruction is so stark. But whatever the form, the image is that of a goal-oriented journey in which the manner of journeying is itself a constituent part of the pilgrimage. "The Way" refers both to the path and the manner of travel. To walk in "the Way" involves a moral style so intimately related to the destination itself that to wander from "the Way" is to miss the goal (a righteous life in a community faithful to God). Destination and means are so intertwined that means are themselves ends-in-process. Lassalle's stanza reflects a biblical notion:

> Show us not the aim without the way.
> For ends and means on earth are so entangled
> That changing one you change the other too;
> Each different path brings other ends in view.[9]

Instruction "in the Way" was not only characteristic of the Judaism which influenced early Christian ethics profoundly. It was also a trademark of other moral patterns in the Greco-Roman world where Christianity took hold in the form of small "house church" communities in villages and urban centers.[10] Non-Christian writers often referred to Christianity as a "philosophical school."[11] That may strike us as odd, especially since many of Christianity's early converts were illiterate and untutored members of lower socioeconomic classes. We do not expect "philosophical school" to designate what, by modern markings, appeared more akin to a religious sect of socially marginal people.

Philosophical schools were a lively part of Greek and Roman public life, but they were identified in a way we no longer readily associate with philosophy. Each school claimed its *bios,* or "way of life." Philosophy was not simply a way of thinking—the enterprise of cognitive metaphysical pursuits. Such pursuits were hardly foreign to the ancient schools, of course. But their critical purpose was to discern, through rigorous discussion, the substance of fitting and proper conduct and to convert that into action. Good philosophy revolved around life-style and ethics, which philosophy sought to embody in a life of discipline and virtue. The reference was not so much to the *study* of philosophy as to the *practice* of it (*askēsis*). Socrates was said to have risen above natural human instincts by "practicing philosophy."

The schools' traditions, while a vigorous part of Roman public life, were Greek in origin, as the reference to Socrates suggests. Philosophy in ancient Greece had included the guidance of souls, or "soulcraft" (*psychogogia*). A chief part of its work was the soul's moral formation. Aristotle himself understood the pursuit of philosophy to include active care for the *polis* (city-state) by nurturing human agency in community and orienting it to the practice of virtue. Aristotle in fact uses a word which becomes a key term for the early Christians—*koinōnia* (community or fellowship). The purpose of government for Aristotle was *koinōnia* and philosophy was to promote it. The philosophical schools, carrying on now under Roman rule, continued as communities of soulcraft.

The schools were popular and highly competitive. When an individual turned from his or her former way to another, the change was called a "conversion." Sociologists today would label it "resocialization." By whatever name, pagan philosophical conversion parallels the accounts of early Christian conversion in striking ways. It was a conversion to a particular community morality, together with the supporting beliefs and the instruction and training necessary to live the new "way." It was resocialization into a new community, learning to behave in ways appropriate to the community. Conversion frequently

23

meant a changed personal identity, and was viewed as a clear break with "the world."

The commonality of moral practice of the philosophical schools and the Christian communities is often striking. Thus Galen, a non-Christian writer of the second century, speaks of "the Christian philosophy" as one which has also led people to lives of self-discipline and strict control in matters of food and drink and sexual conduct; to the pursuit of justice; and to a "contempt" for death, i.e., a lack of fear of death. And Justin Martyr, writing earlier in the same century, presents his conversion to Christianity as a conversion to this particular "philosophy," albeit one in competition with the *bioi* (ways or styles of life) of other schools.[12] But that Justin Martyr would identify Christianity as a philosophy is telling.

Perhaps more telling is to cite non-Christian testimony about a non-Christian movement. This will display some of the qualities the schools shared with Christians and thereby underscore our point that the early Christian communities were communities of collective moral formation around a way of life. The following account is of a well-known Roman senator who was "converted" to the school of the (non-Christian) philosopher Plotinus. The account is relayed by Porphyry, a student of Plotinus who was also one of the ablest early critics of Christianity. Porphyry witnesses to the new life of Rogatianus in an account which has almost exact parallels among Christian converts of the age.

> There was also Rogatianus, a senator, who advanced so far in renunciation of public life that he gave up all his property, dismissed all his servants, and resigned his rank. When he was on the point of appearing in public as praetor and the lictors were already there, he refused to appear to have anything to do with the office. He would not even keep his own house to live in, but went the round of his friends and acquaintances, dining at one house and sleeping at another (but he only ate every other day). As a result of this renunciation and indifference to the needs of life, though he had been so gouty that he had to be carried in a chair, he regained his health, and, though he had not been able to stretch out his hands, he became able to use them much more easily than professional handicraftmen. Plotinus regarded him with great favor and praised him highly and frequently held him up as an example to all who practiced philosophy.[13]

While Christian conduct was often strikingly similar to the ways of those "who practiced philosophy," we must quickly add that not all pagan observers agreed that Christianity was a "philosophy." Some said "the Galileans'" way of life was not intellectually rigorous enough, a charge Christian apologists were already moving to rebut in the second century. Many called Christianity "a superstition." They meant that it was a foreign religious cult, practicing outside the pantheon of Greek and Roman gods and engaging in semisecret practices different from common religious habits. Moreover—and this was occasion for moral condemnation—Christianity showed indifference and sometimes opposition to the imperial civil religion. (For this latter reason, Christians were occasionally dubbed "atheists.")[14]

The salient point remains: Whether early Christian ethics is viewed in terms of the strong sense of community which belonged to ancient Judaism and which permeates the Hebrew Bible, or is seen against the background of classical culture, "the Way"—meaning a way of life with a religious/moral center—is at the core. "The Way" is always a community matter. It is the way of life of a community of faith.

Jewish Trademarks

If we are to understand Christian ethics in its earliest and most formative period, and describe it in ways the first Christians would themselves have recognized, we must turn to the moral patterns of Judaism. It is not enough to note the emphasis on a way of life shared by early Christian communities and Roman philosophical schools. The schools did not emphasize the community *religious* identity which distinguished Christian communities, since the "Way" of the latter was the *bios* of a faith community. Moreover, those social groupings of the Greco-Roman world which were closest of all in form to the Christian gatherings, namely, the religious cults, paid relatively little attention to what occupied Christians considerably—morality and ethics as community tasks. If we are to understand Christian ethics in its early stages, we must recognize that the Jewish legacy is even more important than the Greco-Roman one.

Two of the most striking and tenacious characteristics of ancient Israel and its offshoot, early Christianity, are *the sense of being a "people," and the high place that Scripture eventually acquired in the community.*

25

Peoplehood. To be "a people" does not mean to be a single cohesive community, either for Judaism or Christianity. Israel was a tribal confederation, a small nation, a community in exile, and a diaspora community. At the time of Jesus, Israel had a plethora of community forms: messianic renewal movements like those around Jesus and John the Baptist; semimonastic communities like the Essenes' Qumran community of the new covenant; scattered diaspora communities in cosmopolitan centers such as Alexandria and Rome; and, overridingly important for later Judaism, the growing schools of the rabbis.[15]

This is only a partial list from a period which also witnessed the onset of pluralism in the Christian community.[16] Some of the pluralism is preserved in the New Testament itself. If already in the first centuries of Christian history no one institution or community form endured and represented "the people," what did the term mean? For the Christian church it would soon come to include a certain complex and living set of events, figures, and stories, rituals, beliefs, practices, rules, oral and written wisdom, and institutions. These would be shared across centuries and continents, albeit with extensive modification, addition, and elaboration; they would nonetheless yield a recognizable cohesiveness amidst vast differences of custom, geography, language, culture, race, class, and national origin.

Even more basic to the sense of "a people" was a dynamic which permeated the shared elements and their variations: *the Jewish insistence upon the social embodiment of faith in the one God.*[17] To be a people of God meant to *give communal form to the collective experience of God, first in Israel and then in Jesus and the Spirit.* The communities insisted upon a religio*social,* or religio*communal,* reality as the matrix of their members' lives. Their basic "unit" of human reality was not the *polis,* as it was for the Greeks; nor the empire, as it was for the Romans; nor the individual, as it is for many moderns. It was the people as a religiosocial community. How strong this trait was, and how strong the initial similarity between Judaism and the church, is reflected in the response of Rome. The Romans perceived the Christian "People of the Way" as a variant of Jewish community.

Christian ethics has never entirely lost its sense for the communal embodiment of faith so characteristic of its origins, and will not, so long as it preserves the testimony of its own Scriptures. (One reason is that almost all the biblical images of religious identity are communal ones: Israel, family, kingdom, covenant, a banquet, one vine with many branches, a body with many parts, a chosen race and royal priesthood, etc.) But later developments weakened the religiosocial sense considerably:

• A dualism and asceticism more Greek than Hebrew, and already present in the early centuries, severed material from spiritual reality and located the reality of faith in the unseen, rather than in, with, and under that which was socially visible. Nature/supernature, mind/body, and spirit/body dualisms developed.

• From Emperor Constantine onward (the 4th century C.E.) the extension of church boundaries to coincide with civic ones dissolved the line between the religious community's alternative way of life and the moral and cultural patterns of the wider society. A distinctive way of life characteristic of Christian communities faded from public view, or took a visible but semidetached social form which included only some groups or "classes" of Christians (monasticism is the prominent example).[18]

• The triumph of individualism in matters of morality, most prevalent in the West from the Enlightenment forward (the 17th century and following) and strongest in Anglo-American culture, removed the very sense of a necessary moral community. "The common good" receded as a basic moral notion and morality, including Christian morality, became increasingly a private matter. The formation of morality was left to families, sometimes schools, and to those communities which were voluntarily contracted as the outcome of individual choices. Many people regarded values themselves as expressions of individual tastes and preferences.

Given the cumulative weight of this threefold legacy—asceticism and dualism, Constantinian arrangements, and individualism—we do well to cite biblical instances of the moral formation of "peoplehood." Otherwise the force of Christian ethics as inherently communal is lost. We choose two examples, one from Israel, another from the early church.

The exodus was the initial, formative event of peoplehood. The event itself left the freed slaves in the Sinai wilderness where they were inevitably faced with a question something like this: How do we now meet our bodily needs and show in our life together the freedom won for us by this liberating God who knew our sufferings and heard our cries? "Sinai" inaugurated the answer. The social task in the wilderness

27

was to fashion, amid forbidding circumstances, a faithful community that took its cues from God's mighty presence in their midst. Freedom *from* had to become freedom *for*; freedom had to find social form in the community's life. In effect, a whole set of questions was addressed, both in the wilderness and on into the new land: What would be the community's economics, its governance and political structure? its ritual and worship? its social intercourse and relations to neighbors? Who would perform what tasks of livelihood, and make the rules for family, clan, and federation? How would work be assigned and benefits and burdens shared? What laws would prevail? How would offenders be treated?

The pattern of answering such questions was significant. Attention was given to local conditions and resources, of course; and memory and imagination were mixed with other human skills in charting the way. But all this happened under the conviction that the community should reflect in its own character and conduct the character and conduct of the righteous and compassionate God who knew their suffering and brought them up from the land of Egypt.[19] The collective moral reasoning of these "tribes of Yahweh" went like this: If the majestic and elusive presence we called Yahweh redeemed us, the poor, and knew our sufferings, the suffering of slaves, so too must we show compassion and redeem the victim and the excluded. If mighty Yahweh visited us as strangers in the land of Egypt and extended saving hospitality to us, we in turn must not oppress strangers but take them in and give them refuge. Indeed, we must love the neighbor, including the stranger, as ourselves. If mighty Yahweh identified with us, the powerless and dispossessed, so too should we as the community of Yahweh. Radical love and a caring justice are not optional acts of voluntary piety; they are at the heart of what it means for us to be a people of this God.[20]

The key to this pattern of community morality is the experienced character of God, who is here a God of the oppressed.[21] The outcome of the process is a community which consciously tries to become an alternative to that which it had known in Egypt. Covenant community with the compassionate and righteous God was defined in contrast to the imperial community of the Pharaoh and other great cultures of the ancient Near East, where the power of the nation paralleled the power of its gods. When Egypt was weak its gods were weak, and when Egypt was strong the gods were said to be strong. The power of the gods was measured by the strength of the nation's military might, economic strength and cultural achievement, and access to the gods was mediated by an elaborate priesthood that was in partnership with reigning political and economic power in a society rigidly stratified from top to bottom. The gods clearly favored those at the top of the social pyramid, thus endorsing and reinforcing imperial arrangements.

It was a revolution in gods, then, when one of them heard the groans of the dispossessed and freely entered a covenantal relationship with slaves without standing or power. It was also a revolution in social arrangements when these slaves fashioned a community which was an alternative to that of the nations of the period. We cannot trace the process and outcome in detail here, but we can sketch this effort to give communal form to a people's experience of God.[22]

The legislation that fills the pages of Exodus, Leviticus, and Deuteronomy illustrates this mix of the practical necessities of community formation and people trying to give their religiomoral convictions communal expression. The texts reflect a very strong sense of "peoplehood," even a collective religious vocation as "a kingdom of priests" (Exod. 19:6) on behalf of all peoples, albeit precisely as a community which was not to be "like the nations" (1 Sam. 8:5,20). As in every community, the texts also reflect unmistakable evidence of human frailty and error, and narrow, unjust, and corrupting perspectives and practices. The hated ways of the Pharaoh would in fact find their own counterpart later in Israel itself.[23] It was at least as difficult to get "Egypt" out of "Israel" as "Israel" out of "Egypt." This irony nonetheless does not alter the deep insistence upon finding a way to give social form to the experience of God as a community-creating and community-preserving experience.

Similar dynamics were present in the early church, as we see in Acts. The collective experience of the resurrected Jesus and the giving of the Spirit led to very practical questions: How do we now embody the intense reality of the living Christ among us, in our day-to-day life together? What will we do with our goods, our houses, our land? How will we organize fellowship with one another, locally and across great distances, i.e., how will we "break bread together" as members of the same body in different locales? What should be our form of governance and how do we recognize our leaders, by what measure? How will worship be conducted? How will the rituals and rites and festivals of our former life be treated? What shall we now say to Caesar, now

29

that "Jesus is our Caesar" (Acts 17:8); and what should we do about service in the emperor's army? How do the relationships of parents and children, of husband and wife, of slave and slaveholder change now? What are the requirements of membership in the community? How should transgressors be treated? How should we treat those who take offense at the new gospel and persecute us?

Like the Sinai responses, these efforts bore all the marks of limited human vision and limited cooperation. Factions proliferated. Nonetheless, lives were transformed in new communities that cannot be understood apart from the empowering experience of Jesus and his way, as vindicated by God in the resurrection and vivified in the Spirit. This Christian orientation was distinguished from other Jewish and Gentile communities in that it turned on "following Jesus" (the language of the Gospels) or "putting on Christ" (Pauline language). Upon closer inspection, however, we see that this was the way the Christian communities spoke of their experience *of God,* and this was their form of the Hebrew moral pattern; i.e., a community ethic is inferred from the character of the divine presence they experienced. In this instance, Jesus and the Spirit were the community's experience of God's presence, and the social form of their faith took its clues from that. So when the question was the moral one, "What ought we now to be and do?" the answer of early Christians appealed to Jesus as Pattern, Teacher, or Example; or it looked to other clues from "the Jesus story"—predominately the passion drama of cross and resurrection;[24] or it drew from the continued presence of Jesus in their midst in the Spirit; or, frequently, to some combination of these. The distinctiveness of early Christians was not in the way they answered moral questions—they continued the main lines of the Jewish legacy. Their distinctiveness lay in the conviction that it was in the Jew, Jesus of Nazareth, that God had been seen with compelling clarity and had come to the fullest expression possible in human form. The distinctiveness was not that Christians veered from the sense of being "a people" with a collective religiomoral vocation, but in their contention that this Jesus was both "true God" (a faithful disclosure of God) and "true humanity" (an exemplary model of human life).

We should interject a note about "the Jesus movement" itself. It continues the pattern of which we speak but is not the same membership as that of many early churches—of, for example, the Pauline congregations. The Jesus movement refers to the community immediately around Jesus in his own lifetime and until the destruction of the Temple in 70 C.E. It was made up of those who traveled with Jesus, together with the supporters of "the Way" who remained in their villages, chiefly in Galilee. It was a Jewish movement wholly within Palestine, and was one of the many renewal, or restoration, movements of the period. C. H. Dodd speaks of Jesus' purpose as that of creating "a community worthy of the name of a people of God." [25] In pursuit of this he sought to form "the new Israel under his own leadership; he nominated its foundation members, and admitted them into the new 'covenant,' and he laid down its new law. That was his mission." [26]

This is the Jewish quest. It is stated with precision by Marcus Borg: "Jesus [is] concerned about creating a community within history whose corporate life reflected faithfulness to God." [27]

In sum, both examples—Israel's beginnings and those of the early church, with the Jesus movement as its earliest phase—witness to religious communities which did not so much "have" a social ethic as they "were" a social ethic in the process of formation. Morality was a dimension of shared religious experience; it was communal in form and its communal form was dynamic. The ethics were, to use the New Testament term, *koinōnia* ethics—community-creating human relatedness rooted in a compelling experience of God. [28]

Scripture's Place. The strong sense of peoplehood in early Christian ethics is a prime mark of the Jewish legacy. Closely related is a second, the high authority of Scripture for the moral life.

What place does Scripture hold in the earliest Christian communities? It is not and could not be exactly as ours, since those communities did not have the Bible as we do. Scriptures themselves were in formation as documents of the faith community, first in oral, then written forms which were added to, passed along, and preserved. The Hebrew Scriptures, or *Tanak* (the Christian Old Testament), did not take final canonical form until near the beginning of the second century after Christ. The Law, the Prophets, and other books were already in use 200 years before, however, and the Pentateuch, the five books attributed to Moses, had long been cited in community discourse and took canonical form very early. [29] The Greek Scriptures (the Christian New Testament) were a selection of early church writings which received canonical sanction in the fourth century after Christ. Until that time, varied collections of these writings, together with Hebrew Scriptures, were used as Christian Scriptures. [30]

Yet even before assuming canonical form, these letters from the ancestral faith communities held a place unparalleled among religious and philosophical movements of the ancient world. Their community authority was "a unique characteristic of the Jewish ethos."[31] The writings of the founding philosophers and renowned teachers of the Greek and Roman schools were never accorded such high status in their respective communities, not even already established classics such as the works of Homer or the writings of Plato. None carried anything like the "constitutional" status the Torah did in Jewish communities, or the sacred writings did in Christian ones.[32] In their communities the Scriptures were charter documents with living power.

How such an authority functioned in and for the moral life of these communities is a matter for later chapters. For now, we note only the following: both ancient Jewish and Christian communities were convinced that what is morally significant could be discerned through the careful study of these Scriptures. The Scriptures comprised a reliable guide in matters of faith and life. Not *all* that was necessary for the living of the moral life was found in these sacred pages, however, and the faith communities made no claim that the Scriptures constituted a full ethical system. The direct moral exhortation which *is* present (the Ten Commandments, portions of the Sermon on the Mount, Pauline commendations) functioned more as *exemplary* guidance, rather than comprehensive instruction. Instructions in "the Way" were more akin to strong signals than legislation, even when the language is the lawlike language of moral obligation.[33] What is signaled and exemplified is *the sort of life* expected of the community in view of the presence of God, and with a view to the hopes of God for all creation. Scriptures recount the Way, for the purpose of the community's formation, instruction, preservation, and renewal.

This can be said somewhat differently. The Scriptures were not so much a *fixed moral deposit* for these communities as they were precious community records of what it meant in varied times and places under varied conditions to try to *be* Israel or to try to *be* a Christian people of God.

Still, there is an even more encompassing moral use of Scripture in these communities. Both Jewish and Christian renderings discerned deep moral and theological dimensions in the drama of history itself—not only in their own communities' histories, but in all human history. The one God reigns, righteous and compassionate, and humanity is accountable to this God for all things touched by human power, great and small. A divine goal inhabits the drama: the full flourishing of all creation. Human beings are responsible before God for living in ways which realize rather than frustrate this goal. The Scriptures express and promote this reading of history in theological and moral terms. They place the faith community's life within the overarching context of God's purposes for all creation. God-community-creation are moral realities indissolubly bound together.

Continuation and Conclusion

For all that we've said, it is still too little to conclude only that the *original* context of Christian ethics is community. It is too little even if we underscore the fact that the original *content* is a distinctive community way of life. We begin to say more when we recognize what those original, formative impulses continue to mean. They mean that the faith community is to *remain* the reference point and the ongoing socializing agent for the moral life. In Christianity, moral deliberation and moral formation are to be tied to the shared memory, mission, and continuing life of Christian faith communities.

That continuing life means that Christian ethics, as with Jewish ethics, is always in process; it changes with developments in the community. Scripture itself witnesses to this. Critical, often unique historical events, such as the exodus, exile, and Jesus' crucifixion, gave rise to stories, traditions, and rituals which were called upon, generation after generation, for religiomoral orientation and guidance. Worship, spirituality, and festivity became important observances and, like the varied works of justice and charity, they helped fashion *the kinds of persons* people of the Way were to be. Moral wisdom and resources came from many other quarters as well, including non-Jewish and non-Christian sources. The biblical accounts themselves reflect this very process. Yet the point here is that it continues in Christian ethics through ensuing centuries. In both biblical and post-biblical worlds, then, resources from beyond the faith community's traditions were filtered through the community's own self-understanding and shaped in keeping with its own corporate temper. The community (*koinōnia*) was itself altered in the process of appropriating materials from its wider world; sometimes it was dramatically altered. In turn, it frequently influenced the very world which had deeply affected it.

In summary: Christian ethics not only was but *is* community ethics. It is not only so in origin, but also in continuation. Influences from biblical Judaism and the Greco-Roman world lived on in Christianity, just as Christianity influenced and was influenced by the Roman and Byzantine Empires and their successors. North African, Middle Eastern, Indian, Slavic, and Western societies all shaped the mind, form, and ethos of Christian communities in decisive ways, just as they are presently being shaped by African, Asian, and other cultures. The same community process seen in Scripture itself continues after the biblical canon is closed.

●   ●   ●

The implications of Christian ethics as community ethics will be pursued in due course. For the moment it is enough to step back and recognize the contribution of Scripture to all subsequent discussion of Christian ethics, including Christian ethics today. What the Bible does for Christian ethics is at least this: *It places morality very near the center of the life of the faith community, as the practical expression— or way of life—of community faith itself.* Unfortunately, much study of the Bible to this day fails to recognize Scripture's intense vocation of community moral formation. Just as unfortunately, many common understandings of Christian ethics fail to redress this serious oversight.

But how does the moral life come to be? How is it sustained and carried out? How is a way of life fashioned in the first place, and reformed? How does the faith community itself give form to the moral life? Questions such as these presume we know what "the moral life" means and what the elements of Christian ethics are. Yet these are not self-evident. For this reason, the next chapter is an introduction to the moral life and to essential moral concepts in Christian ethics.

3

CHARTING
THE
MORAL LIFE

The meaning of *moral* is something of a puzzle. At least it is not self-evident. The object of this chapter is to distinguish the "moral" from the "nonmoral" dimensions of our lives, and to provide a common vocabulary for the moral life.

The moral life is not strange to us, nor is the language we use to describe and debate it. Moral matters belong to everyday experience and routine discussion. Yet our common language does not always disclose what we mean by "moral," at least not with the kind of precision that lets us see clearly what we encounter daily.

For example, how would you distinguish "moral" from "nonmoral," rather than "immoral"? To what does "moral" refer? If we look carefully at our habits of mind and speech, we recognize two instances where differences surface. The first distinguishes human from other life forms, the second resides in distinctions within human experience itself. We take each in turn, noting how words which we frequently use in moral matters can have nonmoral meanings as well.

1. "Good" is such a word. It may be the most commonly used word in the vocabulary of morality, with "right" and "wrong" running close behind. "Judgment" is another prevalent term (we commonly speak of "value judgments" or "moral judgments"). Yet if we used "good" when "judging" plants, for example, and said that tomatoes or corn are "good" while dandelions and thistles are "bad," it is not because we consider plants moral creatures whose behavior is subject to moral

judgments. We have used common "moral" terms, "good," "bad," and "judgment," but not to assess plant morality! The notion of plant morality itself strikes us as odd. Why? Because we consider humans, but not plants, to be "moral" creatures. Yet why, for what reasons? Not because humans possess consciousness and plants exhibit none. Plants may not show *self*-consciousness, as humans do, but they certainly demonstrate a highly variegated response to their environment. The particular consciousness they lack, and humans possess, is the awareness of a gap or a difference: the difference of "is" from "ought," the difference of what presently exists from a world which could be better than it is. "Moral" consciousness resides in this distinction of "is" from "ought" and this capacity to choose a different world. Plants do not consciously seek to change the world in order that what "is" might better align with what "ought" to be; people do. The lives of "moral" creatures, as distinct from "nonmoral" ones, are lives which are stretched across this "is/ought" gap and which show the tensions of living across that gap. Differently said, moral creatures live with a conscious sense of both right and wrong, better and worse. They try to distinguish good from evil, give reasons for such distinctions, and then act accordingly (or suffer further tensions if they don't!). Plants, while as vibrant with life as humans, don't display these moral habits.

The line between "moral" and "nonmoral" consciousness fades somewhat as we move from the plant kingdom to the animal kingdom and compare human animals with other animals. Among nonhuman mammals, we frequently observe behavior we readily sense as "moral." Many care for the young and the vulnerable. They seem to show affection and perhaps even "love." They demonstrate hostility. Many exhibit group loyalty. Some have elaborate ways to protect their own kind. All this seems to belong to the universe of "moral" sensibilities. Still, nonhuman animals apparently do not project a different and "better" world, and then with conscious intent try and transform the present one in keeping with this vision. The "is/ought" gap is certainly much wider, and the "is/ought" dynamic much stronger, among humans. So we find it peculiar to ascribe moral vision to nonhuman animals.

The point is not the crispness of the demarcations between ourselves and our fellow siblings across the created order of things. It is to name a fundamental characteristic of "moral" consciousness—the world might be different than it is, and better. Judgments of moral good and evil, right and wrong, belong to this kind of consciousness.

2. Yet not *all* human experience is a matter of such judgments. There are nonmoral dimensions of human experience, just as there are non-moral values and judgments; we use "good" and "bad," "right" and "wrong" in nonmoral ways. An example or two will suffice.

If you pause before Rembrandt's paintings to ponder his artistry, and your art instructor whispers over your shoulder, "Rembrandt is a good painter," you are immediately aware of two things: (1) this is an understatement; (2) the instructor is using "good" in a nonmoral sense. She is not referring to Rembrandt's character nor to moral actions on his part. Those are beside the point for this particular judgment. The value described is not moral, it is aesthetic. The aesthetic is one of the nonmoral dimensions of human experience.

We often describe other capacities and other sensibilities with the same words which we employ in moral judgments. To be a good mechanic, a good scientist, a good chef, a good musician, or a good athlete requires knowledge, skills, training, and a sense for nuance and complexity. But such a rating ("good") is not a *moral* rating in any of these cases, any more than our judgments about Pete Rose's performance at homeplate are, or the liturgical sense with which a priest celebrates Mass. "Good" and "bad" refer to technical capacities here, just as "right" and "wrong" refer to technical execution.

When we shift the vocabulary from "nonmoral" and "moral" to "immoral" and "moral," we shift the frame of reference as well. "Immoral" is markedly different from "nonmoral." "Immoral" is a judgment made *within* the moral universe. It is a moral judgment itself, rendered by us acting precisely *as* "moral agents." The moral world is the generic reality here, and "moral" and "immoral" are distinctions *within* this; they are judgments about human character and conduct as morally good or bad, morally right or wrong. Had your art instructor said, "Rembrandt was of dubious character," she would have registered a clear moral judgment, just as "Rembrandt was a good painter" was a clear aesthetic one.

This book's concern is wholly with moral experience rather than nonmoral. Both moral and immoral already belong to the world of these pages.

37

The Moral World

What can we say beyond these initial distinctions? How might the world of morality be described? What categories and concepts help us to understand ourselves from a moral point of view?

The etymology of key terms offers some initial insight. "Ethics" has a Greek root, the noun form of which is *tō ēthos*. The parallel in Latin is *mos*, from which we have "mores," "morality," and "morale." *Tō ēthos* originally referred to the shelter or dwelling place for animals. In order to provide for society what animals were raised to provide, they needed a place of protection and nutrition. The stall meant sustenance and security. It meant a daily routine that met their needs and a familiarity that gave them a sense of "home." The "stable" offered "stability" (the two words share a common root, meaning to stand, or a firm place to stand).

Eiōtha is the Greek verb form of "ethics." It means "to be accustomed to," a parallel of *mos* ("mores" are customs). One of the oldest meanings of "morality" is behavior according to custom. Customary behavior does for human society much of what the stall does for animals; it provides stability and security, and helps to sustain society. Morality is a kind of social glue (to shift images). It keeps society sufficiently intact to let people get on with the living of life; so whenever it comes morally "unglued," society almost instinctively seeks moral repair, often by force, in order to carry on the business of life in something approaching a workable manner. Without compliance with some minimal moral stipulations, life together cannot happen.[1]

The Greeks came to make distinctions between "morality" and "ethics," however. The distinctions created a certain tension. Morality continued to refer to behavior according to custom. But with the rise of philosophy, ethics came to mean behavior according to reason, or reflection. Ethics then called morality into question and offered recommended changes of behavior on the basis of this analytical reflection. Ethics also confirmed customary behavior in many instances, but now the confirmation required what came to be termed "justification." To justify morality meant to provide publicly accountable, reasoned argument for it.

"Morality" and "ethics" today carry many meanings and the best admonition may simply be to "watch your language" and listen well to what people say when they talk ethics talk. The previous chapter identified both morality and ethics under the common rubric of a "way of life." Later uses in this volume will distinguish Christian ethics from Christian morality, however, and "ethics" will designate the task of investigating morality, assessing it, and making moral recommendations. Throughout most of these pages, Christian ethics is this critical intellectual discipline in the service of the Christian moral life, while morality refers to the standards of character and conduct people use in the living of it.

Whatever the many meanings of these key terms, they are not arbitrary, even in the most casual conversations. It is not a case, as in *Through the Looking Glass*, in which the Queen tells Humpty Dumpty she does with words just as she chooses, and they mean just what she chooses them to mean. But the variety of meanings does underscore the admonition to watch our language.

Even with these distinctions in hand, we lack a description of the elements of the moral life. The chart below is a guide for that, and will serve as the map to the remainder of this chapter and several which follow. Some of the chart's key terms are treated extensively in this chapter (moral vision, virtue, obligation, and value), others are only introduced here and treated in later chapters (character formation and decision making).

MORAL AGENCY

Character Formation	Decision making and Action
the good person and the good society	right choice and action
moral virtue	moral value and moral obligation
the ethics of being	the ethics of doing

moral vision

The overarching notion is that of "moral agency," with ourselves as "moral agents." "Agent" and "agency" are technical terms in ethics, the meaning of which will unfold as we interpret the chart. For the moment, moral agency is simply a way to name that which is necessary to make sense of ourselves as creatures who act "morally." It is a tag for describing human experience, and especially human action, from a moral point of view. It means we are those kinds of creatures who are able to perceive various courses of action, weigh them with a view to various considerations, choose among the actions on the basis of the considerations, and act on the choices. It also means we can be held accountable for our choices and actions.[2] "Agency" encompasses both character and conduct, both our moral "being" and our moral "doing," and thus is comprehensive of the elements of the chart.

The chart includes a horizontal line. This indicates the unity of human agency in the moral life. Moral agency does not separate "being" from "doing," or character from decision making and action. The continuous line illustrates this basic unity. The perpendicular line *does* separate the elements of moral agency, but it does so only for the sake of clear recognition, analysis, and discussion. The perpendicular line should be viewed as tentative. It exists solely to aid understanding. It is not a line which slices from top to bottom through our moral experience itself.

"Moral vision" is placed separately at the base of the chart. Like moral agency it encompasses dimensions of both columns. It is not a synonym of moral agency, however, and requires separate treatment.

An introduction to the chart as a whole is in order before turning to individual elements.

The focus in the left column is on one of the ancient and persisting questions of ethics, "What is the good society, or the good community, and who is the good person?" "Good" refers to *prized qualities of being* or *desirable traits of moral character,* whether these are qualities and traits of a single person or a group of people. The reference is to *the kinds of persons* the moral agents are.

When attention is given to "character" the reference is to moral elements we often consider "internal" to the person or group—motives, dispositions, attitudes, intentions, and perceptions. These belong to moral "being," as aspects of our moral identity. They express our character, individually or collectively. They reflect *who* we are, morally.

Moral judgments about character and moral identity are judgments about "virtue," judgments about what qualities or "excellences" characterize the good person and community. The concern of virtue, however, is not limited to who we are and ought to be as persons and groups of people. It necessarily includes the sort of world that must exist so as to foster the desired qualities. That is, moral virtue pertains not only to qualities of sound moral character but to the social arrangements which make for communities of sound moral character. So virtue and character must ask, What arrangements nurture courageous and compassionate people, honest and just ones? What fosters an ethos of graciousness and a climate of gratitude? What encourages dispositions that prize fair and equal treatment of all social groups? These are "virtue" concerns in Christian ethics (and in other moral traditions).

The column on the right also engages an ancient and persisting question of ethics, "What ought I or we to do?" Here *concrete choices and deeds in particular circumstances on specific moral issues and problems* are the subjects of moral judgment.

Such choices are normal fare in the long stretch of Christian ethics. Should Christians participate in war, revolution, personal self-defense, or other actions entailing violence, often deadly violence? If so, in what way? What is the proper choice in matters of abortion or euthanasia? What about economic policies and choices? What are fair tax laws, the rights of workers and management, employment and unemployment benefits, the distribution of wealth and opportunity in a society? What civil rights are due members of society? What is just adjudication when rights conflict? Who properly attends to health care? How is it fairly delivered? How ought parents, lovers, and friends treat one another? What are the responsibilities of parents toward their children, and vice versa? What is due the stranger? What is due the enemy?

Questions such as these only begin a list of moral queries which reach as far as human concerns themselves do. They are not encountered as a list, however! They are faced daily, as concrete choices in particular circumstances, as matters demanding decisions. They are the living material of moral quandaries and conflicts. In both routine and extraordinary ways, they comprise much of our lives as moral agents.

Judgments on such issues and choices as these are judgments about

41

what is morally "right," as that reflects cherished moral values and sensed moral obligations. Both terms—value and obligation—must be treated separately. We need only recognize that, like virtue, they belong to matters of moral judgment. They refer, however, not to "interior" qualities of character but to decisions and actions themselves. They have their focus on overt behavior, on "doing."

This presents the chart in a brief, broadstroke way. Later discussions build from here, but we emphasize again that, in the actual living of the moral life, the broken line fades in a reciprocity of influences across these columns. A story about the playwright Oscar Wilde illustrates this nicely. When Wilde arrived in the United States in 1882, he was asked by the customs officials what he had to declare, if anything. Wilde, always the wit and somewhat given to pretension, replied: "Only my genius!" Some 15 years later he found himself in Reading Jail, however. There, in a more pensive and humbler mood, he wrote one of his more thoughtful works, "De Profundis." His lines include the confession that he had been "the spendthrift of [his] genius." "I forgot," he said, "that every little action of the common day makes or unmakes character."[3]

Aristotle, the very philosopher who gave us the classic formulation of the ethics of virtue, or character formation, writes much the same in the *Nicomachean Ethics:* "We become just by doing just acts, temperate by doing temperate acts, brave by doing brave acts."[4] Hebrew wisdom literature says much the same, adding that benefits accrue for the life of virtue.

> If you pursue justice, you will attain it
> and wear it as a glorious robe.
> Birds flock with their kind;
> so truth returns to those who practice it.
> (Sirach 27:8-9)

All this is to say that just as character informs actions, so acts form character. Being and doing shape one another. An essential unity of the self, its choices and actions, exists, as choices and deeds help create the very character which finds expression in them. There are daunting complexities in moral formation here which we much later address, but this is the starting point. We can turn now to fuller exploration of virtue, value, obligation, and vision.

Each raises the curtain on a different aspect of the moral life. One test of an adequate Christian ethic is whether all are present and well accounted for.

Virtue. The speaker is Glaucon. Plato has given him a classic ethics assignment. He is to tell how he would recognize a just person. What, Plato asks, would demonstrate the sure presence of justice? Glaucon replies that a truly just person would be one

> of true simplicity of character who . . . wants to be and not to seem good. We must not allow him [or her] to seem good, for if he does he will have all the rewards and honours paid to the one who has a reputation for justice, and we should not be able to tell whether his motive is love of justice or love of the rewards and honours. No, we must strip him of everything except his justice. . . . He must have the worst of reputations for wrongdoing even though he has done no wrong, so we can test his justice and see if he weakens in the face of unpopularity and all that goes with it. We shall give him an undeserved and lifelong reputation for wickedness and make him stick to his chosen course until his death. . . . They will say that the just man, as we have pictured him, will be scourged, tortured, and imprisoned, his eyes will be put out and after enduring every humiliation he will be crucified. . . .[5]

For sheer brutality this description is striking, as is the stark parallel to Isaiah's Suffering Servant and Jesus of Nazareth. Yet the attention of the text does not swerve from Plato's question, In what does justice reside?

Our purpose in citing Glaucon is slightly different from Plato's, however, and poses questions which might be considered "prior" to Plato's own: Why is this passage "ethics talk" at all? What makes it so? And what dimensions of the moral life is Plato uncovering?

"Justice" certainly belongs to "ethics talk." Hardly another word, except "love," recurs more often in Jewish and Christian ethics. They are the most prominent moral norms in these traditions and many others. Yet what does justice refer to here, where does justice reside, to what is our attention drawn? The text bears careful scrutiny, not least for its omissions.

In common parlance justice often refers to some disputed matter that begs resolution. We judge an outcome to be "just" or "unjust." But that cannot be the meaning here. No moral dispute is raised. Glaucon

43

does not ask for moral resolution. He doesn't discuss a single social problem, or call upon different parties and their interests. The moral meaning of justice is elsewhere.

Another possibility is justice as used to describe some specific social system, or even society as a whole. We find justice relatively present or absent as we assess the economic order, the criminal justice system, present political arrangements, or the way education happens. But that cannot be the reference here either. No system is even mentioned, much less described and assessed.

Perhaps justice is Glaucon's label for laudable human actions. We frequently judge what people *do* to be just or unjust. Yet the passage denies any wrongdoing on the part of the person tested for justice. No specific unjust deeds have been alleged, although a severe reputation for wrongdoing has been imputed. In this passage, everything is done *to* him. No clues to his own deeds are given. Not a single one is mentioned. "Just" modifies something else. Justice here is not a judgment of this person's actions, right or wrong.

Glaucon's answer to Plato's question is intimated at the outset: "true simplicity of character . . . [the qualities of one] who . . . wants to be and not to seem good." Justice is a quality, or "excellence," of character. It is, to use the time-honored coinage of moral discourse, a matter of "virtue." It is an attribute of this person's very being.

Other dimensions of justice surface elsewhere in Plato's works. But this suffices to signal what ethics is for Plato and what feature of the moral life he highlights. *Ethics is that artful science which asks after the best kind of life to live and the excellences of character which foster and express that.* The focus is on moral traits, together with the social arrangements which nurture moral qualities appropriate to people's social roles. This is a strong theme in ancient classical culture that is taken up with vigor in Christian ethics. The classic formulation of Roman Catholic ethics by Thomas Aquinas uses Aristotle to supply the basic framework, to cite one example. For Aristotle, too, ethics is about the qualities of the good society, as expressed in the kinds of persons present in the society.[6]

Vexing moral problems and innumerable issues of social justice arose for the Greeks, of course, as they have for every people. Yet the work of morality was directed less to the resolution of moral quandaries ("what would you do if . . .") than to the deliberation of how we should live, with special concern for the sorts of persons we should be. This side of the moral life brings *moral formation* to the fore and accentuates moral education and training for the good life as key elements of ethics. The formation and ordering of society is crucial in this, since society is both the tutor and the living environment of morality. Society is both the teacher and classroom for character formation.

This side of the moral life—virtue and moral formation—is hardly the monopoly of Greek influences in Christian ethics, however. The more persistent force is the Jewish legacy with its sense of belonging to a people of faith who have a vocation *as* a people. To belong to a people of God means *the formation and transformation of personal moral identity in keeping with the faith identity of the community.* This encompasses more than virtue and character formation, but they are indispensable components. Moreover, the *scriptures* of the community are a prime medium for moral formation. (The Greeks had "classics" which they used for moral formation, but not sacred scriptures.) Sometimes particular virtues themselves are encouraged in these writings. Paul tells the communities in Galatia that living in the Spirit brings with it the fruits of the Spirit: "love, joy, peace, patience, kindness, goodness, faithfulness, gentleness, and self-control." (Gal. 5:22-23) Those "led by the Spirit" (Gal. 5:18) are also to do away with vices (vices are settled dispositions to do particular wrongs)—self-conceit, provoking of one another, and envy of one another. (Gal. 5:24,26)

Scripture is used less, however, for *direct* moral *exhortation* than for indirect means to achieve moral formation. Psalms sung again and again in worship or read in quiet devotion foster certain "senses" which take the form of virtues: a sense of gratitude, dependence, responsibility, humility, and awe, for example. These aren't "exhorted," they are nurtured in the course of prayer. Likewise, the recital of the great narrative accounts in Scripture, the telling of parables, and the hearing anew of the oracles and dreams of the prophets, create moral identity. It is not claiming too much to say that Scripture in the life of the Christian community has this moral vocation, to shape the personal moral identity of community members in keeping with the ways of God. Scripture encourages in myriad ways the internalizing of moral qualities which mirror who we are as a people of faith. But the larger point is that both the Jewish and the Greek legacies demonstrate a persistent concern in Christian ethics for virtue and moral formation, and that virtue and moral formation certainly belong to any adequate

45

understanding of the Christian moral life. An ethic which slights them is inherently faulty.[7]

We should reiterate the close tie to action which "agency" connotes. Virtues are "internal," a matter of character, but they are moral goods internally related to *practices;* they are habits of behavior nurtured in conduct, as the earlier references to Aristotle and the writer of Sirach suggest.

We add a closing note: While Christian ethics has had an important place for virtue since its beginnings, it has also been suspicious of it, on theological grounds. The Christian moral tradition understands much evil as the corruption of good, and much vice as the perversion of virtue. Thinkers with a lively doctrine of human sinfulness, like Luther, were almost as wary of the deadly virtues as the deadly sins! The quest for virtue often gives rise to a self-righteousness which is only the smug and perverse side of goodness. Humility, especially religious humility, becomes a form of pride, and false modesty a substitute for the real thing. Moreover, virtue perverted carries with it a sinister self-deception which makes it difficult to discern the evil present in the good (people mean well and think that what they do is in the best interests of all). Perhaps as much human damage occurs from the perversion of good as from conscious vice. Luther's words at the onset of his *Lectures on Romans* include these:

> The exodus of the people Israel has for a long time been interpreted to signify the transition from vice to virtue. But one should, rather, interpret it as the way from virtue to the grace of Christ, because virtues are often the greater and worse faults the less they are regarded as such and the more powerful they subject to themselves all human affections beyond all other goods. So also the right side of the Jordan was more fearful than the left side.[8]

Invariably, Luther says, Christian ethics becomes synonymous with a movement *from vice to virtue.* Sanctification is regarded as moral growth. Such thinking in terms of movement or progress is thinking *ad modum Aristotelis* (in the manner of Aristotle) "where everything depends on what the person does" and where righteousness is "real only to the degree that sin is expelled."[9] Sin is never expelled for Luther, so if there is to be "movement," it is not from vice to virtue, but from vice *and* virtue to grace. We should do away with the propensity to think in terms of law, virtue, and moral progress, Luther insists, and instead participate in a "daily dying and rising with Christ," in the knowledge that "none is righteous, no, not one." Cross the Jordan if you wish, he says, but life on both banks is much the same and equally in need of a fundamental transformation. "Grace," not "virtue," is the key term in ethics.[10]

The Brazilian priest Dom Helder Camara, meditating in the middle hours of the night about the attitudes of the rich toward the poor, and of the so-called "First World" toward the "Third," wrote in August 1962:

> I pray incessantly
> for the conversion
> of the prodigal son's brother.
> Ever in my ear
> rings the dread warning
> "This one [the prodigal] has awoken
> from his life of sin.
> When will the other [the brother]
> awaken
> from his virtue?"[11]

None of this banishes virtue and moral formation from the moral life, nor diminishes its importance. But it does alert us to the human perversion of virtue, and draw to our attention that the Christian life is more than virtue.

Value. Ethics itself is more than virtue and the moral life is more than the playing out of people's character in society. "Value" and "values" expose other aspects. To what do they refer? A true tale from mainland China near the onset of World War II offers a clue.

As the Japanese invaded China, they rounded up the non-Chinese and placed them in civilian internment camps. One of these was Shantung Compound, at Weihsien in North China. Its population was about 1500, overwhelmingly European and U.S. American with some Eurasians, South Americans, and South Africans. Japanese military personnel maintained strict access to the camp and controlled all goods entering and leaving, but they left the basic internal organization, maintenance, and day-to-day functioning of the camp community to the detainees themselves. People little known to one another were thus

47

thrown the daunting task of creating a small civilization at every level (except securing protection, which was provided by the enemy!). As the narrator notes, society was reduced to visible size here, and its fundamental dynamics were plain for all to see.[12] A microcosm of the wider world was forced to fashion a workable community together. As such, it was an enclosed, living laboratory in community creation, social values, and recurring human problems.

An incident from 1945 illustrates "value" as a dimension of the life at Weihsien. On a cold January day a wholly unexpected delivery was made. The guards opened the gates of the compound and donkey cart after donkey cart brought the deprived populace an unimagined gift— 1500 parcels! Each was packed with 50 pounds of rich, fat-laden food which was received by the assemblage as manna from heaven.[13]

The parcels were gifts of the American Red Cross. Many of the 200 U.S. Americans (of the then 1,450 internees) quickly registered special claim to the parcels, on grounds of origin. The Japanese commandant passed down his ruling: Each American would receive one and one-half parcels, all others would receive one each. The mathematics worked perfectly. Nonetheless a number of Americans protested vigorously—the Americans should decide the distribution of American Red Cross goods. The commandant responded by postponing the distribution until the community had discussed the protest.

The discussion included the following exchange between two of the Americans, Grant, an elderly missionary, and Gilkey, a young teacher (and the narrator of the Shantung Compound experience). Grant, Gilkey recalls, wanted to argue the "moral" side of the parcel affair: "I always look at things, Gilkey, from the moral point of view." "Fascinated," Gilkey comments, "I heard him out."[14]

> I want to be sure that there be a moral quality to the use we make of these fine American goods. Now as you are well aware, Gilkey, there is no virtue whatever in being *forced* to share. We Americans should be given the parcels, all right. Then each of us should be left to exercise his own moral judgment in deciding what to do with them. We will share, but not on order from the enemy, for then it would not be moral.

Gilkey, pursuing the meaning of "moral," asked how many parcels the Americans would likely share. Grant replied that each would likely give away at least two. Gilkey noted that this meant each non-American would receive less than one-fourth parcel, rather than the parcel apiece the commandant had initially ordered. Gilkey then put a question to Grant: "Would that be moral sharing when all of us are equally hungry and in need?" He reports the response: "Grant looked at me in bafflement. That was not at all what he meant by 'moral.' " "I don't understand you," he said. "If the Japanese share it *for* us, no one is doing a good act, and so there's no morality in it anywhere." [15]

Gilkey goes on to characterize Grant's understanding of "moral" and contrast it with his own. Grant contended that human actions which are not the free acts of individuals cannot be considered "moral." If we are not acting from choice and do not express who we are in our choices, then "morality" is not truly present. Even actions which yield beneficial social consequences, if they are *compelled* (by an enemy government in this instance), cannot be regarded as genuinely "moral." Moral actions, according to Grant (via Gilkey), are conceived in reference to those who perform them: Good actions express and add to virtue, bad ones detract from it. [16] For Grant the wellspring of morality is in character, free choice, and the genuinely free exercise of responsibility.

Gilkey countered this and went on to say that Grant's theory of morality

completely ignores the fact that moral action has to do primarily with the relations between persons in a community. Thus in reality moral actions are those in which the needs of the neighbor are given an equality with one's own needs; immoral acts are those in which the neighbor is forgotten for the sake of the self. Moral action, then, certainly if it is to be called "Christian," expresses in the outward form of an act a concern for the neighbor's welfare, which concern is, if anything is, the substance of inner virtue. [17]

Gilkey concludes his account: "In such a view all actions which help to feed the hungry neighbor are moral, even if the final instrument of that sharing is an impersonal arm of government. Thus, as I argued to Grant, efforts designed to bring about a universal sharing were moral, efforts to block such a sharing, immoral." [18]

Gilkey differed so sharply from Grant because Gilkey's ethic was centered, not in character and maximum individual free choice, but in the expression of *values as realized in, and tested by, social consequences*. In this case the salient value was the roughly equal sharing

49

of critical goods on the basis of common need. An even more basic value for Gilkey underlay this—the fundamental equality of persons in inescapable relationship with one another. On the basis of this value, each neighbor's welfare is placed in the same frame of reference as one's own, and because Gilkey's ethic is value-centered, the result is to declare that social policy "moral" which gives expression to neighbor love in the consequences of actions, whatever their source.

"Values" in ethics *refer to moral goods to be realized in society.* They function as moral norms by which we judge both actions and the structures of society itself. Or, as we project our hopes into the future, they function as the standards by which we judge the kind of society we aspire to. (The watchwords of the French Revolution were three values—*liberté! egalité! fraternité!*) Value judgments, then, are judgments about which values we want to see realized in society, through our and others' actions. Christian ethics as value ethics highlights and assesses peoples' efforts to purposefully realize the social good in accord with held values.

Recall the Sinai episode we discussed in the foregoing chapter. The community in the wilderness had the task of giving form to a society which reflected their religious experience of freedom from slavery. The vehicle for doing so was primarily the law, as the ordering of society in a way which expressed the values mirroring God's treatment of the slave band. The law was the means, in this case, for "realizing" values as moral goods in society.

As another example and for purposes of comparison, we can cite "justice" as a value and not only a virtue, as it was in the Glaucon episode and as it would likely have been conceived by Grant. Justice as a value is pervasive of the biblical materials and has a long history in Christian ethics. It is frequently invoked as *the* measure of society's well-being and the norm for Christian social striving. We should note that when it is invoked as a value, justice is not primarily a measure of the interior condition and motives of persons (Grant's concern); rather, justice is a measure of the outcome of actions taken, or those projected.

Reinhold Niebuhr's discussion of justice is helpful. For Niebuhr, the discussion must begin with love as *the* moral norm in the Christian life and, indeed, for all human life. This means love is also the moral norm for justice, since love is the very "law" of our being. That is, when we live by it, we live in accord with our true nature; when we transgress it, we transgress our essence as beings who can only be ourselves through relationships of mutuality with others. Yet love, Niebuhr says, is realized most directly by individuals in relationships of intimacy and is increasingly difficult as the scale of human organization increases (nations and corporations don't "love"). At the same time, love has a claim upon us which includes our relationship to everyone, expressed in Niebuhr's language as "the ideal of brotherhood."

> Community is an individual as well as social necessity; for the individual can realize himself only in intimate and organic relation with his fellow men. Love is therefore the primary law of his nature; and brotherhood the fundamental requirement of social existence.[19]

Since we cannot share mutuality and intimacy with everyone, the question becomes: How will love best be approximated in society at large? Niebuhr answers: through the instrumentality of justice. Justice is not identical with love but stands in a positive relation to it as the approximation of "brotherhood" [and sisterhood] under the conditions of sin. How is love as a moral value realized through justice? In two dimensions, says Niebuhr: "The first is the dimension of rules and laws of justice. The second is the dimension of structures of justice, of social and political organizations in their relation to brotherhood."[20] The latter we have already noted in our discussion of the Hebrew insistence upon the social embodiment of faith; here we add Niebuhr's discussion of the former.

> Systems and principles of justice are the servants and instruments of the spirit of brotherhood in so far as they extend the sense of obligation towards one another, (a) from an immediately felt obligation, prompted by obvious need, to a continued obligation expressed in fixed principles of mutual support; (b) from a simple relation between a self and one "other" to the complex relations of the self and the "others;" and (c) finally from the obligations, discerned by the individual self, to the wider obligations which the community defines from its more impartial perspective. These communal definitions evolve slowly in custom and law. They contain some higher elements of disinterestedness, which would not be possible to the individual self.
>
> In these three ways rules and laws of justice stand in a positive relation to the law of love.[21]

Love, then, is a moral good realized in society through the rules, laws, and structures of justice. This gives justice a dimension which is different from its character as a virtue, seen by Glaucon. Likewise, love expressed through justice is more than the motive and virtue it was in Grant's ethics.

An important theological conviction underlies value as a dimension of the moral life. It holds for all values—love, justice, or others. The conviction is that the world is unfinished and human beings are themselves "unfinished" agents. Differently said, creation is a dynamic rather than a static notion, and humans are coparticipants with God in a grand, ongoing venture. (Biblical Hebrew uses verb forms rather than noun forms to speak of creation; this underscores, in the choice of language itself, creation's dynamic and unfinished character.)

Two items follow from this. Christian ethics as value ethics is invariably "teleological" ethics. *Telos* is the Greek for "goal" or "end purpose." Value ethics are goal-oriented ethics; thus the attention to the consequences of actions, and to the social realization of the moral goods we call "values." Teleological ethics have a history far beyond Christian versions, but important strands of Christian ethics are part of this tradition.[22]

The second item is this: Value ethics generally emphasize the possibilities for human growth and development. There is a strong sense of human agency in value ethics (unfinished agents acting in an unfinished world), and there is steady attention to the role of human action in personal and social transformation. Strains of Christian ethics which emphasize value and values in the moral life usually reflect these characteristics.[23]

Obligation.   Consider the following hypothetical case, relayed by Beauchamp and Childress.[24] Close friends go mountain climbing together. You are one of them. Your friend falls. When you reach him on the rocks below, it is apparent he is severely injured. In his dying moments he asks you to make him a promise. You readily agree. He reveals that he has managed to amass a tidy, but secret, sum of money— nearly a million dollars. He explains he acquired it by dint of hard work and prudent investments, he tells you where the money is, and then asks you to deliver it to a relative, an uncle who gave him needed help and support at a crucial moment in the past. Your friend dies.

You know three things. You have made a promise; only you know about the million dollars; and your friend's uncle, whom you know well, is both rich and likely to squander your friend's money. Furthermore, you know better uses for the money, needier causes, and you wonder whether the money should not go to them. Carefully considered philanthropy would serve worthier ends than the uncle's and at the same time would be a fitting memorial for your friend. So you ask yourself whether you should break your promise to your friend. Whether you do or not, your friend will never know; and if you do break it, his uncle will never know either.

The case and the question disclose that side of life characterized by "moral obligation." What are we duty-bound to do? is the question which obligation puts to the moral life. What is right and wrong, good and evil, given the matrix of relationships which register their claims upon us? What do we owe one other, morally? To whom are we obliged, and what are we obliged to do, in view of the investments of our lives and the investment of life itself in our hands? Answering such questions requires judgments of moral obligation. In this particular case, the judgment at issue is whether you should break your promise to your friend in order to use his money for needier causes. Whatever the actual judgment you make, the very existence of a strong nagging sense that you should not break your promise is testimony to obligation as a reality of the moral life. Some variants of Christian ethics have made obligation, or duty, the central reality, just as others have done with virtue or value.[25]

Yet what is obligation about? What underlies its moral power? The case of the dying friend assumes that responsibilities arise amidst our relationships and are part of them. If we are close friends we expect behavior toward one another which is different from that between total strangers. If we are parents we cannot morally act as though our children did not exist. If we are employed we cannot be oblivious to the responsibilities demanded by our jobs. Relationships invariably entail responsibilities which we experience as duties or obligations.

Obligation connotes even more than this, however. There is a deep level of obligation and relationship that accompanies life itself. Living together *at all* requires ground rules. It entails minimum stipulations which are universally binding. Different epochs and cultures offer differing versions of these stipulations; but there is considerable cross-cultural agreement about the basic fact that life itself makes binding moral claims upon us and obligations arise from the necessities of shared existence. This persistent tug in the moral life is what obligation, as ethics talk, tries to illumine.

One example will suffice. Suppose you pick up the telephone and call for the correct time. The reply is "10:20." You hang up and begin to set your watch but are distracted by an incoming call. You converse a few minutes. By then you are again uncertain of the hour, so you call "Time" again. The reply: "6:32." Knowing this cannot be correct, you try once more. "1:15" is given. You know that is wrong as well, so you turn on the radio. The news "at the top of the hour" has just come on, and you quickly set your watch for 11:00 a.m. The time was not actually announced, but since it is forenoon and you're rather sure the original information about 10-something-or-other was correct, you conclude the hour must be 11. Yet when you leave your apartment you encounter a clock on the corner which reads "3:28" and another across the street which registers "9:12." Furthermore, you arrive at your destination only to be greeted angrily by one colleague who says you were to be present an hour earlier, at 2:00 p.m., for an important meeting, and another who says you are embarrassingly late for a 4:00 p.m. committee.

This little episode is surreal. It could not have happened. Why? Because if this were the actual state of affairs, society could not cope. Indeed, "society" would not exist, only chaos would. To muster society at all, reasonably reliable patterns of expectations and behaviors must exist. There must be a modicum of order, a dependable structure. When minimum order crumbles, a deeply human drive sets about to recreate it. The reason is not mysterious: Our lives literally depend upon minimum trustworthiness; it is a requirement of living together at all. In this particular instance, an agreed-upon sequence for a common day together is necessary. "Time" must exist, and time must be given a form which most people will honor often enough to order their comings and goings.

"Time" as an agreed-upon social invention isn't all that is required. A more profound example is the obligation to speak the truth and keep promises. We could retell this same episode with the assumption that every party actually knew what time it was, but no one told the truth. Each fabricated a time and was utterly oblivious to the results. When they literally wouldn't give you the time of day, you quickly concluded you couldn't take them at their word. You couldn't trust them about the current time, their pledge to hold an important meeting, or be present if the meeting were scheduled. In half a day, you would have learned that truth-telling and promise-keeping are simple requirements of daily existence itself, utter necessities of workable, humane expectations and behavior. Elemental trust is an indispensable social requisite. Life cannot be lived in basic distrust.

Truth-telling and promise-keeping only begin the list of requisites. "Respect" is another. Without at least some respect for others, including strangers, society would be engaged in a warfare of all against all; life would indeed be "solitary, poor, nasty, brutish, and short" (Thomas Hobbes).

Minimum respect means respect for bodily needs. Depriving persons of basic nutritional needs damages their humanity. The same might be said about shelter and meaningful work. They belong to first-level needs which must be met if more complex forms of human development are not to be thwarted.

Something similar can be said about equitable treatment of one another. Respect entails similar treatment of similar cases, or some other rendition of fair play. Negatively stated, we cannot live together if our treatment of each other is wholly arbitrary and thus utterly unpredictable. We cannot live together apart from respect as a moral quality and qualification. We must come up with something like the Golden Rule, i.e., treating others in the manner we ourselves want to be treated.

Whatever our particular list of moral requisites, it illustrates the larger point: Moral obligation is that effort of the moral life which strives to articulate *the ground rules,* ground rules which are required by the very nature of human existence itself. We are social creatures who cannot live with one another apart from these rules. Precisely *as* ground rules, these duties qualify and set the boundaries for all the actions we might contemplate. They establish the framework and limits. Judgments of moral obligation are judgments, then, about which actions we are duty-bound to observe as having the most basic claims upon us.

Such claims are often stated in the form of principles, laws, rules, or codes. Jesus' statement of the Golden Rule is an example already alluded to: "So always treat others as you would like them to treat you; that is the meaning of the Law and the Prophets" (Matt. 7:12 JB). Immanuel Kant's second formulation of the categorical imperative is another: "So act in every case as to treat humanity, whether in your own person or in that of another, as an end, and never a means only."[26]

55

The Ten Commandments are also examples of fundamental moral duties: "Honor your father and your mother . . . ; You shall not kill; You shall not commit adultery; You shall not steal; You shall not bear false witness against your neighbor," etc. (Exod. 20:12-16). It should not escape notice that the Ten Commandments were given at that moment in Israel's history when the people had left one intact, albeit oppressive, social order—Pharaoh's Egypt—and were now required to give basic form to another. The task at hand was certainly that of realizing moral values, as we noted above; but even more fundamentally the task was that of stipulating the most basic requisites of life together as a functioning community. It should also not escape our attention that these stipulations—the "commandments"—are considered expressions of a fundamental moral order authored by none less than the God who upholds all that is; the commandments are rooted in an existence which is itself grounded in God.

There are expressions of moral obligation which are considerably less comprehensive than the Ten Commandments or the reigning mores of a society. Many professional or work roles carry obligations specific to them, expressed in the form of ethics codes and rules. Whatever actions a doctor may take, she is to relieve unnecessary suffering and refrain from doing unnecessary harm (a portion of the Hippocratic Oath). A scientist who experiments with human subjects is normally required to obtain the informed consent of participants and provide an oversight committee with reports which are scrutinized in light of an adopted code of ethics. International law mandates that soldiers refuse participation in "crimes against humanity" even when these crimes are commanded by superior officers. Lawyers are to abide by codes of legal ethics, just as many public officeholders are subject to ethics in government codes. Clergy and psychiatrists who are told things in confidence are obliged to hold them in confidence. In all these cases and many more like them, moral obligation takes the form of duties indigenous to the kind of work performed in a specified relationship. The duties themselves are stipulated as rules, laws, codes, and principles which qualify and limit the kind and range of action the moral agent may take.

Most often, however, moral obligation is "sensed" and "intuited" rather than overtly stipulated. It arises amidst relationships so much a part of us that we "know" what is incumbent upon us without asking for formal moral guides. We recognize what a fitting response would be, given the claims of the relationship. Obligation is organic here, as when a friend knows she "must" cut vacation short to be with another friend who has suddenly taken ill; or when a spouse realizes he has been insensitive and must ask forgiveness and make amends. No "laws" or "codes" are cited, and no commandments are invoked. Sometimes no words are even spoken. It would in fact be somewhat bizarre to invoke moral laws, except perhaps as reminders of vows already made and promises given in trust. But, even in silence, obligation is deeply real here, as a dimension of morality intrinsic to the relationships themselves.

The foregoing examples suffice to illustrate that aspect of the moral life which provides the fundamental ground rules for decisions and actions. If it can be said that "value" highlights that dimension of the moral life which reflects the *openness* of our humanity to further development, "obligation" highlights that dimension which emphasizes the *givenness* of our humanity and the requirements which arise from, and for, our life together.[27] The moral life as obligation makes community possible; value makes it meaningful.

It goes without saying that many of our most intense discussions are about the *content* of moral obligation—precisely what is binding upon whom in what circumstances, and what to do when moral duties conflict. (A character in one of Tom Stoppard's plays says, rightly, "There would be no moral dilemmas if moral principles worked in straight lines and never crossed each other.")[28] This common experience in the moral life—moral principles crossing one another—only underscores the meaning and necessity of "judgment" in ethics; we must always strive for a discriminating discernment and decision about what is right and good, wrong and bad, in the particular circumstance at hand.

We add two notes about obligation for Christian ethics in particular. One is the theological grounding of obligation. Obligation is finally to God, just as obligation arises from the requirements of God's creation itself. The other note is that Scripture is a source of lasting, obligatory moral content. This was nicely confirmed on the editorial page of *The New York Times*. The subject was criticism of a presidential candidate who had declared for the 1988 election and who had complained that the press had demanded too much "precision" in his accounts of rather embarrassing episodes in his life. The editorial's concluding paragraph reads: "Telling the truth is not a stern requirement recently imposed by moralizing media; it dates back at least two Testaments. To depart from it as a standard invites a descent into babble, or, as Mr. Robertson might say, Babel." [29]

Vision. The following incident occurred at a conference on the ethics of organ transplants. Participants had been discussing various health care policies and issues with clear moral dimensions—equal access to services, the economic ramifications of increased demand for organs, the role of government regulation. It was obvious when the speaker for the next session arrived—a young Ph.D. in history—that he suffered a severe deformity. His congenitally deformed back required that he be supported in a special way in order to address the assemblage of physicians, lawyers, health care administrators, and professional ethicists.

The young man spoke matter-of-factly about his condition and went on to point out that in ancient civilizations the disabled had been killed for no other reason than their disability. Furthermore, he said, this had also happened in the United States. Even now the disabled were not being allowed to live in certain cases.

The attentive audience responded immediately and skeptically to this claim. Several participants challenged the speaker straightforwardly from the floor. He replied with a question put specifically to the transplant surgeons present: If two persons could avoid death, and could anticipate significantly prolonged life from an organ transplant, and if the only difference between them was that one was disabled and the other not, who would receive the saving transplant?

At first the surgeons defended their practice of excluding significantly disabled persons, all other factors being equal. They did so vigorously, with what the majority considered reasonable, informed, and sophisticated moral and policy arguments. Yet before long they began to realize the actual consequences of their train of mind: The person who had quietly put the question to them would not, by their judgments, have been allowed to live. The surgeons experienced a kind of slow, silent moral shock. Deep down they realized they had not considered the disabled to be fully persons.

Roy Branson, a conference member who reported the event, comments: "In the silences between their sentences the participants sensed that they had passed beyond the discussion of ethical, economic, medical and legal terms to glimpse new horizons of responsibility. Their sense of humanity had expanded." [30]

What had happened here? What, from a moral point of view, had occurred when "[t]heir sense of humanity . . . expanded"?

For conjecture's sake, let us presume the surgeons were persons of normally acceptable character. Some no doubt were more upstanding than others, but let us presume that the majority genuinely cared for the well-being of their patients, were dedicated to the relief of their suffering, and were sensitive as well as skillful in the treatment of those in their care. Most, if not all, demonstrated the moral and technical virtues expected of physicians. Moreover, they indicated that they did not shirk the stipulated moral obligations of their profession. Their spirited defense of their policies indicated that they took their duties seriously. They did so not least when facing very hard choices, choices of life and death.

We have, then, persons of character who show that they take their moral responsibilities seriously. We can also attest to certain values and value judgments which matter to them and which cannot be dismissed as hypocrisy or opportunism. Their goal, they argued, was the best health possible for as many citizens as resources permitted, and their practices were directed to serving this end.

The surgeons had attended not only to virtues and obligations, they had sincerely sought the social good as well; this is our conclusion. Yet something transpired in this poignant encounter which went beyond virtue, obligation, and value. It was something which cast all these against a different horizon and placed them in a new light. The surgeons realized they would have to think through anew the policies governing the designation of transplant recipients. They began to do so almost immediately. At the same time moral self-critique set in; they wondered whether their previous sense of compassion hadn't been restricted and their understanding of the social good prejudicial.

What happened to the surgeons was the intrusion of a different vision, a different *moral* vision. This is the meaning of "[t]heir sense of humanity had expanded." They "saw" things differently; the new perspective now included the disabled, or differently abled, as full persons. For some of the surgeons, it may well have been the first time.

Moral vision is the vision of the good we hold, a part of which is how we perceive and regard ourselves and others. It is our integrated grasp of the moral realm. It is sometimes brought to full consciousness by encounters such as the surgeons', and changed in the course of

59

catalytic events. More often it is the socialized (or internalized) reflection of the communities we move among, as that has taken form over a long period of time through encounters both extraordinary and mundane. Often we are only dimly aware of this internalized community moral vision, but it is effective in our lives nonetheless.

As in other changes of moral vision, so too in this case virtue, value, and obligation had to be reassessed. This in turn led both to self-critique and prospectively altered actions. (Readers should recall that "moral vision" was placed on the chart in a way that includes all elements.)

The past is rife with shifts in moral vision and subsequent shifts throughout the moral life. Slavery is a prime example. For much of recorded history, some human beings made slaves of others. The arrangements and conditions varied widely. Some were extraordinarily brutal, as with chattel slavery. Others were less so, and a few were paternalistic in a way which reflected familial care. Again for conjecture's sake, let us assume that virtue was taught, as indeed it was: the master should show care for the slave, the slave should always respect and obey the master. Let us also assume that obligations were stipulated, as indeed they were: both masters and slaves had rights and duties by law and custom in most societies (including biblical ones), albeit wildly unequal rights and duties. Let us further assume that slavery was defended, as indeed it was: its proponents said it was a matter of social necessity and social good. In fact, they claimed, slavery was rooted in the very order of God's universe and was a matter of nature itself.

The day came, first here, then there, and never without conflict, when slavery itself was condemned as inherently immoral. What caught on among people was the moral vision of the fundamental equality of all persons and their right to be free. The slaves had long known the truth of the yearning for freedom and their dignity and equality in God; but eventually it gained credence among the socioeconomically privileged as well, especially when they were subjected to economic and military pressure! In any case, those who were once dismissed as utopian dreamers, because they had imagined that a society without slavery was possible, were finally vindicated. And despite the fact that many remnants of master/slave morality still exist today—the continuing high incidence of domestic violence against women and children is one brutal example—no one makes an overt moral case for reinstitutionalizing slavery. While for centuries the moral vision of those with power, and even of many without, could not conceive of society *without* slavery, now no society includes it as a necessary part *of* its moral vision.

There have been other shifts in moral vision, some of them still in process. Many people today strain for a moral vision which considers the welfare not only of the human community, but all life. The search is for a "biocentric" ethic in place of an "anthropocentric" one, thereby expanding the sense of obligation, value, and virtue to include all life, not only human life.[31] To cite another contemporary example, virtue, value, obligation, and moral vision itself are being criticized and reconstructed in light of the treatment of women, and with a view to women's reality itself.[32] A third example of one in which the dangers of a technological mind-set bent on domination and control is redressed by offering a new "conceptual frame" for viewing the world. Jeremy Rifkin writes:

Within the old conceptual frame, it is impossible ever to conceive of a nuclear free world or a world without genetic engineering. As long as we continue to believe that our security can only be won by maximizing power, advantage, and control, we will never be able to give up nuclear weapons or the genetic engineering of life. It is only by radically rethinking our ideas about the nature of security that we can begin to imagine a world without the ever present reality of these two technologies. By exchanging empathy for power, equity for advantage, borrowing and indebtedness for growth and expansion, and participation and caring for control and manipulation we establish a new reference point for insuring the security of each individual and the species as a whole. There is no room for nuclear weapons or genetic engineering in a world that defines itself as a single family, living in a single community, inhabiting a common ecosystem, enclosed in a single globe.[33]

We should add that not every shift in moral vision is a major one, as this last example and the ones just preceding it would be. The life of the surgeons might well have gone on much the same as before, with the important exception of their view and treatment of the differently abled.

We should also add that the function of some biblical materials is precisely the reorientation of the moral life which a different moral vision brings. The parables of Jesus do this by recasting conventional relationships and offering a different way of seeing them. The visions of the prophets do the same in their setting.

In conclusion, moral vision establishes the reference point for the other elements in the moral life. It sets the terms for that which will be included and excluded. It confers status upon that which is of greater importance and lesser, and, indeed, of no importance at all. Formation of moral character, together with decision making and action, are pervaded by the reigning moral vision. What comprises good and evil, right and wrong reflects this vision. The most basic moral notions we have—what is good, right, and fitting—make sense or fail to make sense to us in light of the particular moral vision we embrace. Our moral vision is our sense of the total environment within which the moral life is lived.[34]

An image from the world of television conveys the meaning of moral vision as the "framing" component of the moral life. Producers of a television show have a loose-leaf book they term their "bible." It is a basic tool of the trade. The contents of their bible provide the structure, general direction, and basic framework for the series they will produce, though not the exact course for each particular show in the series. The bible includes the baseline character development for the various roles and it lays out the "structural" relationships between them. It is a kind of map to the terrain which will become the home territory of the individual shows. It is the master script which sets the terms for developing the particular episodes.

The bible's own script can be changed, of course. It is not fixed, it is a loose-leaf book. But to rewrite it is to alter the series itself and decisively affect the character of each show in it. "Moral vision" is that dimension of the moral life which functions as its "bible."[35]

Scripture and Moral Agency

This concludes the general introduction to the chart, and to moral virtue, value, obligation, and vision in particular. The chapters which immediately follow provide extensive introduction to elements not yet treated here—character formation and decision making. We close the present discussion with four items important to Scripture and ethics.

1. Virtue, value, obligation, and vision each has its opposite in ethics—vice; disvalue; disobedience, or moral violation; and moral

myopia, or perversion. Just as "moral" and "immoral" both belong to the moral world (recall the discussion at the outset of this chapter) so each of these pairs belongs to the generic meaning of the terms we have used. Both "virtue" and "vice" belong to the discussion of "virtue"; both fulfilling moral duties and violating them belong to "obligation," etc. A fuller account of Christian ethics than we can provide here would necessarily include detailed treatment of each pair, and a look at Scripture would offer resources for that.[36]

2. Virtue, value, obligation, and vision are teaching aids for illuminating dimensions of the moral life which surface daily in our experience. They, like all concepts, are abstractions which can be helpful to understanding, but which do not have a life of their own. They are drawn from the lived moral life and exist only to serve it. Furthermore, each illumines only certain aspects of the moral life, and thus none is adequate as the organizing concept for the whole. This is important to say because in the long history of Christian ethics each of these has now and again been elaborated as *the* form of Christian ethics and as *the* focus of the Christian moral life. To do so is always misleading and gives rise to serious distortions and omissions. These terms belong together as a plural presence; wisdom resists treating them as discrete ethical systems or summations of what the whole of the moral life is about. Christian ethics certainly is an ethic of character formation and virtue; but it is not this alone. Christian ethics prizes social values, some more than others; yet the realization of moral value in society does not exhaust the meaning and dimensions of the Christian moral life. Christian ethics understands full well that moral obligations exist— others make claims upon our lives and we upon theirs; life itself is rife with moral claims. Yet Christian ethics cannot be reduced to duty alone. Christian ethics would certainly not be Christian ethics apart from an overarching moral vision that encompasses all creation. Still, this embracing vision of the good in God cannot of itself substitute for the other elements. Particular virtues, values, and obligations must yet be stipulated and acted upon.

In a word, any adequate Christian ethic includes all these elements and is careful to exclude none. Bringing them to conscious expression is, to repeat, not a task done for itself, but for the sake of the community's moral life.

Dorothy Emmet's helpful image of a moral prism can be borrowed and adapted. The light which enters the prism is the moral life as we

63

experience it in undifferentiated fashion. The prism itself is the medium for separating the elements present in the light (something like our chart and the discussion of its elements). The differentiated light which emerges from the prism lets us see that which comprises the moral life we live. Following the analogy, we recognize that "virtue" is the name we give for what we now experience as the color blue, "value" the color red, etc., until the primary colors of the moral life have been seen and described. We should not mistake the moral life itself for just one of the emerging colors; all of them together blend to make the kind of light initially entering the prism.[37] An inadequate ethic reduces the Christian moral life to one or two colors only and then mistakes its portrayal for the moral life itself.[38]

3. The Bible not only reveals these four dimensions as present in the life of biblical communities, it promotes all four. In ways to be detailed later, the Bible names and helps form and name virtues and values, encourages and specifies obligations, and creates and renews moral vision. A badly truncated use of Scripture reduces the moral use of the Bible to an ethics of duty only, or of virtue or value, or some grand vision as a general moral framework but nothing more. Wise use of Scripture is sensitive to the varied dimensions of the moral life embedded in the biblical texts themselves, and in our own lives. We should read our lives in the light of Scripture and Scripture in the light of our lives, with the expectation that in both quarters—Scripture and our experience—the moral life is considerably richer than we commonly perceive.

4. The Bible emphasizes some dimensions of the Christian life which our chart does not. The chart works only with a limited set of formal concepts which are shared by Christian and other versions of the moral life. It is vital that the neglected dimensions be discussed later. Most important are those of theological substance, chiefly the understanding of God and the symbols through which God and world are understood in relation to one another. For the moment, we mention only the following. A vital base point of every Christian ethic is the understanding and interpretation of God. In terms we will develop later, every Christian ethic views the Christian moral life as set within a "story" grander than its own, namely "God's story." We intimated this earlier when we spoke of the habit of Jews and Christians to read all of history in theological/moral terms, as part of the drama of all creation. Now we must underscore that a *particular* understanding and interpretation of

God is always present in any Christian ethic and is always important to it. Of special significance are the christological choices, since the Christian claim is that God has come to clearer expression in Jesus Christ than anywhere else. To illustrate: If "God's story" is that in Christ God is bringing about the divinization of humanity and the transfiguration of all life (the teaching of Eastern Orthodoxy), the understanding of the Christian moral life will line up with this theological claim.[39] If God-in-Christ is the liberator from evil in the hearts and minds of human beings as well as in the structures of human society itself, and human beings are themselves empowered by God as co-participants in the drama of redemption (the teaching of liberation theologies), then the ethical implications will move along lines appropriate to this rendering of "God's story."[40] If, by way of contrast, God-in-Christ is the preserver of an immutable moral order reflected in traditional patterns of social arrangements (as in some earlier versions of Christian natural law ethics), then the moral life will have a very different face on it than the liberationist portrayal.[41]

This is not the time to draw this discussion forward, beyond recognizing, with Tom Driver, that "when we do Christology we are doing ethics, and when we do ethics we are doing something or other with Christ. . . ."[42] For the moment what is important is to alert readers that for Christian ethics the moral life is always set within theological claims, and the theological substance of these claims will always affect all other terms. The particular rendition of the God story will give particular content to the understanding of virtue, value, obligation, and vision. When basic theological changes occur, there will be ramifications for the whole of the moral life. For this reason, the meaning of key Christian symbols such as cross, resurrection, and the sacraments, are always important for Christian ethics; they carry the God story which frames the Christian life.

Having posted this, we must return to the chart to discuss the formation of moral character.

4

THE ELEMENTS OF CHARACTER FORMATION

It was far and away the worst carnage ever—60,000,000 casualties. But it was over, and the last of the Axis powers, Japan, was surrendering. As he received the surrender of the emperor, Gen. Douglas MacArthur included this among his remarks: "The problem [of an enduring peace] is basically theological and involves spiritual recrudescence and improvement of human character. It must be of the spirit, if we are to save the flesh."[1]

Decades later, in 1985, *The Public Interest* printed its 20th anniversary issue. Its lead article, by Professor James Wilson of Harvard, was entitled "The Rediscovery of Character." The opening lines were:

> The most important change in how one defines the public interest that I have witnessed—and experienced—over the last 20 years has been a deepening concern for the development of character in the citizenry. An obvious indication of this shift has been the rise of such social issues as abortion and school prayer. A less obvious but I think more important change has been the growing awareness that a variety of public problems can only be understood—and perhaps addressed—if they are seen as arising out of a defect in character formation.[2]

Wilson does not list any of the "variety of public problems" for which defective character is a cause. The absence of an enduring peace would certainly be on MacArthur's list, and perhaps Wilson's.

We certainly agree with MacArthur and Wilson that, for good or ill, the state of public life mirrors the quality of character in the citizenry. We further agree with MacArthur that improved character includes spiritual and even theological dimensions. Yet this chapter's attention isn't to public issues as such, but to the more general subject of the elements and dynamics of character formation. We nonetheless agree with the assumption of both Wilson and MacArthur, that public life and character formation are inseparable. Our treatment of character will thus place "community" at the center of the discussion of character formation itself. Our thesis is that character formation and community dynamics go hand-in-hand.

As we noted in chapter two, communities are simply the varied forms of human association. Most are associations which share a history. A community's history provides a common set of interpretations for its members. This in turn is the basis for common actions. Indeed, this history and these interpretations and actions socialize members into a pattern of life identified as the community's way of life (*bios*). The identity of the members is influenced as they take on the identity of the larger group to which they belong.[3] The formulation is correct: "Our *identities* are formed precisely as we *identify* with the various social forms which bestow meaning on a society and its participants."[4]

For purposes served later, we insert our definition of Christian community here. When we speak of Christian community (or *koinōnia*, to recall the New Testament term) we mean that *community-creating human relatedness which is a consequence of the impact of Jesus.* We postpone extensive discussion of this for the moment, but only because meaningful discussion of Christian community assumes what we must first show—how persons are formed as moral creatures amidst communities.

Primary Words

Martin Buber wrote a famous treatise in 1922, published in English as *I and Thou.*[5] For human beings there are two primary words, said Buber: "I–Thou" (subject to subject), and "I–It" (subject to object). The primary word is not "I," of itself. It is "I–Thou" or "I–It."

We cannot imagine "I" utterly by itself, for a human self does not exist apart from others—human and nonhuman others. It is even literally impossible to imagine a socially disembodied "I," since we conceive, think, and imagine through words, pictures, and gestures

67

which are cultural in origin and social in transmission. Language, both verbal and nonverbal, is already present in the world we enter, and belongs to it. Language is no individual's creation "from scratch"; it is the product and legacy of social relationships of which we are a part from the time we leave the womb, and which far antedate that. Any powers "I" possess are gathered from the worlds of which I am part, including the powers to imagine, reflect, and communicate.

Yet even if we could conceive the "I" by itself, with no help from society, it would still be a secondary word, not a primary one; it would be derived from something more basic. What is more basic is human relatedness. It is foundational for our sense of self, for personhood, for identity. "There is no 'I' taken in itself, but only the 'I' of the primary word 'I–Thou' and the 'I' of the primary word 'I–It,'" Buber writes.[6] "We are, therefore I am," is the way an African proverb expresses it, only to go on: "I am, therefore we are." The *primary* human word is a *relational* one. "In the beginning is relation."[7] "All real living is meeting."[8] Relationship is constitutive of our being.

Since anyone who can read this has already long since lived with the firm sense of being a "self," the idea that we do not begin life that way is initially a strange one. We come to these pages with a strong awareness of ourselves, and we relate all the detail of the world to this center. This is already so much a part of us that we regard it as "natural." That is, while we are aware that we exist amid networks of both stable and changing relationships, we nonetheless tend to exaggerate our separateness and independence because we assume the firm reality of our own "self" at the center. Our consciousness of self is the "given" and the solid point of reference; the remainder is secondary and related to it, or so it seems to us. This is delusory on two counts, however. It inverts the order of consciousness, and it exaggerates the independent existence of the individual.

To get a truer grip on the process of development, we must understand how the sense of "I" arises in the first place. The infant does not begin with a strong consciousness of self. The infant acquires it as she or he notices other realities. There is little more at the outset than that which is "not-I." There is only "other." What "other" is, has to be learned. One other is "mother." Another is "father." Yet another is "breast" or "bottle." Still another is "hot" or "kitty" or "ouch!" We are drawn from the embrace of the womb forward into the family and then into ever-widening circles. The world becomes more and more differentiated through a complex, enormous, and amazing learning process; and the sense of self, of "I," *is part of the differentiation.* "I" is not the sure, centered, self-conscious reality *prior to* and *independent of* all this "other." "I" *becomes,* and continues to become, amid living relationships which affect the "I."

The relationships aren't only with other human beings. Our mention of "kitty" and "bottle" indicates more. Buber writes movingly of an "I–Thou" relation with a tree. Even inanimate realities may be subjects as well as objects to us, and the ingredients of living relationships. In fact the key words "social" and "society" do not connote human-to-human relationships only. What humans do with the nonhuman environment is part *of* society. Indeed, one of the characteristics of the modern world (from the Renaissance forward) is the increased power to affect more and more of the world. The fate of both nature and history is tied in ever greater measure to the fate of humanity, as nature is gathered up into history. Readers should be aware that when we use the words "society" and "history," or speak of "human relatedness," these terms include *all* that humans touch, not only other humans. A critical implication is that the world of human welfare, narrowly defined, is not the only sphere of moral responsibility. Human/nonhuman relations are morally crucial as well. The wider environment is the subject of ethics.[9]

In summary, then, becoming a self never takes place ". . . through my agency (alone), nor can it ever take place without me. I become through my relation to the Thou; as I become I, I say Thou."[10] (To complete Buber's own line of causation, we must add: "As I say Thou, I become I.") Consciousness of self grows in tandem with the consciousness of others, including nonhuman entities.

Two important implications follow. First, we exist only in relation to something outside ourselves. Apart from social relatedness—or "community"—"we" do not exist. Neither do "I." This basic fact is vital to the discussions of moral formation. Moral relations are *always* dimensions of social relations in which "personal" cannot be separated from "social," nor "individual" from "community." Here—in social relations—is where ethics talk is at home.[11]

Second, there is already something profoundly "moral" in the very structuring of human relatedness. Our existence is so ordered that we are realized, or fulfilled, *only by taking care of that which is not us.* If we do not care for that which is *not* us, our own self is stunted, injured, lost, even destroyed. There is a deep paradox here, one which surfaces often in biblical materials: Human wholeness arrives as a gift which happens in the unguarded openness of our lives to the lives of others and theirs to ours, and in meeting their needs as they meet ours. Paradoxically, an intense and deliberate focus upon our own self-fulfillment reduces the possibilities of reciprocal relationships, and thus of fulfillment itself. These dynamics give credence to Jesus' word that those who seek to "save" their lives lose them, and those who "lose" them find them. (Matt. 10:39) The paradox reaches a certain pitch in the prayer attributed to St. Francis, and in the call of Jesus to "take up the cross."

> O Divine Master, grant that I may not so much seek
> to be consoled, as to console
> to be understood, as to understand
> to be loved, as to love;
> for it is in giving that we receive,
> pardoning that we are pardoned,
> dying that we are born to eternal life.

That we have given our lives in caring for that which is not us, in giving ourselves over to others, leads Christian ethics to ascribe high moral status to sacrifice, not least self-sacrifice. (Jesus' cross is the potent symbol of this in Christian ethics.) Self-sacrifice is sometimes called for, to be sure. But it is crucial to remember that self-sacrifice is not the key term for Christian ethics, nor is suffering—*community* is, and community is extended to encompass the well-being of all creation. A Christian ethic is an ethic of receiving care and giving it, in ever-widening circles. Self-sacrifice is the offering sometimes necessary, and the price sometimes exacted, in order to create or preserve community. Sacrifice exists for the sake of mutuality and community and has no meaning apart from these. It accepts suffering in order to forge or retain redemptive bonds. The cross is the hard road sometimes necessary for reconciliation.

Social Dynamics and the Self

We must say more about the dynamics of our formation as moral creatures. How is moral agency itself acquired? What is the role of community in character formation?

There is a considerable and growing body of literature on moral development. The concern itself is hardly new to Christian ethics. The "catechesis" of the second and third centuries (instruction in "the Way") included moral nurture as a dimension of learning the Christian story. Monasticism and other spiritual disciplines have long sought to cultivate Christian character and a life of virtue. John Wesley's "societies" and other pietist and revivalist conventicles have pursued the same end. Jonathan Edwards described the "religious affections" and "the nature of true virtue" at great length, and Horace Bushnell cast the Christian life in the terms of "nurture." Recent attention to moral development in Christian ethics draws less from its own historical examples, however, and more from newer work in cognitive and developmental psychology, especially theories which posit distinct stages of human development.[12] This new literature is certainly worthy of study but we cannot review it here. What we offer instead are names for facets of the moral self, together with a description of key factors in their formation. Studies in developmental psychology and social psychology would add detail to what we provide in these next pages.[13]

Social World.   There are two meanings of the phrase, "social world," and both are important to ethics. The social world is, on one plane, simply the total material environment of a people at any given moment in its history. The make-up of the population, the kind of economy, the level of technology, the arrangements for governing, the manner of education, the contact with other peoples and their worlds—all these belong to the social world. On another plane, the social world refers to the socially constructed reality of a people—the shared meanings that comprise a culture and way of life. Worldview is part of this—the picture people have of the way things are; and so is ethos—the tone, quality, and character of people's life together.[14] These two together—the material and nonmaterial environments—make up the total environment we call the social world. The significance for character formation, and thus for Christian ethics, can best be understood by looking at both planes together under the rubric of "social location." Social Location is a way of talking about our *particular* social world.

Social Location.   All our knowing is socially located, including moral knowledge. Our knowledge of good and evil, and right and wrong, belongs to the groups of which we are a part, and reflects their

71

particular social worlds. Moral knowledge is embedded in group identifications we all have, associated with such distinctions as socioeconomic strata, race, age, and gender; it is embedded in nationality, cultural heritage, religious experience, family experience, and the institutions to which we belong. It resides in the larger patterns and systems of society that make up the material environment and cross over to the nonmaterial one: the economic order—local, regional, national, international; the governance system, and wielding of political power; the cultural system of social communication, with its major sectors in education, the mass media, and the numerous informal ways by which wisdom and instruction are passed from one circle and generation to the next, not least via family and friendship. In all of these, moral knowledge mirrors specific structures of dominance and subordination as well as mutuality, and of various and varying levels of privilege and deprivation as well as equality and reciprocity.

The more visible aspects of the social location of moral knowledge are only the more noticeable ones, but not necessarily more influential. Moral knowledge is always a vital aspect of the nonmaterial environment of any particular social world—the reigning ideas, the broad frameworks of meaning and orientation, and the half-hidden worlds of heart, mind, and imagination that make up a certain worldview and ethos. All these have their home in our social world. They express that world and mold it, and *in* that world they are a force for character formation.

The role of language in our particular social world and in our moral formation requires special mention. Language isn't "external" to our social reality, as though it were a neutral tool for expressing experience which is somehow separate from language. Language carries our sense of how the world is. It transmits the experience of our relations and the social patterns of which they are part. It mirrors our place in society and conveys our sense of who we are. It either reproduces our social reality or reinterprets it so as to alter it. "Language is the main bearer and transmitter of 'social structure.' "[15]

The renowned professor of psychology Jerome Bruner reports in *Child's Talk* that even before learning words the infant learns what language is for. In the small interactions between the child and its caretakers, especially mother, conventions are learned which differentiate and transmit "the world." In mastering language, Bruner argues, children learn the ways of their culture and their place in it. He goes on to say that the words and images learned, and the ways they connect and frame the seemingly disconnected experiences of our lives, shape the way we experience life itself. Language actively determines what we look for, what we find, and what it means.[16]

Among other things, this tells us that the social world we are born into is already saturated with moral judgments which are embedded in language itself. We appropriate them as soon as we learn words, gestures, and other forms of communication—well before we become moral decision makers and actors ourselves, well before we become active "moral agents." Specific words encode judgments which are widely shared and socially powerful. Thus "everyone knows" that "murder," "rape," and "cruelty" are wrong, and "loving," "sharing," and "keeping your word" are good and right. As soon as we speak, our vocabulary is replete with moral content and connotation.[17]

All these elements—language, group identities, ideological and institutional patterns—compose the complex, dynamic reality of our social location. They supply a highly particular world. We are part of *this* world, rather than another. Our moral agency can only be understood with a view to this specific world, its development, and its impact upon us.

The impact is not one-way. Persons, whether belonging to groups or acting almost solitarily, fashion the varying elements of their social world together in their own ways. We "work on" the substance of social experience in a manner that it is genuinely our own rendering. We order the various elements and their meanings into patterns that make them ours.

In this process we do far more than simply "take on" society. We inject that which we fashion "back into" society. Our own subjective meanings and the ways of life which express them become part *of* society itself. These meanings and their social embodiments thus take on public character. They have a life both inside us and among us, and extend well beyond our immediate reach. In a word, we are always in society; society is always in us; society is always more than our lives alone.

Society and self are, then, twin-born. We could not exist apart from our highly specific worlds. We are also co-creators of those worlds. Our social location forms us, and we contribute to it.

The salient point is that *moral character is formed in this interactive*

73

process. It occurs in a communal process of specific, changing, and continuing social relations. *"Character" is the name given to the moral being of a person or group as that is forged into a distinctive constellation.*[18]

The etymology of "character" is helpful. The English term is a 14th-century word taken from the Greek *charaktēr,* which means "engraving tool." By extension it also refers to the mark made by an engraving tool. Eventually it came to mean the distinctive mark of a person—the person's "character" exhibited those qualities which distinguished that person from another. This is the meaning just given. But there is a second meaning. A person "with character" is someone with judgment to know what is right and courage to do what is good. "Character," in other words, is the mark of those who are morally discerning and committed to acting on their convictions.[19]

All this leads us from the crucial factor of social dynamics and character into the elements of character itself. For the moment we will focus on the first meaning of character just given, and describe the following elements: perception, dispositions, and intentions. "Faith" must be discussed as well, for reasons which will become obvious.

Faith and Perception

James Gaffney begins his article "Values, Victims and Visions"[20] with an account of Robert Browning's poem "The Ring and the Book." The poem is about a celebrated murder case in Italy. A married teenager and her elderly parents were killed by the young woman's middle-aged husband. The husband believed that his wife and a young priest had each been unfaithful, together! Because the priest had taken religious vows, his case was transferred from a civil to an ecclesiastical court and was eventually decided in a criminal tribunal of the Vatican.

Gaffney's fascination with the poem, however, is with Browning's telling and retelling of the tale. Time after time it is retold, by different people of varying social backgrounds and ambitions, and varied degrees of involvement in the case. The bare facts remain the same throughout, but they are seen from many perspectives. As Gaffney comments:

> We discover that what one account presents us as momentous appears trivial in another. We find motives not even suspected in one taken for granted in another. We see heroes transformed into villains and villains

into non-entities. Virtues turn into vices, bystanders into participants, and neutral circumstances into compelling influences. Each account is a peculiar mosaic of lights and shadows, and the pattern of vividness and obscurity constantly changes. Hence, for the reader, even though a definite fabric of facts remains substantially unaltered, the moral picture is repeatedly transformed. What causes the transformations are the different human view-points from which it is perceived.[21]

Even the most ordinary moral cases appear differently to different people. "It all depends, it all depends . . . " we say about judgments offered in most any controversial case, even one with "a definite fabric of facts" which "remain substantially unaltered."[22] We mean that it all depends on your point of view. Yet we don't always recognize that differences of perspective depend on how viewers "are enabled and accustomed to do their seeing."[23]

How *do* people come to see, in moral matters? Rabbi Heschel confirms Gaffney's observation:

Facts of personal existence are not merely given. They are given through self-comprehension, and self-comprehension is an interpretation, since every act of self-comprehension involves the application of value judgments, norms, and decisions, and is the result of a selective awareness, reflecting a particular perspective. . . .[24]

But why "a selective awareness?" Why inevitably "a particular perspective?"

At birth each of us enters fresh into a moral and social world already rich and crowded. Society is a fellowship not only of those now living and those soon to be born, but those who have gone before. The moral legacies of the past and the creations of the present live on. They reside in the ways of culture and its institutions, in the habits of heart and mind and the memories and hopes of the people. They are expressed in the varied objects and symbols of human love, trust, allegiance, and commitment, and manifest themselves in the forms of religious devotion, in the choice of cultural heroes and heroines, in the direction of a nation and its people, and in people's causes, creeds, and ways of life. Moral legacies are passed along in the traditions and rituals people practice, the stories they tell, and the songs they sing. All these are effective conveyers of the moral world we enter as we enter our social world.

The moral legacies, expressed in these varied forms, display what is valued in a society. They hold aloft what is deemed of overriding worth, and locate what the society, or sectors of it, esteems as "the good." The priorities among the moral legacies are the society's own moral priorities.

Yet our internalizing of our social and moral world is selective. We integrate some, but not all, of society's objects of trust and devotion; some, but not all, of the images, stories, and other carriers of meaning which are present in our world; some, but not all, of the reigning commitments and perspectives.

The selective internalization and integration forms our moral character. The internalized meanings interpret events, order experience, and form our expectations. In the process they yield considerable moral coherence and continuity as we move through life's experiences. (Jerome Bruner, cited above, listens carefully to people tell their life stories. He notes especially those images and words which seem to connect otherwise disconnected events. He mentions that this "internalized guidance system" goes far to shape the way people will experience future events as well.)[25]

Incidentally, there is considerable evidence that after the transition from adolescence to adulthood, basic traits of moral character do not alter much. William James, who had only the powers of his own observation at hand, thought character was "set in plaster" at about age 25. This does not mean that behavior does not change thereafter. It means that, for more-or-less morally formed adults, change is more likely explained by changed roles, responsibilities, and circumstances, than by basic change in moral character itself.[26]

The foregoing can be summarized: Our selective internalization of society, and our selective integration of its morality, molds *the way we see the world, think about it, and respond to it.*

The language of "faith" is appropriate here. "Faith" indicates both the fact of having dominant objects of trust and centers of value, and the content of these. Thus a person, or group, not only "has faith" (trust in something or other) but also has "a faith" (beliefs which help order experience).[27] Martin Luther put it as follows:

> To have a God is simply to trust and believe in one with our whole heart.
> As I have often said, the confidence and faith of the heart alone make

both God and an idol. . . . Whatever your heart clings to and confides in, that is really your God.[28]

When we enter society, it is already alive with its own functional "deities" (those which are earnestly trusted and believed). What these "gods" have to say is communicated in the myriad ways to which we have already referred. The functional deities tell us how our lives are to be lived. More to the point, the selective internalization of the "gods"—making society's most prized loves and loyalties our own—largely determines what we see. For this reason, two people of different character witnessing the same event may very well perceive, understand, and respond differently. "Seeing"—or perception—is far more than simple observation, then. It is selecting, interpreting, and evaluating. Some horizons become the horizons of the person's, or the group's, interest, and some never appear as matters of interest at all. Some data fall within the range of vision, some go unnoticed altogether or are ignored. Some issues are deemed morally significant and others are not. Some fail to register at all as moral matters to us, while our neighbors regard them as issues of burning immediacy. "It all depends, it all depends . . ." upon our view of things. In short, who we are and are becoming, in accord with the faith we hold, largely determines what we see. *How we come to be* heavily influences *what we come to see.*

To return to *The Ring and the Book* murder case: Even while the jury knows that "the definite fabric of facts remains substantially unaltered," nonetheless "the moral picture is repeatedly transformed" with each account, as each account "is a peculiar mosaic of lights and shadows."[29] The transformation of moral perceptions reflects varied perspectives; and these are finally best explained by the tellers' own social location and experience, by the formation of their character in their communities.

It is difficult to exaggerate the significance of faith and perception for the moral life. A Chinese proverb expresses it well: "Ninety percent of what we see lies *behind* our eyes." And there is W. I. Thomas's axiom: "What we define as real is real in its consequences." Our perceptions aren't mental photographs, they are highly active images. Our faith and perception "define" our reality. They help set the direction and limits of our conduct, generating certain choices and actions rather than others, underlining some issues as more significant than

77

others, and disposing us to some responses rather than others. Why we do one thing and not the other, indeed why we do something rather than nothing at all, depends on our apprehension of things. At the end of specific responses dangles our faith. In a word, *believing is seeing.*[30]

If it is difficult to exaggerate the moral significance of faith and perception, it is equally difficult to exaggerate the importance of particularity and social location. *Which* objects of faith and *which* social experience, *which* images and stories, have been internalized and integrated, matter immensely for morality. Each of us has only a selective awareness and a particular perspective. We are an expression of some communities, but never all; and we carry only some aspects of the communities of which we are part, never all.

Implications for Ethics. We interrupt the discussion of character elements to make two comments important for Christian ethics in particular.

1. There is a normative faith claim for Christian ethics, the biblically based claim that God as seen in Jesus and experienced in the Spirit is the final source of moral goodness and the object of ultimate trust, love, loyalty, and commitment. There are innumerable other "goods" in our moral world, of course; but they are to take their place in keeping with the will of God as the definitive moral measure.

Within its social world the Christian community has the task of forming perception and character in accord with this faith. The community is the socializing agent for the faith. A major part of this work consists of immersing members in the particular stories, traditions, symbols, and lessons (both positive and negative) of past and present faith communities. These become essential content as the community helps to define moral goodness.

2. *Critical social analysis* is an indispensable requirement of an adequate Christian ethic. Without it we simply fail to uncover the social-moral world. The reason is this: Our provincial world is often so powerfully present that we effectively identify it as *the only real world*, and act accordingly. We assume that the reigning moral standards of our world are *the* standards, and we treat them as though they were universal rather than parochial. Critical analysis uncovers the "particularity" of morality and exposes its limited dimensions. Differently said, critical social analysis is necessary because assumed moral notions go largely unnoticed until they are challenged. Any adequate

ethic challenges, of course—recall our earlier "Greek" distinction of "ethics" from "morality," and the tension created by the refusal of ethical reflection to accept morality on the grounds of custom and habit alone, or any other authorities. Critical social analysis is helpful and necessary in order to effectively investigate assumed moral notions and hold them up to criticism. It belongs to the task with which Christian ethics, as a species *of* ethics, is charged.

Critical social analysis is needed for another, quite different, reason. A Christian ethic which does not have routine ways of investigating concrete social-moral reality—i.e., does not undertake social analysis—will not have credibility when it makes specific moral judgments and offers recommendations. It will be too far from life as it is actually lived, and people will instinctively recognize its irrelevance. In short, social analysis is vital to Christian ethics for both critical and constructive tasks.

We return to the discussion of the elements of character.

Dispositions and Intentions

Dispositions are our *persisting attitudes,* those character traits we possess over a long enough time that they become part of our temperament. Intentions are *expressions of character which show aim, direction, purpose;* they express the volitional side of character. We will take each of these, dispositions and intentions, in turn.

Let us say that our conduct is regularly characterized by hopefulness and compassion in some areas and by resignation and contempt in others. We care deeply about the condition of the neighborhood and the welfare of the people on the block, for example, but we "can't stand" politicians and don't think voting makes a whit of difference. When these attitudes are not simply episodic but carry over from one situation and circumstance to another, then we become "disposed" to these responses; we act and react in particular and relatively consistent ways.

This point—recurrence, consistency—is important. One greedy act does not a greedy person make. Conversely, an occasional friendly gesture does not make a genuinely friendly person. What makes greedy or friendly people are internalized traits which dispose them to a consistency of expression. We are "attitudinally" greedy or friendly (or

79

both). We display these as characteristic inclinations, as our "bent" or character. Or, recalling the etymology, these are the engravings of character.

These persisting attitudes are, then, the *habits* of heart and mind in the moral life. They constitute the customary patterns which provide continuity as we move from one decision to another. Dispositions often become so "natural" to us that we make many of our decisions reflexively. We don't confront most choices by asking: "Now what do we (or I) believe in, and what does that mean in this case?" Rather we just "know," or intuit, what our response will be.

We may occasionally act in ways which are out of keeping with these habits. What is significant, however, is that this is recognized, often with a comment as direct as "That is not like her at all!" or "It was so uncharacteristic of him to act like that."

Dispositions are synchronized with the way we see life. They are the attitudinal expressions of our basic perception of things. They are also "in character" with our intentions. But intentions are distinct from dispositions. Intentions signal deliberately chosen and self-conscious activity. They are volitional in a way attitudes are not. They express the will. They manifest purposive, goal-oriented determinations. Thus we plan a course of action and intend to achieve a certain goal, or avoid a particular fate. We vow to live in line with a basic commitment, and willingly take on a specific set of responsibilities.

Like dispositions, intentions ward off fragmentation in the moral life. They provide coherence as we move from situation to situation and decision to decision. Consecutive and even widely separated choices line up with our intentions, at least our basic and broad intentions. Our basic intentions thus provide coherence, provided they are not wholly at odds with one another!

If intentions give direction to choice, and dispositions provide some patterns of response, then our choices and actions are not wholly situation-driven. Together with moral perception, dispositions and intentions set the boundaries and direction of our conduct, determine what we consider morally significant, craft the nature of our responses to issues, and provide stability in our behavior.

A fuller account of character and its formation would discuss other elements. Motives and motivation are familiar aspects. They are the springs of intentions, the internal factors that move people to act. Moral "style" is another facet of character; it refers to the manner in which moral traits are expressed. We speak, for example, of the "sensitive" or "insensitive" way someone responds to a person in need.[31]

Conscience. We list conscience separately because it isn't a discrete element of character so much as the form taken by moral character as a whole *when character functions as an ethical compass.* Conscience orients us to proceed in a certain direction, and registers when we deviate or when moral perplexities and dilemmas appear on the path we have taken. Conscience, then, is closely related to moral perception and does most of its work there, even though it is most conscious to us when we face specific and morally troublesome choices. Roger Shinn, at a conference in Washington, D.C. on public service and public morality, commented to the participants: "Conscience works not primarily by bringing moral standards to bear after policy options have been offered. That is, we do not first shape up a possible program, then judge its morality. The effect of conscience is on our perceptions of a situation and the course of action that we envision. Long before the actual decision, we have been moved by conscience to give attention to some evidence, to envision some possibilities and to exclude others. For that reason, some of the most conscientious people talk least about morality."[32]

Conclusion

Character will be discussed further in later chapters, but we have said enough to arrive at the first half of an important overall conclusion: (1) *Character is the chief architect of our decisions and actions.* Yet this conclusion should not overshadow the point with which we began; namely, that community is the agent of moral formation. So we must amend the conclusion to supply the second half: (2) *Community is the chief architect of character.* It is certainly true that individuals' characters are sometimes better than the communities which formed them; but not often, and never apart from materials which they have gathered from their social world.

Firsthand Accounts

This chapter has been heavy with theory. We would be well served to give some credence to theory by concluding with firsthand accounts which illustrate moral character in action. The illustrations are both negative (showing inadequately developed character) and positive. They include the first meaning of character discussed above—community-influenced moral traits—as well as the second meaning—character as sound moral discernment and commitment.

Often, character is not well formed, and reflects the flaws of morally maldeveloped communities. People's ethical compasses either do not register true north, or do not exist at all. Lacking such a compass, many, in effect, contract out their moral judgments to others. The following is John Ehrlichmann's testimony. Together with Bob Haldeman, Ehrlichmann headed the inner circle of Richard Nixon's White House staff. After his release in 1978 from prison, Ehrlichmann testified to what he had learned on his moral journey.

At the White House the President is the boss, and in 1969 I found myself working for him, taking orders and shaping my schedule to his convenience.

I gave the President advice when it was asked for, but, like everyone else there, I was expected to be faithful to his decisions whether I agreed with them or not.

I reposed vast confidence in Richard Nixon, partly because he was President and partly because I had watched him make a number of thoughtful and sound decisions in times of crisis.

As the Watergate noose tightened in early 1973, I felt instinctively that it was vital for President Nixon to make a clean breast of everything he knew about Watergate and its aftermath if his Presidency was to survive and be effective. (I didn't realize at the time that his full disclosure would have included a confession that in June 1972 he had tried to use the CIA to obstruct the FBI's Watergate investigation.)

When the President declined to "come clean" with the American people, I did what I had been doing for nearly five years: I fell into step with his decision, rather than to chart my own course by my own ethical compass.

I intend never again to abdicate the moral judgments I am called upon to make. I hope I succeed. Nothing I've learned is more important to me.[33]

Similar testimony comes from an earlier administration. At issue was the need for a basic, internalized moral reference point, a guidance system that functioned reasonably well under stress. Chester Bowles was under secretary of state when John Kennedy was president. He wrote the following a month after the unsuccessful attempt of the Kennedy administration to sponsor an invasion of Cuba at the Bay of Pigs and after a period when Kennedy contemplated an assassination of Fidel Castro.

> The question which concerns me most about this new Administration is whether it lacks a genuine sense of conviction about what is right and what is wrong. I realize in posing the question I am raising an extremely serious point. Nevertheless I feel it must be faced.
>
> Anyone in public life who has strong convictions about the rights and wrongs of public morality, both domestic and international, has a very great advantage in times of strain, since his instincts on what to do are clear and immediate. Lacking such a framework of moral conviction or sense of what is right and what is wrong, he is forced to lean almost entirely upon his mental processes; he adds up the pluses and minuses of any question and comes up with a conclusion. Under normal conditions, when he is not tired or frustrated, this pragmatic approach should successfully bring him out on the right side of the question.
>
> What worries me are the conclusions that such an individual may reach when he is tired, angry, frustrated, or emotionally affected. The Cuban fiasco demonstrates how far astray a man as brilliant and well intentioned as Kennedy can go who lacks a basic moral reference point.[34]

A third case shows the presence of a community's character. In this case it is rather strong, positive moral character, though not unambivalent.

The events occurred in a small Minnesota town in November 1987. The night before a high school class reunion, the telephone rang for Dean Lechner. The caller told him that if he attended the reunion, people would leave.

After years away, Lechner had just come home. He had AIDS and was slowly dying. The local paper ran a banner headline, "AIDS has moved into Waseca County." Friends called Lechner from San Francisco to ask how he could possibly live in a little town that had no experience with anyone openly gay, to say nothing of someone infected with the AIDS virus. The *New York Times* account continues:

> The answer would come at the grocery store, the lunch diner, the post office, the barber shop.

The owner of a hair salon here, which Mr. Lechner had stopped patronizing for fear he would chase away customers, spotted him downtown and wrapped her arms around him.

"We miss you," said Susan Burn, the owner of Classic Cuts.

"Who are we to judge?" asked Florence Lohmann, the 57-year-old owner of the Busy Bee Cafe, who does not throw away the dishes Mr. Lechner has used. She washes them with the rest.

"That could be my kid or brother," said Dave Condon, 32, who runs the Condon Farm Service feed store. "You don't kick a guy when he's down."

Nearly 200 cards of support were mailed to Mr. Lechner. People sent books, poems, prayers, money. "You're going to need something to read," said a card clipped to a $5 bill. "Take this and buy a magazine."

The account continues and eventually returns to the phone call, with Dean Lechner asking whether the call meant he had given Waseca too much credit. Then he was called by a former classmate who asked him to join her and her husband. They would attend the reunion together. Word of the call "uninviting" Lechner got out. Kent Huntington, a barber and a member of the reunion committee, told the *Times* reporter: "This is horse manure. This poor guy is dying, and now we're shunning him? Dean Lechner went to school here for 12 years and never hurt anybody."

Dean Lechner attended the reunion. No one left.[35]

Even with all the material of this chapter, we have still not said enough about character and community. The next chapter continues the discussion, but in a quite different vein.

5

CHARACTER FORMATION AND SOCIAL STRUCTURE

Our lives are irreducibly social. They are lived and fashioned amidst large-scale social entities and small-scale ones, amidst relationships of intimacy and intensity and those of geographical and psychological distance, amidst domains and degrees of privacy and of public engagement, amidst institutional patterns and social configurations of all kinds. Any assumption that we can talk of Christian ethics apart from these is blind to the nature of human "being." Moral relations are always dimensions of social ones.

There is a level of complexity here which we must honor. If we do not, our discussion of character will mislead badly. In turn, we will misunderstand the moral life. The issue is a particular, serious twist—or several twists—in the relationship of social structures and character. The discussion of community and character has not faced this complex relationship.

In *Moralities of Everyday Life* John Sabini and Maury Silver report two diary entries from a "Professor Dr. Hans Hermann Kremer."

September 6, 1942. Today, Sunday, excellent lunch: tomato soup, half a hen with potatoes and red cabbage (20g. fat), sweets and marvelous ice (cream). . . . in the evening at 8.00 hours outside for a Sonderaktion.

September 9, 1942. This morning I got the most pleasant news from my lawyer, Prof. Dr. Hallermann in Munster, that I got divorced from my wife on the first of the month. (Note: I see colors again, a black curtain is drawn back from my life!) Later on, present as doctor at a corporal punishment of eight prisoners and an execution by shooting with small-calibre rifles. Got soap flakes and two pieces of soap. . . . In the evening present at a Sonderaktion, fourth time.[1]

If readers do not already know, the doctor's diary is from Auschwitz, and "Sonderaktionen" ("Special Actions") were the more spectacular atrocities. A not uncommon one was the burning of live prisoners, often children, in pits 20 x 40 x 50 meters, on banks of wood soaked in gasoline.[2]

How is it, Sabini and Silver ask, that "a Sonderaktion and soap flakes (can) possibly be mentioned in the same breath?"[3] "How could someone participate in mass murder without showing some emotion—distress, anger, or even glee?"[4] At the end of the paragraph they conclude: "What needs explication is not so much how the sadist could murder, but how the murder could come to have the same importance as soap flakes."[5]

How indeed? A wholly satisfactory answer eludes us. Evil so massive as this, yet so "minute" (down to the last detail), so intimate and at the same time so categorically impersonal, escapes the capacity to fathom. It can be remembered in the horror of the stories and their blinding images—and there may be no other way. Generations can also be imbued with the plea, "Never again!" but the evil will always defy explanation. Theologians have a phrase for it—"the mystery of iniquity." It means that the magnitude of evil in human life is enormous and exists as part of a human condition so fundamentally flawed that we feel as much victim as perpetrator, and are often both.[6] Furthermore, this enormous evil seems in the end not only beyond our comprehension but beyond our ability to redress. Yet even this sober realization is inadequate as an explanation of monstrosities of holocaust dimensions.[7] Perhaps only silence can communicate.

Still, we must try to make our point. The alternative is a disabling impotence.

Is Professor Kremer evil? Yes, unequivocally. But is he only evil? If he is, how should we understand him, *as* evil? Sabini and Silver tell us no more of Kremer. We cannot therefore make an informed judgment about his character beyond what we might infer from his diary. Let us conjecture, however, that he was not unlike other administrators in the camps. Let us posit that he enjoyed Bach, Mozart, and Wagner, and that he was a disciplined and good student. ("Professor Doctor" *was* his title.) Let us also speculate that he was known among his friends as loyal and helpful. He was even willing, amid the frequent scarcities of the war years, to share his goods with friends when their needs clearly exceeded his. Let us say further that he enjoyed a good party and wasn't without a sense of humor. He was not handsome but he took care to be neat in his appearance. He was especially conscientious about regular exercise and pursued as good a diet as wartime conditions permitted.

One area of his life often distressed him—the ruined relationship with Lisa. He in fact felt more emotion toward her, despite time and distance, than he felt toward any of the camp personnel. Sometimes he felt hate and anger toward her, sometimes the last remnants of real love, emotions he felt toward no one in the camp. The divorce came as the lifting of a burden, a welcome ending.

Would this knowledge of Hans Kremer's character and personality explain the brutally routine accounts of September 6 and 9? Certainly not on the face of it. Even a direct encounter with Kremer might well fail to muster an explanation. If we are to understand him, we have to look elsewhere.

In their own search for an explanation, Sabini and Silver discuss mob violence. In mob violence deep and destructive emotions run to the surface, and take the form of fury. Inevitably there is destruction— of goods and property, often of lives. But emotions eventually run their course. Even blood lust is temporarily stated. Hatred cannot be sustained without pause, without relief.[8] Too, emotions are fickle and quickly change. The pleading cry of a child may stop the assailant's club in midair above her mother's head. People can flip from rage and anger to compassion and pity and back to anger again.

Committing genocide requires something far more efficient and reliable than transient and uncertain emotions. Bureaucracy must replace the mob. Shared rage must give way to routine compliance with steady, socially legitimated, effective authority.

The requisite bureaucracy would be effective whether staffed by extreme or tepid anti-Semites; . . . it would govern the actions of its members not by arousing passions, but by organizing routines; it would make only distinctions it was designed to make, not those its members might be moved to make, say, between children and adults, scholar and thief, innocent and guilty; it would be responsive to the will of the ultimate authority through a hierarchy of responsibility—whatever that will might be. It was *this bureaucratization of evil . . .* that marked the Third Reich.[9]

This is "systemic evil" in which, as Richard Rubenstein writes: "The bureaucrats drew up the definitions and decrees; the Churches gave evidence of Aryan descent; the postal authorities carried the messages of definition, expropriation, denationalization and deportation; business corporations dismissed their Jewish employees and took over 'Aryanized' properties; the railroads carried the victims to their place of execution."[10]

The face—or facelessness—of this banal organization of evil is reported by Hannah Arendt in her famed account, *Eichmann in Jerusalem.* Eichmann was the long-sought, high-ranking Nazi officer who coordinated the transportation to ship Jews, gypsies, homosexuals, Communists, and others to the death camps. To the surprise of many, he was an utterly bland personality as he went on trial in Israel after being extradited from Argentina. Eichmann seemed to have neither a grand destructive vision nor the requisite vicious values. If there was passion in him at all, it was not to be seen. Much less was there evidence of the conquering, history-creating emotions of the Nordic superrace he had claimed to be part of.[11] There was only

> the colorless bureaucrat, replicated two million times in those who assembled the trains, dispatched the supplies, manufactured the poison gas, filed the paper work, sent out the death notices, guarded the prisoners, pointed left and right, supervised the loading-unloading of the vans, disposed of the ashes, and performed the countless other tasks. . . .[12]

To consider Kremer, like Eichmann, evil, is surely a correct moral judgment. Yet to conclude that by character structure Kremer must therefore have been a sadist, a virulent racist, and a passionate anti-Semite might well miss the point altogether. Maybe it wasn't even true. The evil of the Holocaust, whatever else it was, was monumentally insipid and horrifyingly routine.

None of this implies that no connection existed between the bureaucratization of evil and the collective passions loose in Germany during the Third Reich. Hitler's malignant charisma is legendary, and it inflamed the bigotry and hatred already present in the history of German anti-Semitism. No doubt there is a close link between the emotions of German life and the lockstep efficiency of the millions of dull bureaucrats who worked to carry out the Final Solution. That is a link we must investigate soon, but the question about Kremer is this: Is the issue here an issue of character at all? And if it is, how do we explain his actions with a view both to what we know of his character and what we know of his context? On one level, the answer is yes, Kremer's character is somehow deeply involved here. It must be; Nazi atrocities cannot be explained apart from the kinds of persons who committed them. At the same time, we probably would learn little by confronting Kremer straight-on, as an individual abstracted from his communities and their structure and character. We must treat Kremer with a view to the society and organization of the Third Reich, and see him as part and parcel of the ethos of German life and its social-institutional form—in education, career, workplace, family, clubs, civic and professional organizations, and church. What must be displayed is the way character was shaped within this context; we must look for the particular *interaction* of character and social structure that permitted and nurtured the institutionalization of murder.

Channels

The point of this involved introduction is not to conduct a tirade against "bureaucracy." That, too, would distort the interaction of moral character and social structure. It would isolate character from structure, perhaps in the manner of romanticism and existentialism. There the innocent, alienated, and solitary self is set defiantly over against the inhumanity of great, grey institutions. No, Nazi Germany formed Kremer; and Kremer formed and "performed" Nazi Germany. The personal is political and the political is personal—but in a complex way, and our quest is to recognize the reciprocal influences which move between social dynamics and character formation. When we abstract either social dynamics or character from the other, we understand neither. They are twin-born. Good and evil belong to both, and to both together.

Consider Kremer's setting. A primary social value for Germans decade-in and decade-out was disciplined, thorough work. *"Arbeit macht*

89

frei" was a common proverb—"In work is freedom." Another basic social value was moral responsibility understood as the subordination of personal, individual desires to community obligations and the carrying out of these obligations in meticulous detail. The practical moral instruction was: Be obedient to your superiors and show respect for rank and office. In his 1943 Christmas essay, written as a gift for fellow conspirators against Hitler, Dietrich Bonhoeffer notes these traits.

> In a long history, we Germans have had to learn the need for and the strength of obedience. In the subordination of all personal wishes and ideas to the tasks to which we have been called, we have seen the meaning and greatness of our lives. We have looked upwards, not in servile fear, but in free trust, seeing in our tasks a call, and in our call a vocation. This readiness to follow a command from "above" rather than our own private opinions and wishes was a sign of legitimate self-distrust. Who would deny that in obedience, in their task and calling, the Germans have again and again shown the utmost bravery and self-sacrifice? . . .[13]

At home, through school and church, into the workplace and beyond, there were few corners of German society which did not endorse, encourage, and even glorify disciplined work and obedience to authorities, coupled with a sense of vocation and national pride. Social structures reflected this complex of moral values, benefited from it, and actively encouraged it. Character was formed in ways which rewarded these values, internalized them as virtues, and returned them to society in the form of everyday actions. Kremer contributed his share, in exchange for what he had been given.

These prized social values, which were simultaneously desirable traits of character and crucial to social organization, were essential elements of "the bureaucratization of evil, the institutionalization of murder."[14] The moral slogan which is crafted in sturdy, imperishable iron and arches across the entrance of Auschwitz, reads as follows: *"Arbeit macht frei."*

There are several observations to be made about the case of Kremer and the Holocaust.

First, the reciprocal influences of social values, social organization, and character traits is shown in this brief examination of two social values and virtues (thorough work and obedience to authorities). In this case they interacted with literally deadly results. Blessedly, social values, organization, and character traits often interact in life-giving ways as well. A sound Social Security system, for example, expresses the values of people's contribution to society and a society's responsibility for its members, and provides for people when their powers to provide for themselves have faded, or when society must make room for others in the ranks of the employed. The point is that there is always significant interaction, for good or ill.

Secondly, we underscore what the Kremer example does—the power of social arrangements to channel character and conduct. There were vehement anti-Semites aplenty in Germany, but the Holocaust happened because all manner of tepid anti-Semites and utterly noncommittal people were present and cooperated with evil in numbers even greater than those of the rabid Jew-haters. To which group Kremer belonged we do not know. But all three—the rabid anti-Semites, the tepid ones, and the blandly noncaring—were incorporated into established Nazi institutions which channeled their behavior with an efficiency approaching that of Eichmann's trains. The routinizing of evil happens because social arrangements have the capacity to be conduits of behavior in ways which direct and encourage some character traits and ignore or obstruct others. Happily, the routinizing of good occurs in like manner. This again underlines the need to strive for those social arrangements which make for righteousness (the Hebrew quest for justice) and virtue (the Greek endeavor). It also underlines the fact that any full and true definition of "the good person" and "the good society" can never refer *only* to internalized qualities of character. Rather, "good" refers to the *convergence* of virtue *and* morally right action, and is a convergence which is sometimes promoted by social arrangements and sometimes obstructed by them. But social arrangements are never neutral. Walter Rauschenbusch's insight about the power of social structure, although excessively optimistic and Christian-triumphalist, is still timely.

> An unchristian social order can be known by the fact that it makes good men do bad things . . . a Christian social order makes bad men do good things.[15]

The third observation, or lesson, is this: to understand social structure and character formation in modern, highly differentiated societies, close attention must be given to what in ethics is called "role morality."

91

Some of Kremer's character no doubt carried over from one setting to another. He was likely recognizable as the same person in several different settings. But his roles and tasks varied widely as he went from one assignment to the next. He was trained to be a doctor in one, a student and professor in another, perhaps an athlete in yet a third, and a soldier in a fourth. His social roles included learning the arts of friendship, of being a son, a lover, and husband, and perhaps a father, uncle, or brother as well. In any case, like most who live and work in industrial and technological societies, he found his roles to be differentiated. Different behaviors were required in different settings and were evoked by the way those settings were organized.

In such societies the same personality, possessing the same basic character traits, may in fact exhibit a bewildering range of moral conduct. Why? Because different roles carry different moral content, together with considerable moral pressure. When we step into roles, then, to some degree we accept or take on their moral content, or at least we feel pressure to do so, whether or not what is expected of us in these roles accords well with who we are and wish to be. When we simply "do our job," we are the effective moral agents of these roles, whether we heartily approve or not, and whether we even give it much thought.

The outcome is that sometimes actions in one sphere are totally incongruent with those in another. Many holders of public office and business executives in corporation suites have sanctioned actions in these posts which they would never condone in their roles as parents, friends, or members of their neighborhood civic organization or church. To cite one instance: the most prominent Wall Street figure arrested in the 1986 insider trading scandals was the major contributor to the seminary library of his religious communion; another was the lay leader in his congregation.

None of this means Kremer's character was not evil; it was. Nor does any of this imply Kremer was not morally culpable; he was. Certainly none of this means that character doesn't matter as we move between different roles; it does. But Kremer's was evil action *in conjunction with and as part of a larger, socially structured evil,* and must be understood as such; it was encouraged and made possible by his assigned role. Had Kremer emigrated to New Zealand in 1930 and taught and practiced medicine in Auckland, in all likelihood he would have done none of the despicable things he did as a functionary in

Germany, even though we can well imagine his basic character might have been much the same. His conduct in New Zealand would have reflected the social and work roles there, and the ethos and organization which they reflected and helped create.

We must not finish Kremer's case without citing that of Kurt Waldheim, who was United Nations Secretary-General for eight years and as such was the chief international diplomat for human rights. In June 1986 Waldheim became President of Austria. Not long before his election, but after his term at the U.N., evidence came to light about his links to Nazi atrocities in the Balkans during the time he served as a liaison officer in the German Army Group E. Group E was responsible for sending thousands of Jews, civilians, Partisans, and Allied commandos to forced labor camps and to concentration camps. (Article 6 of the Charter of the International Military Tribunal, adopted by the United States, Britain, the Soviet Union, and France in August 1945, defined "ill-treatment or deportation to slave labor or any other purpose of civilian population of or in occupied territories" as a war crime.) An international commission of military historians, appointed by the Austrian government, concluded that Waldheim had to have known of the atrocities committed by his army unit, that he had done nothing to stop them, and that he had subsequently kept his wartime activities secret. "He repeatedly went along with unlawful acts and thereby made it easier for them to be carried out," the commission's report stated. The commission went on to say, however, that it found no evidence Waldheim was directly guilty of war crimes. On the basis of additional documents not yet released, the U.S. Department of Justice differed on this last point and says that in May 1942, Waldheim must have facilitated the deportation of Yugoslavs in Operations Rogatica and Foca. Waldheim has been placed by the Justice Department on the list of persons barred from entering the United States.

Waldheim himself, after having admitted that he consistently withheld the truth of his whereabouts in WWII, acknowledged to the Austrian people in a nationally televised address that he was not among "the heroes and martyrs" of the war. He went on to say that he had no intention to resign the presidency, and should not. He then pointedly asked Austrians to make a definitive assessment of him and his conduct under the conditions of war and in view of later service:

> You can judge for yourselves whether your President is the young lieutenant—or even the distorted picture of this officer of the Wehrmacht—

or whether your President is a man who, for decades of his life, worked for justice, tolerance and peace. I ask you to form your own judgment.[16]

Waldheim's posing of the choice as an "either/or" forecloses on a third possibility, one for which the evidence is strongest. Namely, he was both the lieutenant who actively complied with evil, and the diplomat who gave years to international human rights and welfare. What helps explain contrary behaviors during decades when there is very little indication that Waldheim's character itself changed is this: His roles and context were markedly different and carried contrasting moral content and behavioral pressures. Our hypothetical emigration to New Zealand for Kremer had its counterpart in Waldheim's actual move into the circles of international diplomacy.

Again, this does not imply in any way that character is neutral. Waldheim's display of character in the 1988 controversy gives credence to an analysis which says his character continues quite capable of being the cooperative lieutenant, the diplomatic UN Secretary-General, and the stubborn President who is not ready to admit guilt, but only regret, about the exigencies of war. Waldheim's character remains a party to all the twists and turns. Different character may well have meant different response to the roles and to the demands he and others faced. In this case, what comes through is the character of a morally shallow individual who is all too susceptible to the pressures, evil as well as good, of roles and their contexts.[17]

Any adequate Christian ethic must, then, be attentive to role morality as roles interact *with* the character of persons in them. Much Christian ethics has ignored role morality, either by giving insufficient attention to social structures and social analysis, or by wrongly assuming that the basic character of the person would straightforwardly determine moral conduct in the roles played. The latter is the naive assumption that good persons will, *ipso facto,* mean a good society, while morally corrupt persons *ipso facto* generate a corrupt society. The pressure and content of roles markedly qualify—and complicate—this assumption, an assumption often held by a too consistent character ethic.

We can conclude that good character is a *necessary* condition for the good society, but not a *sufficient* one. A critical mass of good people is required, but virtue must find its channels in policy and established structure—and this requires more than virtue and character *per se* can provide. It is vital to strive for a society so ordered that it is easier for people to be and do good.

A final lesson follows from the limitations of character ethics: Effective morality requires skills, many of which are quite independent of character. James Fallows makes this point well. Fallows, who was a speechwriter for Jimmy Carter during the first two years of his administration, and a keen observer of the president's character and his abilities, says this about Carter:

> Carter is usually patient, less vindictive than the political norm, blessed with a sense of perspective about the chanciness of life and the transience of its glories and pursuits. I left his service feeling that when the moral choices faced him, he would resolve them fairly; that when questions of life and death, of nuclear war and human destruction were laid upon his desk, he would act on them calmly, with self-knowledge, free of interior demons that might tempt him to act rashly or to prove at terrible cost that he was a man. One factor in our choice of Presidents is their soundness in the ultimate moments of decision, when the finger is poised over the button and the future of the race is at stake. Of all contenders on the horizon, none would be saner or surer than Carter in those moments. In his ability to do justice case by case, he would be the ideal non-lawyer for the Supreme Court. If I had to choose one politician to sit at the Pearly Gates and pass judgment on my soul, Jimmy Carter would be the one.
>
> But if he has the gift of virtue, there are other gifts he lacks.
>
> One is sophistication. It soon became clear . . . Carter and those closest to him took office in profound ignorance of their jobs. They were ignorant of the possibilities and the most likely pitfalls. They fell prey to predictable dangers and squandered precious time.
>
> The second is the ability to explain his goals, and thereby to offer an object for loyalty larger than himself.
>
> The third, and most important, is the passion *to convert himself from a good man into an effective one,* to learn how to do the job. Carter often seemed more concerned with taking the correct position than with learning how to turn that position into results. . . .[18]

Any adequate Christian ethic must promote effective action as well as good character.

Implications

What can we say about the marks of an adequate Christian ethic, drawing from this chapter's discussion and that of the preceding one? Some of the qualities of a good ethic concern its form, some its specific moral content. We discuss the first as elements of an ethic, the second as an insight about human nature.

Elements. An adequate Christian ethic has at least three formal components: 1. A good ethic must demonstrate *conceptual adequacy.* Conceptual adequacy is the way an issue is approached, analyzed, and deliberated. *How* we think about any given matter, and how we do *not* do so, is crucial. The categories we think *with* as we think *about* something are vital for the moral content and outcome. The comment of French theologian-novelist George Bernanos is appropriate: "The worst, the most corrupting lies are problems poorly [or wrongly] stated." [19] Why? Because the functioning moral concepts and notions, and how they frame issues and shape decisions, always have profound moral dimensions themselves. How Kremer's basic moral perception functioned and what moral "grid" he used as he thought about Jews, German society, and his own duty, was vital for his actual behavior. In his case the conceptions were, from a moral point of view, disastrously inadequate and, in the end, criminal. But the larger point is the importance of sound conceptual adequacy in ethics. Without it we do not grasp the meaning and implications of our actions.

"Metaethics" is the technical name for the branch of ethics which investigates the categories people use when they "do ethics." Metaethics tests the adequacies of ethical categories and makes any recommendations for their revision.

2. *Social requisites,* or requirements, comprise the second component which must be in place or created if desirable moral outcomes are to be realized and undesirable ones prevented. Thinking well (conceptual adequacy) is done in vain if institutional forms and policies for channeling character and enacting decisions are absent or deficient. Even if our ethical positions were conceptually sound, without the earthen vessels of systems, institutions, and policies, they would be too short-lived to matter much. Recall James Fallows' complaint that taking the morally correct position is of little value if it cannot be turned into results. Policies, strategies, tactics, institutions, and systems

turn positions into results. They are crucial to an adequate Christian ethic.

We must add that without the social requisites, decisions cannot even be made, or character formed, in the first place. They are the active media for these. Nothing happens apart from them.

3. The *moral character* of sufficient numbers of people is the third component. Sound investigation, analysis, and deliberation of moral issues (conceptual adequacy), as well as sound channels for public action (social requisites), are impotent if the kinds of people who dare to venture morally sensitive actions on weighty matters are not present, or if their numbers are too few. To adapt an idea from physics: A critical mass of moral character and conviction is necessary. Without sufficient moral commitment, nothing will happen to prevent the nightmare of a holocaust, or to realize positive social good. An ethic which does not foster character in our second sense of the word—people of discerning judgment who are committed to act—is an inadequate ethic. Sound moral formation is a major element of any good Christian ethic.

None of these elements—right thinking, social requisites, personal moral character—is finally separable from the other. But neither can any be substituted for another, and none is dispensable. Right thinking can never take the place of good character, and good character, even on a large scale, does not of itself provide the institutional ordering of the good society. All are essential to an adequate Christian ethic, none dare be neglected.[20]

The Recognition of Evil.   The attention to the *formal* components of a Christian ethic can have its own neglect, namely, the failure to speak of particular substance, or content. A later chapter will offer more than we can here, but we include a comment relevant to the discussion of Kremer and Waldheim. John Yoder writes about "a positive doctrine of human fallibility."[21] The reference incorporates Paul's experience, familiar to all of us: "I cannot understand my own behavior. I fail to carry out the things I want to do, and I find myself doing the very things I hate" (Rom. 6:15 JB). "A positive doctrine of fallibility" means that we must radically qualify some distinctions we commonly make, such as "a good person" or "an evil person." Moral character differences *are* real and important—that is not being contested. Yet even more basic, however, is our active capacity for *both* good and evil, a capacity which is considerable, whatever guidance character may provide.

97

The sobering realization which emerges from studying nazism—and Scripture—is not only that we might have been those Germans, *but that we are always capable of becoming them.* Something deep within us, which Christians call "original sin" and Jews "the evil impulse," simply gives the lie to the common conception that the world is made up of good people and bad people. Rather, "every outer evil inevitably attracts from our own depths parts of ourselves that resemble it."[22] Likewise, and thankfully, so does every outer good. For nearly inexplicable reasons, we tend to become, as the psalmist knew, like that which we love *and* that which we hate.

The evil impulse is the subject of Thomas Merton's letter to Pablo Antonia Cuadra:

> We must be wary of ourselves when the worst that is in [us] becomes objectified in society, approved, acclaimed and deified, when hatred becomes patriotism and murder a holy duty, when spying and delation are called love of truth and the stool pigeon is a public benefactor, when the gnawing and prurient resentments of frustrated bureaucrats become the conscience of the people and the gangster is enthroned in power; then we must heed the voice of our own heart, even when it denounces them. For are we not all tainted with the same poison?[23]

A debate at the Constitutional Convention of 1787 makes the same point Christian ethics would make here: It is wise to be sober and realistic about human behavior, and acknowledge the evil impulse, while yet refusing to set limits to the good which can be accomplished. The debate was over the New Jersey Plan for the contemplated U.S. Congress. That plan proposed a single house, with each state casting one vote. It granted the house considerable power and provided no internal mechanisms for checking or balancing that power. James Wilson of Pennsylvania, opposing the plan, commented: "In a single house [there is no check but] the virtue and good sense of those who compose it." And everybody, he went on, "knows that check is an inadequate one."[24]

"Virtue and good sense" are necessary but insufficient guarantors of good. They are only part of the mix of good and evil within us, and fragile realities at best. This gives pause to all hopes that character can be created so as to guarantee good. At the very same time, it underscores the importance of structures and ethos as nurturers and conveyers of good, and as checks upon destructive actions.[25] (Witness the difference of character and conduct in the immediately neighboring nations in the 1930s and 1940s—Germany and Switzerland, or Germany and Denmark.) Still, Wilson of Pennsylvania didn't believe that proper structural arrangements could guarantee social salvation either, only a "checking and balancing" of power which, if unchecked, would invariably lead to injustice. In short, "the positive doctrine of human fallibility," or recognition of the evil impulse, means we must attend with the greatest care to the complex interplay of character and social structure so that virtue is not only cultivated, but far more important, that virtue and right action converge.

However important character and social structure are, they do not yet tell us about decision making on moral issues. The importance of decisions is obvious, and we turn to them next. It is one thing to know the elements of character formation and recognize the importance of social structure, still another to make concrete decisions on moral issues.

6

DECISION MAKING

The Question

"What should I do?" "What do we do now?" "What's right in this case?" We face questions like these every day.

"This case" varies as widely as the circumstances we face. The decision may be an excruciatingly difficult and painful one—whether to instruct the attending physician to withdraw the life support systems for a terminally ill parent or child; whether to close a financially troubled business important to the welfare of the local community; whether to negotiate with insurgents holding hostages and demanding land reform. Or the case at hand could entail happy choices (but not necessarily easy ones). Your organization has $85,000 to give to the cause or causes of its choice, but which? Or you face the proverbial fork in the road and can choose but one of two careers, as posed by different job opportunities. Both are acceptable, but they force you to ask what you most want to do with your life.[1]

The choice at hand may not be as momentous as any of these: Should we sign this petition, buy that book, take a day off to visit a friend, volunteer for the tutoring program, reprove a neighbor about an unsettling remark, look for a different part-time job? What all these and other plausible examples have in common is one thing: They call for decisions. They all press the irrepressible question, "What should I, or we, *do*?" That simple question moves us from the left side of the chart to the right (see p. 39 above) and draws us into matters of ethics which we have not yet given consideration.

It is readily apparent that decisions are a critical part of the moral life, but it is not immediately obvious why we must give decision making separate attention. Why not trust that good character and sound social arrangements will result in right decisions? What else needs attention, beyond character formation and the general ways in which our lives are socially ordered? What is it about decisions that requires special consideration?

The answer is that decisions entail questions and require information which character and social structure do not supply: What data are important for this particular issue (whatever the issue may be)? What factors weigh most heavily in the decision? What moral criteria should be brought to this decision, and what norms should guide us? How should we make the decision, using what process? Who has authority in this matter? What sources do we consult? What means should be considered? What strategy and tactics should we use in order to see our choice realized? Character, even good character, cannot of itself answer such queries. Dispositions, intentions, and perceptions do not tell us *which* of several plausible actions is most fitting, nor does moral vision. Nor do they tell us how to get from here to there. Qualities of character do not "decide," even when they are vitally important to any and every decision. Social arrangements and roles do not of themselves "decide," either, even though, as we have seen, they are powerful determinants. The right-hand column of our chart must be consulted on its own terms even as we continue to emphasize the indissolubility of "being" and "doing" and even as we lodge a protest against any version of Christian ethics which would reduce ethics to decision making and moral problems only.[2] Ethics as decisions *only* is too reductionist; ethics as character formation is too simplistic. Separate but complementary attention is necessary.

Practical Moral Reasoning

Not all decisions are decisions of morality, nor is every judgment a moral judgment. Whether Rembrandt chooses yellow or gold pigment for the fabled light of one of his canvases is an aesthetic decision, not an ethical one. Whether you purchase model X bicycle or model Y has more to do with economic and technical judgments than moral ones. But when moral decisions *are* made, and they are made *in every case* which involves virtue, obligation, value, or vision, then an enterprise vital to the moral life is joined. That enterprise is *practical moral reasoning*. Practical moral reasoning is *the manner by which people arrive at their moral choices*. How it happens in a Christian context is the primary concern of this chapter.

With few exceptions (very young children or adults who are severely mentally incapacitated) everyone engages in practical moral reasoning. Often it is an exercise so mundane and habitual as to be hardly noticeable. Indeed, "reasoning" isn't the most precise term for what is frequently a reflexive exercise done without conscious deliberation. We don't consciously consider whether or not to hold up the clerk and empty the cash register as we pick up a gallon of milk at the store, or whether we should care about a friend as she faces an important appointment with her physician. Any number of moral judgments have been so internalized that we make them intuitively and quite apart from conscious and prolonged deliberation. (Recall our discussion, p. 72-73, about the force of language and the presence of moral content in the vocabulary we have made our own.)

Still, our decisions entail a process of some kind. This is true even for many decisions made reflexively, or intuitively. We may, for example, make a particular decision because others, whom we respect, have so decided. Or we may respond as we did in the past, relying upon the cumulative wisdom of our experience. Or we may choose to act in keeping with a moral maxim on which we have been weaned and which we have made our own: I will act in the way I would want others to act toward me.

None of these decisions entails practical moral reasoning in the form of involved argument or weighty deliberation. They are, nonetheless, common ways by which people arrive at moral choices—and they are more complex than their reflexive nature initially signals. They are in fact rudimentary forms of moral reasoning: in the first example, we decide through appeal to *example* as the operative moral authority; in the second, through *tradition and experience* as trustworthy guides; in the third, through a form of the Golden Rule as a *universal principle*. Each is a different escort through decision making, and each entails a process which is learned.

Practical moral reasoning often takes more complex forms. For difficult decisions, several sources of guidance are usually drawn upon, many factors are weighed, and various points of view and consequences are considered. An examined decision is made, rather than a reflexive and intuitive one. Yet whether moral judgment is simple or complex, reflexive or examined, we employ practical moral reasoning. We move through a process in order to make a decision on the moral issue before us. The choice is never whether to engage in this process; it is only what *form, context, and content* it will have.

Community as Context. Since the chief concern in this chapter is the form, context, and content of decision making in Christian ethics, we begin with an organizing thesis: *The nature of Christian ethics as community ethics determines the form and context of Christian decision making, and the biblical story and the impact of Jesus determines much of its content.*

As a general subject, "community" has been notably absent in the literature of ethics in the West since the Enlightenment. Authors of works in ethics have largely written as individuals set within intellectual traditions, rather than as organic representatives of living communities. They have thus failed to see that as a practical matter there is no place more at home for moral choice than the communities of which we are a part. We cannot get "below" or "beyond" or "behind" communities, in order to decide "from scratch." There is no "scratch" to get to! No single universal moral community with a clear and discrete language exists. We are historical creatures whose moral rootedness is in particular communities and their particular traditions. Any effort to evade these, in order to ground moral judgment elsewhere, only ends up creating another community, usually of the writer's imagination. Much literature in ethics works this way, referring to the fictive community of "all rational persons of good will." This, it turns out, is a community of individuals located nowhere in particular and stripped of all human characteristics except rational self-interest.[3] More precisely, however, the writer unwittingly presents the disguised influences of a particular social location he or she reflects, but does not acknowledge.

Cornel West's description of how moral knowledge happens and how deliberation occurs parallels our own. He describes knowledge as understood in pragmatist philosophies.

> Knowledge should not be a rummaging for foundations but a matter of public testing and open evaluation of consequences. Knowledge claims are secured by the social practices of a community of inquirers, rather

than the purely mental activity of an individual subject. The community understands inquiry as a set of social practices geared toward achieving and warranting knowledge, a perennial process of dialogue which can question any claim but never all at once. This self-correcting enterprise requires neither foundations nor grounds. It yields no absolute certainty. The social or communal is thus the central philosophical category of this pragmatist conception of knowledge. It recognizes that in knowledge the crucial component is not intuition but social practice and communal norm.[4]

We modify this slightly to claim that for the Christian community there are foundations and grounds, accepted as a matter of faith. One image which conveys this is taken from Scripture, the image of a covenanting God who is part of an ongoing dialog of which the faith community is a part. In this dialog no moral knowledge or action is ever wholly "finished," in the sense of belonging to a completed past. Rather, the past is part of the present, and both belong to an ongoing covenant between God, a people of God, and the creation as a whole. We participate in an unfinished conversation like that described by West and understand our place to be located in the continuing drama of creation as gathered in God. The community's moral search occurs within this framework and on these grounds.

Having made this one change, we agree with West's description of the role of community in "knowing," and turn our attention to the Christian faith community and the way it affects how people arrive at moral choice. From this point forward in the discussion, *the decision making context refers to a group of people whose collective identity arises from the impact of Jesus.* This is a people who, *as* a people, share a history, a set of stories, symbols, interpretations, ritual forms, and other traditions which influence moral character and moral choice. We identify practical moral reasoning itself as the detailed process by which these people do make, or might make, particular choices. We want to see how such a community of faith would serve as a forum for moral judgments and a base for moral actions.

The process we propose is the playing out of the contention that practical moral reasoning is less a matter of how moral *ideas* work than how moral *communities* do. Rules for decision making are important, but certain community *roles,* or tasks, are even more so.[5] Before we describe those roles, however, it is important to show that the faith community is already positioned for this kind of decision making by the biblical story itself.

The Impact of Jesus. The genesis and baseline of Christian identity is the impact of Jesus.[6] God is understood via the Jesus account within the broader biblical account. Claims about Jesus are what distinguish Christian ethics from other streams of ethics.

The Jesus story is many-sided, to be sure. Even in its most immediate telling—the Gospels—there are four variations, and others beyond the New Testament. Nor are the Gospels the only important materials. Hebrew Scriptures are so vital a part of the story as to be Christians' First, or Old, Testament. Canonical materials other than the Gospels appear later in the Second, or New, Testament. All these together comprise a highly diverse set of materials. The biblical canon canonizes pluralism.

Already a many-sided story, the Jesus story has also been an interpreted story from the outset, and remains so for us. The high priestly Jesus of the letter to the Hebrews is markedly different from the spare, compelling figure in Mark's Gospel. John's Jesus is not the clone of Paul's or Peter's, even when strong common themes weave their way through the apostolic witness. Or, to jump the centuries, the Jesus of the Renaissance is not identical with the Jesus of the Reformation, or with the Jesus of diverse communities around the globe in the late 20th century. There are many faces of Jesus and an inexhaustible reservoir of meaning in his story.[7] That is hardly a surprise since, if the faith community is a living one, changing perspectives are the norm; and changing perspectives always discover new facets in the legacies they have inherited. Our point is that this living, developing, changing Jesus story is *the* formative story for the Christian community, not only for its identity, but as the framework for decision making.

Story. But why do we call it a "story," and what does story yield for the kind of decision making we commend? We choose story for a double reason: Christianity as a faith has a narrative character about it, and so do our own lives. What narrative does is bring order to what otherwise might be a chaotic stream of events, impressions, insights, memories, and emotions. *Narrative gives form to experience* in ways which tie the past to the present and anticipate the future. Or, from another angle, *narrative discloses an order* which may already be there, but which comes to expression as we tell of it. Psychologist Jerome

Bruner, whom we cited earlier,[8] asks his clients to tell their life *stories*. It is through story that people create their own plot lines and establish the framework in which they presently live, and will live in the future. The particular ways people relay their experience through narrative, Bruner has discovered, "become so habitual that [the stories] finally become recipes for structuring experience itself, for laying down routes into memory, and, finally, for guiding one's life."[9] The last-mentioned point has obvious, direct import for ethics. A way of life and a narrative go hand-in-hand.[10]

Religious narrative is a special case. Religions are "comprehensive interpretive schemes"[11] which are expressed in narrative and myth and are heavily ritualized. What the comprehensive interpretive schemes do, *via* story, myth, and ritual,[12] is "structure human experience and understanding of self and world"[13] in ways which relate them to matters of *ultimate* significance and meaning. Comprehensiveness and ultimacy are the distinctive characteristics of religion.[14]

Returning to the Jesus story in particular, we note that Christianity is, in its essence, a religious story. As Frederick Buechner says, it entails "a time, a place, a set of characters, and the implied promise . . . that something is coming, something interesting or significant or exciting is about to happen"[15] which is of ultimate significance. Moreover, it shares what is apparently a deep-seated human habit to turn to narrative in order to communicate the most important things. Buechner continues:

> If we whittle away long enough, it is a story that we come to at last. And if we take even the fanciest and most metaphysical kind of theologian or preacher and keep on questioning him [or her] far enough—Why is this so? All right, but why is *that* so? Yes, but how do we know that it's so?—even he [or she] is forced finally to take off his [or her] spectacles and push [the] books off to one side and say, "Once upon a time there was . . ." and then everybody leans forward a little and starts to listen. . . .[16]

With good reason, Jewish ethics has always assigned a major role to stories as wise guides for practical moral reasoning. It is a biblical habit that mirrors our own experience as we probe moral issues.

What all good stories do is draw us into their world. And what powerful stories, like the Jesus story, do is mold people's identities and their sense of the world and reality. Powerful stories create a basic orientation for those who are drawn into them. They foster and hone sensitivities. They help form commitments and convictions. They yield insight, and inspire. They create and shape virtue, value, vision, and obligation. And not least, they solicit our involvement—we want to hear more! All this creates a certain framework for decision making.

We add that good stories not only create frameworks, they often change them, and even explode some. The parables of Jesus are an instance of stories which recast the familiar world of the hearers so as to present a still recognizable, but radically different, world. This different world means a different way of life in which social relationships are altered, and thus decisions as well.[17]

The Christian Claim. Can we describe the content of this formative story? Any crisp attempt is admittedly foolish. The story is many-sided and each rendering is already a limited interpretation. Yet we must offer some statement, since we hold that decision making is affected by the Jesus story. For the moment what is important, however, is not the particular interpretation itself so much as the crucial connection of practical moral decision making to the narrative about Jesus.

The most general Christian moral claim is a double one which in its simplest form is this: (1) God is like that which is seen in Jesus, Jesus in the Spirit is a disclosure of God; (2) and God, the source of all being, is on the side of life and good. The details are critical here— God in the flesh of a particular Jew in Galilee during certain years of a human epoch under Roman rule, announcing a specific message, joining certain people for table fellowship, asking of followers a certain way of life, meeting a certain kind of death on a given Friday, rising from the tomb of another Jew, breaking bread together with his community, etc. The Christian claim is bound to this particular story, since it understands that the way of God is paradigmatically present in the way of Jesus as a way of life, and is carried on among those who strive to make this life their own. Here in Jesus, Christians claim, we find the flesh-and-blood clues to the cosmic drama of which we are part and here we perceive a compelling model for human life.

Each generation needs to reinterpret the clues from Jesus for its own moral struggles. Each has to see God, through Jesus, anew. The Scriptures are the decisive texts for this. This means that some of the materials for continual interpretation are constant: the parables, Jesus' table fellowship, his teachings, his encounters with the parties to his own struggle, above all the passion narrative of the cross and then the resurrection. These, together with other New Testament Scriptures and the Hebrew Bible, become revelatory detail through which Christians grapple with the decisive claim that "the heart of the universe is unqualified love working to befriend the needy, the outcast, the oppressed." [18] They are the materials from which the claim arises that God is like what is glimpsed in Jesus.

There is an "upside-down kingdom" here, [19] and we must recognize it if we are to understand the moral norms which the Christian claim delivers to Christian ethics and Christian communities. For what is glimpsed in Jesus is a different God, a God who is "uncredentialed in the empire, unknown in the courts, [and] unwelcome in the temple," a God whose history begins in attentiveness "to the cries of the marginal ones" (recall the discussion of the exodus) and whose nature is presented "as passion and pathos, the power to care, the capacity to weep, the energy to grieve and then to rejoice." [20] God is "hidden" in the humanity of Jesus, and what we see in that humanity shows us the heart of God, a heart which is one of compassion. This is the tale and the claim which orient and embrace the faith community's moral deliberations.

Roles

After this necessary excursus on story and the Christian claim, we turn directly to the style of moral reasoning appropriate to a community which makes this claim. Because the community's materials for decision making are not only those of the biblical story, but also members' own struggles, interests, passions, concerns, and traditions, moral knowledge happens subjectively rather than objectively, or by immersion rather than detachment. Basic moral knowledge in Christian ethics is existential, and is a collective effort to draw connections between the issues at hand as community members encounter them and the community's faith as the context for deciding them. Other sources of moral experience and knowledge, beyond the community members' own experience, beyond even boundaries of the faith community and the biblical story, may, indeed *must*, be drawn upon as well, for the sake of good decisions. The church learns from the world, and community members should freely use any sources which illuminate their decision making. Yet even when assistance comes from elsewhere, moral knowledge happens as part of a Christian story-in-process in which those who use that knowledge are a part of the developing tale itself. It is their story.

There are specific roles required for decision making in a Christian context. Carrying out these tasks requires a certain community morality. The requisite morality is minimal, but essential. It is this: The environment must be open and tolerant. Persons very different from one another must be free to express themselves without recrimination. There must exist a basic respect for persons, all persons, as bearers of the image of God. All must be accorded a fundamental dignity as creatures of God, and heard as children of God.

Assuming this ethos of frank but respectful exchange, what are the crucial roles? What facilitates a community's decision making?

Agents of Vision and Identity. We have already indicated one essential task: Some members—we will title them "agents of community vision and identity"—must call attention to the vision within which moral deliberation occurs. These members help the community articulate the faith it confesses. Raising that faith to shared public consciousness is not itself a pronouncement on the particular decision before the gathered body. (For the sake of illustration, let us say the group is discussing a neighborhood housing issue.) Nor does consciousness of the faith delineate a specific course of action for the community. (Should the church sponsor local, low-income housing? Should it lobby city council? Should it join a community alliance around the issue? Should it ask its members who are in finance and construction, and those who are in need of low-income housing, to pursue a certain strategy together?) What consciousness of the faith does is locate the essential *context* for deliberation. It reminds the community that discussion here happens as part of the Jesus story, rather than some other. It surfaces the identity of the community so as to consciously ask, What action on our part expresses who we are as a people of God?

Agents of Memory and Analysis. If there must be agents of community identity present, there must also be some who are "agents of memory and analysis." Their role may well include recounting their own experience as that may inform and illumine the discussion, but their chief task is remembering, representing, and analyzing the *community's* experience. This will overlap the work of the agents of identity, for it will recount the community's story surrounding the issue at hand. Still, remembering alone is not enough, for it is not moral *analysis*. Analysis is a taking apart, a sorting, a probing and puzzling, and an assessment: How have Christian communities addressed this issue before? What have we learned from these previous struggles of faith? What do we find that is worthy of emulation? What were the moral failures around this issue? What history of the Christian community on this issue should be repented of rather than eulogized, and resisted rather than repeated? How are other faith communities addressing this issue at present? What key theological themes—covenant and creation, law and gospel, nature and grace, conversion and sanctification, the Trinity and community—might be constructively probed and appropriated? How have they aided moral stands on this issue before, or failed to do so?

Agents of memory and analysis should draw not only from the storehouse of the faith tradition and analyze its resources. They should also know how the particular issue has been and is currently being addressed by others, beyond faith communities, and what the resources are there.

Analysis also includes use of specific tools. They are often present within the community but may need to be gathered from elsewhere—skills of social and psychological analysis, historical and cultural analysis, and any number of other approaches which might illumine. We reject the elitist assumption that such skills are the province of trained professionals. Most are already present in some form in most communities, even when not named. Illuminating analysis using varied approaches can be accomplished with the resources available to most communities.

Memory and analysis must include special attention to Scripture. Indeed, in many ways the process we describe is, in its simplest form, the gathering of believers around Scripture in the face of a given moral challenge in order to discern the way forward together. This includes at least two exegetical "moments" which involve Scripture.

1. One "moment" is the community's effort to understand the scriptural text at the point of its origins and its place in the canon. Matters of historical context, the literary nature and organization of the text, its theological dimensions—these are all pertinent to the decision-making process. (They are also part of a later chapter's discussion; we postpone further treatment until then.)

2. The second "moment" is the meaning the texts cast upon the

community's current deliberation. The community moves between perceptions of the original meanings within the canon and perceptions of meanings for later and current concerns. This movement is akin to what Luther called "living Word"—a genuine encounter with God-in-Jesus Christ, as mediated by an encounter with Scripture, while grappling intensely with the realities of some important present concern. Agents of memory and analysis bring this scrutiny of Scripture into a community discussion, according Scripture a central place at the same time that other resources are used as well.

Agents of Clarity and Direction. Vision and identity, and memory and analysis, are critical elements; the community needs those who give them expression. But the community also needs those who can clarify and guide the discussion itself. These are "educators" in the literal sense of the term—those who can "draw out" (*e-ducare*) from the people what they know about the issue and how they feel about it. These agents raise to awareness the moral and religious dimensions of people's speech and guide these in the direction of a decision. They are "agents of clarity" or "agents of direction" who steer the deliberation, simultaneously encouraging the widest possible participation and giving it status as genuine moral deliberation. They are, in a word, agents of community "due process" and moral focus.

To clarify the tasks of these agents, we must interject a note about four levels on which moral conversation can and does occur.

Levels of Moral Discourse

1. The first level is a simple expressive, or *emotive*, one. We straightforwardly register our feelings and judgments, without reflection or deliberation. "Good!" "Terrible!" "You're bloody right!" "We can't do that!" Such feelings and judgments may well express our most deeply held convictions and express our innermost character. For this reason such emotive responses are very important to moral deliberation.

2. A second level is reached when a *reflective* dimension intrudes. Emotive responses are replaced by pondered questions: "What should we do?" or, retrospectively, "What ought we to have done?" Henry David Aiken[21] calls this the moral level because it involves a reflective turn to precedents and principles, or other moral guides and gauges, to help answer such questions. People reach for moral norms to help

them decide what to do. We encountered this earlier in a simple form when example, tradition, and the Golden Rule were called upon to answer the "ought" question.

On this reflective level, some *factual* base is brought into the discussion, or some *presumed* understanding of what data are important is present. This is hardly surprising, since factual claims are always critical to moral ones and no on wants to recommend a stand which flies in the face of the facts. This level, in sum, is one on which people undertake factual appraisal and moral reflection for the practical purpose of determining the right course of action.

3. As people answer the "ought" question they are sometimes challenged. Their facts, their moral norms, their line of argument, or the results they expect, may be challenged. This challenge may move the discussion to a third level, the "ethical" level, to use Aiken's distinctions, or what might be called the "critical" level, in the sense of "critique." Some discussants might, for example, have answered the "ought" question by suggesting, "We ought to do what most others have done in similar circumstances." Then they go on to say what that has been. If they are challenged at the "critical" level, the return comment would be something like, "But why is the behavior of others the grounds for ours? Why is their example our guide?" This is Aiken's "ethical" level. It asks *justification* for the moral appeals being made at the "moral" level. It asks why and on what grounds we answer the moral dimensions of the "ought" question as we do, and it calls us to give a public account of our working morality and its grounds.

4. There is one further level. Aiken calls it "post-ethical." We can adapt it somewhat and call it the "religious" level, or the level of "ultimacy." While one sign of moral maturity is to be cognizant of the grounds of one's morality and be able to give an account of it at the level of critique, at some juncture a plateau is reached, and little more can be said in the way of reasoned justification. Discussion at the ethical level has made its contribution and has reached the point of diminishing returns. At this juncture the conversation is best helped if people are drawn to articulate their most fundamental and cherished convictions and concerns, their root assumptions and most basic perspectives. Deliberation is now aided by knowing people's *ultimate* loyalties and interests, their "final" beliefs and commitments, what Justice Oliver Wendell Holmes called his "can't helps." These deepest convictions

underlie the reasons given at the critical and reflective levels and usually ground the feelings shared at the emotive level.

A sound discussion should not rush to this religious level. Often the decision-making community need not move to it at all. Yet a discussion which never emerges on this plateau foregoes the precious opportunity to connect moral and ethical deliberation to the basic faith convictions of the community and its assembled members. Etymologically, "religion" means "that which binds us" or "that to which we are [finally] bound." A faith community needs those who skillfully provoke this level of discourse. Under their guidance the religious life becomes an *examined* life in the very same moment the moral life does, and recognizing the relationship between them can often move the community to a confident decision.

Agents of clarity and direction are skilled at moving deliberation onto these different levels and at the same time maintaining focus on the moral agenda. As a matter of community due process, they encourage open conversation and draw out maximum participation. The eventual outcome is a community decision and directives for action. The directives may pertain to the community as a whole, acting as a moral agent in its own right, or to the members severally, in dispersion, or to both. They may be directed to the "internal" life of the community (what it does in its life together with its own collective resources); or to its "external" life (what it does in the wider world which is the setting and subject of the community's decision and action); or the directives for action may apply to both.

We should add that such decisions and actions will invariably include dimensions of vision, virtue, value, and obligation. Vision is the decision context itself as faith identity is brought to bear on the issue. Character and virtue express themselves in the being of the decision makers and the community itself, together with the way moral identity affects all considerations. Value is present in the community's attempt to effect actions which contribute to a desirable social goal. Obligation is seen in the effort to set the moral boundaries—some choices fall outside consideration because they violate fundamental moral commitments, other choices must be included because failing to do so would also betray basic commitments. The decision process is enriched when there are people present who bring these dimensions to community attention and use them to enhance moral deliberation.

To summarize: We have sketched a style of practical moral reasoning as a communal process governed by three elements: faith identity as the chief context for decision making; awareness of moral resources both within faith communities and beyond their boundaries; and "reason giving" in a communal conversation that moves freely among emotive responses, reflective and critical ones, and ultimate convictions and commitments. Such deliberation requires people who are agents of vision and identity, memory and analysis, clarity and direction. While it is important to recognize that these roles require knowledge and skills appropriate to each, the roles are not located in particular offices and are not matters which require highly specialized professional training. Most communities already have capable members in their own ranks, or can learn what is necessary for effective community process. Often the roles are interchangeable, and many people in the course of deliberation perform more than one. In any event, it is the tasks themselves which are crucial. To emphasize our earlier point: knowing how moral ideas work is less important than knowing how moral communities do; knowing how to facilitate the flow of moral conversation in the context of faith is the key.[22] We have also said that the "storied" nature of both our own experience and the broader Christian one commends this highly participatory and ongoing style of decision making.[23]

All this together is the process which in ethics is called "moral discernment." Theologically, it is understood as both the work of the Spirit and "testing the spirits" in the moral life.[24]

An Alternative Style

The style just sketched may be our recommended one, but it is hardly the only one possible. Nor has it enjoyed particular prominence in the literature of Christian ethics. We would be remiss not to acknowledge more prominent alternatives. We present a common and influential one, both for its own value and because it corrects some structural weaknesses in the style we have just proposed.

What we have offered assumes impassioned ethical reflection among people committed to one another in a faith community. It assumes shared ties and "grass roots" engagement, and it works with community members' own highly particular identities, interests, and traditions, experienced with a sense of immediacy around specific events and issues. When the details of members' own personal stories are

114

linked to the biblical story, we have the material of decision making itself.

Yet much ethical knowledge and reflection, both in Christian ethics and beyond, has *not* proceeded from immersion in local community experience, or has not readily acknowledged this experience as formative. In fact there has been a deliberate effort *to disavow the importance of provincial influences in making moral decisions.* The goal of the alternative style is nonprovincial rational and moral autonomy. The search is for moral choices which can be formulated by anyone of rational mind and applied to all. In this effort, which has been prominent in ethical theory since the Enlightenment, moral choices should not be dependent for their validity upon the truth claims of particular communities and traditions. What is precisely to be ruled out is reliance upon experience which is exclusively bound to the unique time and place of the moral agents. The peculiarities of people's own stories— their communities, class, race, gender, nationalities, creeds, etc.—are to be avoided as significant sources. The influence of such particulars is to be checked and minimized. An entry in the *Encyclopedia of Bioethics* summarizes much of modern ethics in this way: "Most contemporary ethical theorists agree that correct moral judgments are those that would be arrived at by impartial rational persons (sympathy is no longer regarded as necessary)."[25] The person making moral judgments "cannot use any fact about himself that distinguishes him from any other person" and "must make his moral decision as if he knew nothing about the identity of the various parties involved."[26] This is the modern effort to achieve a "nonprovincial," and universal, ethic.

The desire by "most contemporary ethical theorists" to proceed in this manner is motivated by two important convictions. (1) There is, they contend, an essential human nature we all share. It exists quite apart from the peculiarities of time, place, and circumstance. This nature can be apprehended with the shared faculty of human reason and should be the basis for deriving common moral postulates, which would then be universal and more trustworthy than any principles grounded in the arbitrary and contingent nature of people's highly distinctive beliefs, character, and stories. (2) We have good reason to be deeply suspicious of individual and group interests. Precisely these interests are what distort and corrupt moral judgment. They cannot be eliminated, but their influence should be held in check as far as possible. From Augustine to Reinhold Niebuhr writers have underscored the profound skewing and self-serving impact of peoples' particular loyalties and locations upon their perception and judgment. Sound moral judgment therefore requires that we do all we can to minimize the consequences of the inevitable self-deception into which we are drawn by our passions and parochialisms. In short, "good" ethics makes every effort to be rational and universal, working from a human nature we all share.

What style of practical moral reasoning follows from this view of good ethics? A common style is one we will call "juridical"—that ethical reflection is best which resembles the operation of good law. Good "ethicists" resemble good lawyers, judges, and juries. We could also use the analogy of good science, with good ethicists resembling good scientists. Much of what we call the juridical style is akin to a science model, however, so we will not develop it separately. Readers will recognize the parallels.

The juridical style fits much that is commended in the literature of recent Christian ethics and moral philosophy: All persons and cases of a like character ought to be judged alike, as good law insists; the materials of judging are principles which are at their best when they are generalizable and can be agreed upon by all on the basis of "disinterested" reason; and those doing the judging are at their best when they set aside the passions of their own histories and seek instead to view the case at hand from the point of view of an impartial observer. Objectivity and detachment, infused with enough empathy to understand people's feelings and probe their motivations, are the key virtues for those who are called upon to render moral verdicts (and that is all of us).

For the juridical style, great attention is given the facts. Evidence must be sound and thorough, including what can be known about motives, conditions, and extenuating circumstances. The use of impartial and universal moral norms is matched by a search for all pertinent data.

The decision-making procedure moves, then, from a high level of objectivity, where moral norms exist apart from individual and group identity, to application in specific cases, with all their particularity. It proceeds by way of careful argument with appeals to a "jury" which tries to keep the interests of its own members from intruding in ways that would distort a fair and objective outcome. The juridical style invariably focuses on *rules* and *cases,* with studied attention to even-handed application.

A strong case for this mode of ethical deliberation has often been made, and we will call upon its strengths shortly in order to supplement our earlier proposal. For the moment, it is apparent that it does not wholly fit the style of close-knit faith communities, even when they do use it; nor does it fit the nature of a "storied" faith which asks for deep personal involvement. After all, it is precisely the *particular* beliefs, experiences, symbols, loyalties, and commitments of the faith community and its members which are the sources of moral vitality and the strongest influences in decision making. Highly specific interests and intimately held symbols, part of the community's own story, are what animate moral deliberation. And at base the Jesus story—a particular identity-forming story that cannot be exchanged for another—sets the framework for the community's ethics and offers a highly partial, "upside-down kingdom" content of a radical justice and a radical love. To bracket or somehow "transcend" the particulars of the biblical story, the community's specific expression of it, and the members' own life experiences, is to scuttle precisely that which is regarded as morally most significant.

Synthesis

Can these styles be combined? Yes, although not by placing them side-by-side as separate but equal. Rather, elements of the juridical style can and should be grafted onto the main stock of *koinōnia* ethics. The result would be as follows.

Basic Christian moral knowledge is acquired in intense engagement. It is rooted in the experience of caring and being cared for, of acting and being acted upon in close community. It is filled with the texture of life itself, of touch, voice, gesture, and symbol, of eating, drinking, playing, working, and worshiping. All the senses are engaged, traditions are honored, attitudes and dispositions are formed and reformed, outlooks are fashioned and refashioned, decisions are made, and actions taken. This is moral knowledge which is affective and even mystical, as well as cognitive.

This kind of moral knowledge is where Christian ethics itself is rooted. It is the ethics of an impassioned story, of God glimpsed in

Jesus. As mentioned earlier,[27] what matters is the passion and the details—God in the flesh of a particular Jew in Galilee, etc. The formative story is inseparable from the details and from the concreteness of life in community. So are the ethics. Power is lost when ethics is cut loose from community, and moral principles are left to somehow take on a life of their own, without reference to particular communities.

If the foregoing is the ground level of community moral knowledge, is there a place for the specifically cognitive style of juridical (or scientific) decision making? Moral knowledge which roots in passion and moves to compassion can still turn out terribly wrong as an actual moral judgment. More is involved, and more is necessary, in making sound decisions. Powers of analysis and adjudication, the ability to stand back and view matters with a critical eye, and give dispassionate attention to differing interpretations, are hedges against collective sentiment gone awry. Furthermore, the juridical style's procedures for testing fairness (treating similar cases similarly) and its checks upon the constant tendency of individual and group bias to distort and corrupt, secure for communal moral deliberation what the ethics of passion and collective conviction often neglect. A persistent socratic and juridical strain thus complements a *koinōnia* ethic. The *koinōnia* ethic, however, knows far better the grounds of moral vitality, the moral resources in people's experience, and the power that moves people to action.

The implication is not that *koinōnia* ethics is uncritical or without powers of analysis and logical argument! All ethical reflection is inherently critical and analytical. By definition ethics pushes the probing questions of justification: "What ought we do, on what grounds, toward what ends?" "Which course of action best reflects who we are as a people of God, for what reasons?" Thorough community moral deliberation insists that we scrutinize moral content and the grounds of moral authority. It promotes examination which is open to public debate and vigorous argumentation. And when the community as a whole does it, the possibility that moral authority will reside, uncriticized, in only certain offices and persons is foreclosed.

Nonetheless, the danger remains that any close community will be subject to distorted perceptions based in shared interests and commonality of mind and argument. For this, even the juridical and scientific styles are not of themselves sufficient correctives, even though they are helpful. Juries can be extremely provincial, and are always so to some degree, as any good trial lawyer knows and counts on! But correctives are available to Christian ethics and we should note them. One is membership in the world church itself. The Christian faith community is a global as well as a local reality. This translates as an openness to, and exchange with, other understandings of the biblical story and other styles of the Christian life. The pluralism and cross-cultural diversity among Christian faith communities, and across sub-cultures within the same culture, can check the persistent tendencies of a close community to be sectarian. The other check is openness to the wider world as a constant partner in conversation and a locus of the presence of God. Resources of moral wisdom and guidance come from beyond the faith community itself, as does corrective criticism. They should be eagerly and systematically sought.

Even with these correctives, the beginning and end of moral wisdom rests in the realization that we can discern only partial meanings and only partially realize the meanings we discern. Grace, as both pardon and the power to begin anew, remains the basis of the Christian moral life and the environment for decision making.

This discussion of decision making, together with the preceding discussion of character, brings to a close our commentary on moral agency. We have put in place the formal elements of Christian ethics which made up our chart of the moral life. The next task is to relate the entirety of the chart to the faith community itself, specifying the church's roles in the Christian moral life. Thereafter our attention will be upon biblical materials, their authority and use.

7

THE CHURCH AND THE MORAL LIFE

What is the place of the faith community itself in Christian ethics? What practical roles does it play, in order to form character and conduct? This chapter discusses four roles: the church as an agent of identity, tradition, deliberation, and action.

A Community of Moral Identity Formation

The place of human communities in forming moral character has been underscored often in these pages. Thus we can turn directly to the church as one of those communities and ask about its place in Christian ethics.

The American Roman Catholic bishops' 1986 pastoral letter on the U.S. economy says that "it is not the church's role to create or promote a specific new economic system." [1] So the letter does not propose one. Instead, its purpose is to "help Catholics form their consciences on the moral dimensions of economic decision making. . . ." [2] and to influence public policy on economic issues by promoting public debate. The latter purpose, influencing policy, will be treated when we discuss the church as a community of moral deliberation and action. The former, the church as a community of identity and conscience formation, is the subject now.

Conscience formation is only one way to talk about the development of moral identity. The bishops speak as well about "the need for moral vision" to sustain "a common culture and a common commitment to moral values."[3] They are keenly aware that we do not acquire a moral vision—or a conscience, either—simply by being reckoned among the quick rather than the dead! Nor can a vision, common culture, and commitment be simply and suddenly *willed* into existence, even when their necessity is recognized. They must have a source in our communities and be nurtured over time. They must be learned and passed along from one generation to the next since they are social rather than genetic. Mature conscience and moral vision express *formed moral identity,* and formed moral identity relies upon living communities of character[4] that have longevity. For Christians that community is the church.

What such communities do is internalize moral vision and qualities as a kind of "moral guidance system." (Conscience as the voice of character is part of this.) The means for creating this guidance system are many. The bishops' letter includes sections which discuss some of them—"Conversion," "Worship and Prayer," "Call to Holiness in the World," "Education," and "Supporting the Family."

A Matter of Time. This necessary internalizing (or socializing) takes continuous effort. It is the work of creating and sustaining "a common culture and a common commitment."[5] These are by definition generational in nature. Here the bishops are wiser than U.S. society at large. Our society is enamored with technique and addicted to short timeframes. A typical approach to a social and moral challenge is a problem/solution "fix"—usually a technological, legal, economic, or martial fix. When we recognize a serious case of public moral disorder—Wall Street insider trading and other cases of business collusion, violation of the public trust by our highest elected officials and their appointees, outrageous legal and medical costs in a system of maldistributed services, growing disparity between rich and poor at home and abroad, loss of the sense of the common good in tandem with the pampering of private interests, and addiction to a hedonistic affluence, just to begin the list—we tend to see the solution as some kind of "ethics fix." Codes of ethics are drawn up for professional groups, laws are drafted, and ethics committees are appointed for public officeholders, new regulations are set for industry, and rules are made for consumer and environmental protection. Or we reach for a solution by assigning responsibility for moral education to certain institutions—schools and churches, for example. While all these measures serve important purposes, they are still "fixes." With the possible exception of the last-named—schools and churches—none faces the deep reality that moral identity formation is everyone's business, can only be done over the long term, and can only be pursued effectively in a variety of ways. Identity formation is not a fix, *it is the quiet social vocation of soulcraft.*[6] And if it is not attended to by society as a day-in, day-out task, even the truly necessary social fixes themselves, such as good laws, will not work. Law itself, Chief Justice Warren liked to say, "floats on a sea of ethics."[7] In any case, a society is simply not viable if everything that should or should not be done needs to be spelled out in laws, rules, and regulations.[8] Moral formation must undergird and supplement these.

The generational nature of moral soulcraft must be underscored emphatically. Collective moral identity is long in the making. The shattering experience of Israel in exile is illustrative. In 587 B.C.E. the Babylonian army broke through the walls of Jerusalem and hauled the prominent citizens into exile, leaving the city in ruins, including the temple. But the subsequent exile was far more than a brutal relocation. It was a cultural, political, and religious catastrophe as well.[9] All the sure marks of a national religious identity were shattered, and the land was gone. The prosperity many had come to regard as a birthright in Israel's heyday as a nation was destroyed, the Davidic kingship was toppled, and the center of the faith itself, the temple, was leveled. Israel's way of life, its leadership, and its faith, were all radically called into question.[10] The implied answer to the plaintive psalm, "How shall we sing the Lord's song in a strange land?" (Ps. 137:4), was that the people could not sing the Lord's song. Into this despondency the exilic prophets came with a word of judgment and of hope. It was judgment in that Israel's catastrophe was related to its own arrogance and injustice during its years of prosperity. It was hope in that God had yet another word, a word of forgiveness and of a future beyond exile. But what grabs our attention in this mighty struggle of the people to come to terms with the worst crisis to befall them is the *way* in which it becomes possible for them to "sing the Lord's song" again. The prophets call up images of the people's identity as these are rooted in their deepest memories, and then recast these images as images of hope and renewal.

> Look to the rock from which you were hewn,
> and to the quarry from which you were digged.
> Look to Abraham your father
> and to Sarah who bore you.
>
> (Isa. 51:1-2)

Isaiah speaks of "a new exodus" and "a new creation," and Jeremiah and Ezekiel both speak of "new covenants of the heart." These are the long-held orienting images of Israel's own identity, and they now reestablish it as a community of faith existing in a drastically changed setting. The people are able to combat resignation and despair, to hope, and to begin the task of a new form for their life together (the birth of the synagogue happens in exile).

> They who wait for the Lord
> shall renew their strength,
> they shall mount up with wings like eagles,
> they shall run and not be weary,
> they shall walk and not faint.
>
> (Isa. 40:31)

The larger point is that "peoplehood" didn't happen (and doesn't happen) solely by sharing common geography, events, or experience. Another ingredient is necessary—a collective memory which augurs hope and fashions a common story from shared experience. In this case, surviving the exile was rendered possible by the newly dispossessed retelling and recasting their stories, stories of their own identity. Their collective sense included the memory of themselves as brickmakers and houseservants who knew they were the children of Abraham, Isaac and Jacob, Sarah, Rebekah, Rachel, and Leah. It included Moses and covenant-making, and David and Solomon. In short, becoming a people was not a sudden event, and never is. Neither was (nor is) surviving as a people.

But let us jump across millennia to a contemporary example, to the songs and stories of slaves and ex-slaves that made possible the vocation of Martin Luther King Jr. Marching together for freedom, as a people, certainly did require the charisma and intelligence of a leader such as King, just as Moses was necessary to the saga of the Hebrews. But the civil rights movement also required generations of spirituals and the cultural and moral power of the black churches and their memory

123

of slaves who kept the faith. It also required a certain constellation of events and consolidation of powers at a certain point in U.S. American history. Yet the larger point remains: The moral formation necessary for overcoming oppression (or any of the other goals in the Christian life) cannot first be willed in the moment of its need; it must be nurtured for generations.

A third example surfaced after World War II in southern France, with the story of the small village of Le Chambon. During the Nazi occupation, and in violation of the laws of the Vichy regime, Le Chambon gave refuge to hundreds of Jews and smuggled them by night across the border to Switzerland and safety. Neighboring villages did *not* risk their lives for the sake of strangers who were desperate to escape the ride to the slave labor camps and the death camps. So the question arose, why did Le Chambon do so, especially since no Jews were native to the village itself? Le Chambon did have rather extraordinary leadership, centered in the household of Pastor André and Magda Trocme and their friends, and that was important. Le Chambon's distinctiveness, however, was that it was a Huguenot community with a long history of suffering as a persecuted religious minority. It knew full well what such identity meant for moral action when persecuted strangers sought saving help. The Chambonnais, by conviction both pacifists and resisters of evil, recognized in the Jews a persecuted people of God in grave need, and they responded in a way they said they "had to," a way they said was simply "natural," despite the opposite reaction throughout the neighboring countryside. When, decades after the war, Philip Hallie, a student of Holocaust studies who went to Le Chambon to learn "how goodness happened" there, posed the oft-asked question to one of the surviving leaders: "But would your kind of resistance have worked in Nazi Germany itself, or in the USSR today?" the reply came back immediately, "Oh, no, no. You see, it takes generations to prepare."[11] Communities of character learn to develop their spirituals, to tell their stories, and to say their prayers. They take "generations to prepare." They practice moral soulcraft in season and out of season.

The bishops were intuitively correct, then, to begin a pastoral letter on a public policy issue with materials which give substance to a moral vision and to end it with recommendations which help to craft moral identity through a varied process of nurture happening in many arenas at once. They know that these materials must be internalized by communities of moral formation who will care for them and pass them on like precious heirlooms. They also know that one of the church's chief roles is to *be* precisely such a community.

Tasks. This role is carried out as two quiet, steady tasks. Both were necessary to the outcome of the exile crisis, the civil rights movement, and Le Chambon as a city of refuge.

1. The faith community's first task is *to directly nurture moral capacities,* with its own indigenous resources. These capacities take the form of individual and collective qualities of character. Sensitivity and empathy are examples of such qualities, as are compassion and courage. They exercise decisive influences on our conduct *prior to* our deliberation of specific choices around given issues, inclining us to respond in certain ways when we are confronted with specific choices. They exist as expressions of moral identity which we *bring to* our reflection on possible courses of action. The people of Le Chambon knew "intuitively" that one suffering people of God rescues another, despite the danger. This action "had to" be taken because certain dispositions had already been formed among them as moral capacities. The faith community can nurture moral identity directly and continuously with materials of its own collective story and identity, forming moral capacities.

This can be done in many ways. We point to only a few. The church is a story-telling community and can form moral capacities in just the ways our examples from Le Chambon, the civil rights movement, and the life of the biblical communities illustrate. The form taken is often the educational program of the church, at all levels. Worship life and the liturgy is of equal importance. Even more important, the nurture in worship and the nurture in education go hand-in-hand as the key Christian symbols are "lived into" and their meanings explored. Baptism, for example, is drawn forth into dimensions of discipleship, including moral dimensions; and the Eucharist is understood in its relationship to the hungers of the world and as the sign which mandates an inclusive community in the presence of God. The Bible itself is a continuous resource for both worship and education here. Scripture belongs at the heart of the church's task of directly nurturing moral capacities, using its own resources. (This is discussed in a later chapter.)

It must be added that many other church gatherings, beyond the set occasions of formal worship and formal education, are also places where moral capacities take form. Very often members' work together, making common cause around specific issues and tasks, is the unnamed, and important, laboratory of moral formation.

2. The community's second task is to be the *integrating community*, a place of moral "centering" for materials from social worlds which lie beyond church boundaries. The faith community gives perspective and place to the images, stories, pressures, and events that reign in our lives, whatever their source. This shapes moral identity by facilitating "integrity" (a moral integration at the very core of our being).

Such integration occurs in keeping with the community's basic claim, that God as seen in Jesus and experienced in the Spirit is the center of value and the ultimate source and measure of goodness and power. The competing claims for allegiance and commitment that permeate our everyday world fall into line and have their influence in accord with this claim, when the community functions as an integrating one.

This ordering and integrating assumes that there are numerous sources of moral influence and wisdom. Some lie outside the faith community, some within it. The issue is not the origin of sources or the diversity of content, however. Plural sources and diverse content formed the biblical materials themselves, and the church has always grafted influences which were non-Christian in origin onto its own traditions (Augustine used Plotinus, Aquinas used Aristotle). So the question for any present community facing a moral choice is not whether the moral content is in the Bible, in the church's traditions, or in the Jesus story itself; the question is whether a center exists to which varied materials can be related, and whether a criterion exists which can take their measure. While we cannot discuss this question in full here, we can offer this guideline: The materials of any Christian ethic must take account of the prominent lines discerned in Scripture. That is, content from whatever source must complement, rather than violate, the ancient message of the gospel. Determining compatibility and complementarity is, of course, an ongoing task and cannot be done once and for all.[12]

What was said earlier about the place of education and worship, and making common cause together around various tasks and issues, holds with equal force for this second task.

These two tasks together, the formation of moral identity from the church's own resources, and the integrating of materials from other quarters, comprise the first major role for the faith community, that of helping to craft moral identity. But they presuppose a second major role.

The Church as a Bearer of Tradition

Stories other than pure fiction are lived before they are told. They are multifaceted social and historical events before they are given the coherence of narration. Yet the effort at coherence happens almost simultaneously with events themselves. Raw experience no sooner occurs than we give it reference, framework, and interpretation. We insist upon making sense of what, to an observer, might appear disparate and fragmented, even nonsensical. We are story-making creatures, compelled to make sense of our experience through recollection and narrative. Narration, as we have noted, gives form and meaning to our experience.

But we don't come to experiences empty-handed. We already have a stock of stories in hand and stand amidst traditions which channel our response and become part of our interpretation of new experience. Therefore the important question, both for moral identity and moral action, becomes: "Of what stories am I a part, and of what traditions?"[13] How are they also a part of me? For I am already born with a past, situated within a matrix which is both social and historical, and alive with carriers of myth and meaning. My identity is already shaped by the living traditions of the communities to which I belong. Even if I reject my past, I invariably do so on terms supplied by it. In my quest for a different identity, I almost always draw on traditions, many of them traditions I no longer want to honor in full.

But how do traditions "work," as living components of a community which bears moral tradition? We cite three functions: (1) moral tradition as an aid for moral development; (2) as a source of content for an ethic; and (3) as a framework of accountability in the moral life. The church provides each of these. We take them in turn.

Roots. For moral development, as for personality development in general, we must be able to situate ourselves before we can go anywhere in a way that is not aimless wandering. And knowing who and where we are means knowing the tradition or traditions in which we live, move, and have our being. Moral growth and maturity require being

127

part of a history and being aware of it as part of us. Lack of traditions, and lack of consciousness of them, result in moral drift and limbo.

But how do traditions work, and what is their authority? The question persists, and we must digress for a moment if we are to understand dynamics which are important to moral development and the church as an agent of it.

1. First we must underline the *living* character of moral traditions. To speak of the "authority of tradition" is badly misleading if we think of tradition as "a settled reality"[14] for which the task is to figure out how the whole complex works, as though it were some kind of single fixed unit.[15] There is a certain "givenness" about tradition, of course. "That which is handed on," whatever it may be, is the generic meaning of tradition. But tradition includes the dynamic process of handing on itself, of continuous sense-making, and appropriation, of the past. This process includes sorting and assessing traditions, honoring some and repudiating others, and recognizing different meanings in them at different times. It includes retrieving portions of the past which have been neglected or rejected by current myths, and gathering for present and future generations human moral experience which has been forgotten, denied, or denigrated. It also includes creating, in the present, that which will become part of a past which will in turn shape future moral identities and give guidance for future moral action. "Traditioning" is a dynamic process, a continuous reworking of the past. It is more verb than noun.

One illustration must suffice. The Society of Friends, or Quakers, began by recovering an early and strong, but later neglected, tradition, namely, the Christian life as essentially a nonviolent way of discipleship. The Quakers sorted and assessed traditions, and gave new forms to the ones they gathered into the Friends' way of life. They continue to work from these living traditions as they engage the new issues of a nuclear age. The Quakers represent one example of the church as the bearer of a living and select tradition which gives guidance for their individual and collective action.

2. If it is important to recognize the dynamics of Christian traditions, it is equally important to recognize the diversity of traditions which belong to myriad Christian communities. Coptic Christians of Egypt or Ethiopia possess very different legacies from those of Southern Baptists in the U.S. Orthodox Christians in the USSR, Syria, or India share much between them, yet are markedly different from one another,

not to say from Lutherans in Scandinavia, who in turn differ from Lutherans in Namibia or Tanzania. Mennonites of the western plains of Canada live the Christian life differently from Roman Catholics of Nicaragua or Brazil, despite shared Scriptures and the common formative Christian story itself, centered in Jesus.

Or, from another perspective—historical rather than geographical—first-century Christian ethics changed markedly after its deep encounter with the Greco-Roman philosophical world in the second and third centuries, and its establishment as the imperial faith after the fourth century. The Christian moral life was different after the Renaissance and Reformation, and after the rise of the bourgeoisie and democratic capitalism, from what it was in the world of medieval and feudal Christendom. And it is still different today, in the wake of Marx and Freud. Yet there are family resemblances throughout, and "Christian" remains a meaningful designation for widely and deeply shared elements.

We are not stuck, then, with inherently static and fixed moral content. Moral traditions are not intrinsically rigid and they are not univocal. (When they have been treated as such, as they often have, they have impeded moral maturity.) The issue, in a word, is not to accept or reject "tradition," but to decide which criteria, in an ecumenically dynamic traditioning process, we should use to sort those traditions we should identify with, from those we should not. How should we choose from among the many voices and diverse moral traditions of the faith community, including those traditions now in the process of creation? Much past morality is, after all, morally dubious, some even outrageous and utterly deserving of abandonment.[16] (We have mentioned slavery and abusive treatment of women; campaigns of slaughter in the name of God can quickly be added.) The makings of an answer to the question of criteria are discussed in later pages, but it begins with a cue from the church's own testimony and experience: to accord high place to Scripture as a common authority and, within Scripture, to give the Jesus story a normative place, as discerned together in the Spirit. The necessary moral discrimination will then follow from what is and what is not compatible with the Jesus story, rather than from what is dictated by a single subtradition. Yet the point we must grasp is not only that we must sort diverse traditions. It is the function of such moral traditions themselves and the role of the church. Traditions in the church help situate us, they give us rootage, and are thereby an

129

indispensable aid to moral development. Indeed, even when we break with certain strains of tradition, we usually take them seriously as heritage and as a point of orientation, just as we usually draw *on* the tradition for the reform *of* it. A rediscovered, or newly uncovered, understanding of Jesus has often served in this way in the life of the faith community, as have other turns to Scripture.

Content. The digression about diversity and dynamics has the virtue of introducing the second function of moral traditions in the church, a function which also aids moral development: Moral traditions supply many of the materials for fashioning the ethic by which to live and die. Diverse interpretations of Christian faith, together with their diverse moralities, are included within the expansive Christian tradition. This means that wide-ranging views on a virtually endless number of moral issues are included in the tradition, as are embodiments of different life-styles and a wealth of portraits, symbols, images, stories, rites, and rituals.

For an adequate ethic there must also be scrutiny of different moral claims and different interpretations, of course. We must make judgments. As we do this, there will be important—and ceaseless—debate about the rights and wrongs of particular stands and particular patterns of living. But precisely this reflection and critique is an essential part *of* Christian moral traditions themselves. The faith tradition as a whole combines content *and* criticism. Both can help fund the ethic we fashion together. Both belong to the church as a community of moral development.[17]

Framework. Finally, moral traditions provide a framework of accountability. As part of a tradition, we are set within a matrix of moral claims and concerns which provide a guiding influence. The faith tradition, functioning as a moral tradition, mediates the claims of others upon us and we upon them.

This framework of accountability can be very specific and direct. The subtitle of the bishops' pastoral letter which we cited earlier is: "Catholic Social Teaching and the U.S. Economy." The bishops addressed Catholics and self-consciously worked from an official body of church teaching as their framework for moral deliberation. The Catholic tradition supplied parameters even as the bishops sought to modify and expand the very legacy which functioned in this way, and even as they drew upon resources from beyond the Catholic tradition. "Catholic social teaching" was an identifiable and authoritative point of reference.

Moral traditions are sometimes less clearly defined as a framework of accountability, but are nonetheless real and effective. The Hebrew understanding of immortality provides an extended illustration: In this understanding my life continues as part of the ongoing life of a people of God living toward a vision of harmonious creation. This sense of corporate personality and immortality nurtures a sense of responsibility towards both ancestors and posterity. In a certain way, I am responsible to Abraham and Sarah and their lot. I am part of the fulfillment of the story that was theirs, is mine, and will be that of those who come after me. They bequeathed a legacy and vocation to me. The legacy and vocation continue, and I am responsible to the ancestors through the heritage placed in my hands. They depend upon me.

This notion of immortality and of a goal for creation means that the past is not only not dead, it is not yet finished; and I am part of its ongoing development. The early church shared just this consciousness of an ongoing covenant. The letter to the Hebrews says as much: It calls the roll of the communion of saints and attests to their living by faith (chap. 11) for a future promised them by God but which they could not yet see. The perils they knew were sometimes dreadful.

> Some had to bear being pilloried and flogged, or even chained up in prison. They were stoned, or sawn in half, or beheaded; they were homeless, and dressed in the skins of sheep and goats; they were penniless and were given nothing but ill-treatment. They were too good for the world and they went out to live in deserts and mountains and in caves and ravines.
>
> (Heb. 11:37-38 JB)

Then the writer concludes: "These are all heroes of faith, but they did not receive what was promised, since God had made provision for us to have something better, and they were not to reach perfection except with us." (Hebrews 11:39-40 JB)

There is an emphatic accountability to the past here. The faith community is charged to carry forward the hopes of the ancestors and the dreams of their God, and to realize those hopes and dreams as best it can.

The same accountability stretches off into the future. Indeed, the best part of Jewish and Christian moral tradition *is* the future, in this understanding. There is a moral *telos* (goal) which is reached when "justice and peace kiss" (Psalm 85:10, author's paraphrase). Our present actions are to be congruent with that which makes for a just and harmonious future creation. We are responsible to coming generations. Their claims to well-being are claims upon us. The conditions that would make well-being possible for them are therefore ours to create as best we can. In a word, the church's moral tradition itself presses accountability for future generations.

This does not neglect present generations. For both Jewish and Christian ethics love of neighbor is obligatory *in the present moment* and is not vitiated by obligations to ancestors and posterity. Furthermore, "neighbor" is universal. *All* are neighbors, whether near at hand or far off, whether friend, stranger, or enemy. The whole community of life is embraced, "all that participates in being,"[18] including nonhuman life.

The tradition itself, then, fosters moral accountability and functions as a framework for it, just as it aids moral development and contributes to the content of an ethic.

Summing Up. We can summarize as follows.

1. The faith community is a major source and resource for moral development. It is this as it sets members within a moral tradition with which they identify.

2. The faith community is the source of rich and varied content for members' ethics. As the community embodies and passes on its own traditions, and helps locate, appropriate, and integrate sources from elsewhere, it supplies such a fund.

3. The faith community is the framework of accountability for the Christian moral life. As its moral traditions form and inform the ongoing life of its members, it functions as this framework.

These three functions together make up the role of the community as a bearer of moral tradition. Indeed, members of a faith community are already, by virtue *of* membership, part of a collective tradition which provides both substance for a present and future Christian ethic, and a process for appropriating it. The earlier example of the Quakers, and the recurring one in this chapter of the American Roman Catholic bishops, show two quite different ways of addressing both substance and process. But the differences reflect the liveliness of the tradition itself.

There is yet more.

The Church as a Community of Moral Deliberation

The preceding chapter devoted extensive space to the church as a community of moral deliberation. We need only highlight some matters not yet covered. The Roman Catholic pastoral letter again provides an extended example of the church's role for individual and collective decision making on moral issues. In the letter, moral deliberation includes several different roles for the church.

New Knowledge. The church is an arena for learning about issues. The process the bishops used is noteworthy, even though it is but one of many possible ways to gain significant knowledge. The bishops arranged hearings at which a spectrum of views were aired. Numerous economic analyses received careful attention by the bishops' staff and committee, who drafted a statement and issued an open invitation to respond to it. Thousands did—members of the business community, the academic community, government, and labor, as well as church groups. Reams of replies appeared and scores of commentaries were published. The bishops took all these into account and made major revisions in what became the second draft. This, too, was published and circulated. The hearings themselves were continued to cover areas previously neglected or in need of additional testimony. Further written responses from home and abroad were forthcoming. Eventually a third draft was written which the bishops discussed, amended, and finally adopted as their own position. It then became a basic teaching document used widely in the American Roman Catholic Church (and far beyond) as well as the basis for the Church's stands on economic policies.

In short, the bishops used the format of hearings and revisions, drawing from a wide spectrum of participants and critical response, in order to help form Catholic conscience and to join a public policy debate on an important issue.

Yet this is an example, and not the point itself. The point is that the faith community is a place of learning on moral issues. Members learned much about economic life and its intersection with Christian faith as the church formulated a stance on a complex set of issues, and issued a call for action. The United Methodist bishops used a similar

133

process to draft their pastoral letter on peace, *In Defense of Creation: The Nuclear Crisis and a Just Peace.*[19] It was also an effective vehicle of learning, both in the process of arriving at the moral stands themselves and as an instrument for ongoing study.

Citing official church statements as examples should not mislead us. They are only one form of many which might be used by the church as a community of moral education. And the issues need not be as global as these. The issues might be strictly local ones in which the congregation, rather than the denomination, is the forum of learning, and the style of interchange is informal, even conversational, perhaps in the manner described in the previous chapter. A congregation or a coalition of neighborhood religious communities might grapple with a housing issue, an action on health care, a response to some item of proposed legislation, etc. The salient matter is to expect the faith community to be an arena for learning about significant issues and their moral dimensions.

Learning *about* issues is necessary. But it is not sufficient. If the Catholic bishops' letter were only a document *about* economic realities, it would, as a *church* document, have been very curious indeed. The church has no economic data to which only a faith community, and not the wider public, is privy. Even when the church is the place where people first learn some essentials about important matters, that knowledge is still public knowledge. (For many people in the U.S., awareness of world hunger and of Central America issues came via church-related education.) Rather, the distinctive mark of the church's role is its formulation of a moral perspective drawn from Christian faith.

Normative Perspective. This introduces the second component of the role the church plays in moral deliberation. The faith community can and should be the arena in which a moral perspective on an issue is fashioned. The bishops used a two-step process. The first was to clarify where and how Christian faith and teaching intersect the matter at hand (economic issues, in this case). The goal was to provide a religiously grounded moral perspective. The second step was to enter the wider public debate, indeed, to promote it where it wasn't already under way. There the moral stance joined a dialog in which church members who held this perspective not only learned more about the economic issues being debated, but provided both moral critique and moral construction in the course of debate. The moral stance itself was modified in the course of debate, as is frequently the case in open exchange.

While the formulation of a moral perspective is quite complex, the process is not difficult to follow in the pastoral letter. The trail goes like this.

(1) The bishops first point to the religious and moral aspects of economic life. This can be seen in paragraphs such as the following:

> Every perspective on economic life that is human, moral, and Christian must be shaped by three questions: What does the economy do *for* people? What does it do *to* people? And how do people *participate* in it? The economy is a human reality: men and women working together to develop and care for the whole of God's creation. All this work must serve the material and spiritual well-being of people. It influences what people hope for themselves and their loved ones. It affects the way they act together in society. It influences their very faith in God (§1).
>
> Anyone who sees all this [the bishops have just described signs of hope and signs of failure in the U.S. economy] will understand our concern as pastors and bishops. People shape the economy and in turn are shaped by it. Economic arrangements can be sources of fulfillment, of hope, of community—or of frustration, isolation, and even despair. They teach virtues—or vices—and day by day help mold our characters. They affect the quality of people's lives; at the extreme even determining whether people live or die. Serious economic choices go beyond purely technical issues to fundamental questions of value and human purpose. We believe that in facing these questions the Christian religious and moral tradition can make an important contribution (§5).

(2) In this belief, the bishops go on to identify perspectives of Christian faith which should orient our approach to the economic realities and issues of the day. Their list includes " . . . the dignity of the human person, the unity of the human family, the universally beneficial purpose of the goods of the earth, the need to pursue the international common good, as well as the good of each nation and the imperative of distributive justice" (§251). These and other themes from biblical faith and Catholic social teaching generate a certain orientation for the church's address of economic life. In fact, they issue in a specific moral test: "The fundamental moral criterion for all economic decisions, policies, and institutions is this: They must be at the service of *all people, especially the poor*" (§24, emphasis in the original).

135

Yet there is more to the faith community's address of a public issue than awareness of religious and moral points of contact and the formulation of a basic orientation and criterion. A way must be found for the church to carry on public moral discourse in a pluralistic society. The faith community must be able to make its views intelligible to parties which do not share the religious premises. The bishops know they cannot say, in effect: "We recommend the following policies because they represent a Christian perspective." For a pluralistic world, "Christian" is not a compelling and sufficient reason. So the bishops make the next move (3) and call to attention the nation's *own* moral claims (recall that this is a debate on national policy). Here the bishops bring on stage moral commitments and promises made since the founding of the American republic—freedom from oppression, both political and economic; equality of opportunity; liberty and justice for all. These claims function as the framework of national moral accountability. Then (4) the bishops point to common ground shared by norms from the Catholic faith tradition and the nation's own moral claims and aspirations. On the basis of this common ground, they next (5) establish "moral priorities for the nation" (see §§85ff.). These priorities in turn (6) enter the deliberation of specific economic policies. There they serve the double purpose of providing both criticism of current conditions and practices, and direction for more just policies.

The faith community is only one of many participants in the public debate of moral issues. But this example shows a way by which it can carry on public moral discourse. The bishops have demonstrated how the church can articulate its own moral perspectives, consciously grounded in its own faith claims, and simultaneously carry these perspectives into the public square in terms that are intelligible on other than Christian grounds.[20] The faith community as the place where a Christian moral stance is formed and the terms are found for public moral discourse, is the second component of the community's role as a community of moral deliberation. We add that the form need not be the one we have tracked here for illustrative purposes (the bishops and the use of official church offices). A local congregation can play exactly the same role, as can any number of informal and ad hoc networks formed to address specific moral issues.

Moral Representative.   The third component of the church's role in moral deliberation is the church as a community of moral proxy.

The Catholic pastoral's subject is the U.S. economy. But as a *church* document, the discussion cannot be bracketed by national boundaries and cannot limit its moral reach to the welfare of U.S. citizens only. The Christian faith community is simultaneously local and global. It is not "national" by any definition of faith. (The gospel knows nothing of the nation-state system.) Since the notion of "neighbor" is a universal one, church discussion of moral issues entails representation. Neighbor means *all,* including enemies and unborn generations, and "proxy" means the faith community must amplify those voices not normally heard. These are invariably voices of the powerless. In the case of the economics pastoral, this means the poor within the nation itself, the poor of other nations, and the prospective poor of future generations.[21]

The people who need representation will often change as moral issues change. But the proxy role remains the same: always to strengthen the voices of those who are not otherwise heard. It is a vocational consequence of Christian faith itself. Again, it can happen in ways large and small, and through both official and ad hoc institutional means.

In sum, the church is a place to learn about issues, to formulate a Christian moral perspective and bring it to bear on the issues, and to represent the under- or unrepresented. All are aspects of the church's function as a community of moral deliberation.[22]

The Church as an Agent of Action

The formation of moral identity, utilizing moral traditions in the process, is a crucial role of the faith community, as is moral deliberation, also using these traditions. Yet conscience and character formation, and deliberation of issues, aren't ends in themselves. They exist to serve concrete action. The faith community is to be an agent of action.

There is an important theological point here. In both Jewish and Christian traditions, faith's truth is finally a "performative" one. We *know* it when we *see* it, or experience it. It is real when it is embodied, and only then. The test of any moral truth is in the social form it takes, and the difference it makes in society. Moral truth and a way of life always go hand in hand.

This "performative" understanding of Christian faith and moral truth necessarily assumes, then, a commitment to action. Literally nothing happens without it! Apart from action, moral identity and deliberation are without consequence, and are thereby rendered meaningless. Their verification is visible only in their outcome.[23]

But what does "action" refer to, precisely, as "Christian ethics talk?" Not every event is a moral action, nor every occurrence a moral act. A bird flying across the sky, or a leaf falling to the ground, is not a moral act; nor is the beating of a heart or the blinking of an eye. Moral action partakes of moral agency and thus includes a range of mental activities we have discussed—choice, deliberation, discernment, disposition, motivation, intention, responsibility. Moral action assumes that agents are aware of what they are doing, have some knowledge they feel is appropriate to the action, have some purpose in mind for the action, and have some possibility *of* acting (i.e., a degree of freedom, or choice, exists for them). When deeds have these characteristics, and include aspects of virtue, value, vision, or obligation, they belong to moral action.

With this qualification in mind, what shall we say about the church functioning as an agent of action? Deeds of faith take place in two zones.

Home Turf.   The faith community itself is the first zone. It is both the subject and the object of the social ethic it claims and proclaims. Its own internal arrangements should reflect the morality it espouses. If, in the celebration of the Eucharist, it invites all to "the welcome table" (a term used in many black church traditions for the communion table), then it cannot contradict this by failing to welcome all into the membership of the community itself. If it pictures the world as a place where we share the same loaf, drink from a common cup, and belong together as members of a single family in God, then it must find the means to share lives and resources for the community's own life together and with the world around. Or, harkening back to the bishops' pastoral, the church as economic agent should turn to its own economic activity and decide what ought to be done in its own organization. The bishops themselves cite five areas of concern—wages and salaries (of church workers); rights of employees; investments and property; works of charity; and working [as an institution] for economic justice. In other words, the church has a role as moral agent on its own institutional turf.

The Wider Public.   The second zone of moral action is the world beyond the boundaries of the institutional church. The actor is still the faith community, but now its attention is focused externally, to the public arena and its condition, rather than internally. The most obvious way the community acts here is through its membership as that is dispersed throughout society. The ministry of a people of God in the workplace and home is of the greatest importance here. It is under-developed as a conscious form of *church* action and reflects the general neglect of the laity's ministry. Role morality, as we've noted, has been badly slighted, only exacerbating the moral wasteland that characterizes many sectors of public life. To its credit, the economics pastoral in-cludes sections on "Working People and Labor Unions," "Owners and Managers," "Citizens and Government" (§§102-104), just as the ear-lier peace pastoral included role morality for "Educators," "Parents," "Youth," "Men and Women in Military Service," "Men and Women in Defense Industries," "Men and Women of Science," "Men and Women of the Media," "Public Officials," and "Catholics as Citizens" (§§304-326).[24] Here, then, the community's presence is a dispersed one, via participation of its membership throughout the social order.

The complement of this is action of the church *as* a gathered com-munity. We do not mean now the attention internally, to the quality of community life there; we mean the church's action as a corporate agent making corporate witness to what ought to happen in the world beyond its bounds. Where, for example, does the church invest its money and how does it use its property? What does it undertake, as a body, on neighborhood issues? Not least, what kind of life is reflected in the way the community is present in its world? The moral form of the community itself and the way in which it embodies its ethic is itself one of the ways the church is an agent of action in the larger public. The theological rationale is expressed by Karl Barth.

> The decisive contribution which the Christian community can make to the upbuilding and work and maintenance of the civil order consists in the witness which it has to give to it and to all human societies in the form of its own upbuilding and constitution. It cannot give in the world a direct portrayal of Jesus Christ, who is also the world's Lord and Savior, or of the peace and freedom and joy of the kingdom of God. For it is of itself only a human society moving like all others to [God's] mani-festation. But in the form in which it exists among them it can and must

be to the world . . . around it a reminder of the law of that kingdom of God already set up on earth in Jesus Christ, and a promise of its future manifestation. *De facto,* whether they realize it or not, it can and should show them there is already on earth an order which is based on the great alteration of the human situation and directed towards its manifestation.[25]

This is action in the form of corporate witness, as the quality of a life together. Here its presence is not only that of an exemplary community, as the Barth citation calls for, but as corporate witness which shows itself in direct, goal-oriented actions of church bodies in the public arena. Congregations, denominations, and ecumenical coalitions of all kinds have been part of civil rights efforts (or, earlier, abolitionist ones), in forming and expressing public opinion on foreign policy issues (Vietnam, Central American, USSR, and South African issues, for example), and in lobbying at local, state, and national levels on proposed legislation (abortion, health care, and other human services issues have received much attention). Corporate action supplements the action of both the church as a community witness on its own turf and the action of members severally as they are dispersed throughout the public arena in their work and social roles.

In sum, the Christian moral life involves the church in four distinct roles: as a community of moral identity formation; as a bearer of moral tradition; as a place of moral deliberation; and as an agent of moral action. Each aids the other and none can be dispensed with, without stunting the Christian moral life. All are imperatives which follow from the substance of Christian faith itself.

What remains to be said is how a faith community which accords its Scriptures the high authority the Christian community does, understands that authority and uses those Scriptures.

8

THE NATURE AND ROLE OF BIBLICAL AUTHORITY

At several points we have mentioned the problem of authority in relating the Bible to Christian ethics. What is the nature of biblical authority in shaping moral character and in the making of moral judgments? The Bible is not the only source of identity-shaping authority. It is certainly clear that the Bible is not authoritative for Christian ethics at the point of making ethical decisions for us. The shaping of both Christian character and conduct involve many influences and sources of insight. What is their authority in relation to one another? It is time to address these questions directly.

Christians cannot escape the question of biblical authority because it is inherent in the claim that the Bible constitutes Scripture for the church. It is not possible to regard the Bible as simply one of many possible influences or sources of insight in ethical matters. When the Bible is claimed as Scripture by the church, a special status or authority is being claimed for it. Scripture is understood as somehow normative for the life of the church and those individuals who identify with that historic community.[1] To be sure, there are many ways of understanding that normative character of Scripture, but Christian ethics, since it shares the scriptural foundations of the church, is not free to regard the Bible as only one among a myriad of historic and modern cultural factors to be taken into account in the doing of Christian ethics. The particular authority of the Bible as the church's Scripture must be considered.

Authority in Christian Ethics

The word authority refers to that which an individual or a community acknowledges as a source of decisive influence in its life. *An* authority may be a document or a body of material (e.g., the Magna Carta), a person, or a community. Strictly speaking, an authority is what authorizes or empowers us. The matter of authority focuses not on some inherent quality in a source of authority but on the process of authorization that takes place in the interaction of that source with ourselves as individuals and communities.

As an example, the Gospels frequently say that Jesus spoke "with authority." The Greek word used is *exousia* which literally means "out of, or from, being." It refers to Jesus' speaking in a way which related to his listeners (and by extension with us, the readers) at the deepest levels of their being. His words went to the heart and have been passed on by the church because they correspond with our most profound realities and concerns. *Exousia* is sometimes translated in the New Testament as "power." Jesus' power is not in his words, as such, but in their ability to call forth in people power they may not have known they had, but can hardly resist because it issues from their very being. Just as Jesus speaks "out of his being" (with authority), so also Jesus' hearers find power "out of their being" (they are authorized, empowered to new life).

In the church we speak of the authority of Scripture as a way of referring to the acknowledged position of the Bible as normative for the Christian life. Authority is not a property inherent in the Bible itself. It is the recognition of the Christian community over centuries of experience that the Scripture is a source of empowerment for its life in the world. Authority derives from acknowledgment of a source's power to influence us, not from absolute power that operates apart from the affirmation of the community. James Gustafson, in a paraphrase of H. Richard Niebuhr, wrote, "Authority . . . is the kind of power that is exercised over us by consent, and voluntarily negated by dissent."[2] To raise the question of biblical authority in matters of ethics is to ask, "What is the nature and degree of influence to be given the

Bible in shaping Christian character and conduct in light of its continued acknowledgment by the historic church as Scripture?''

In moral matters authority is not something possessed solely by Scripture. The claim to be Scripture establishes an authority for the Bible that must be taken into account, but its authority is not absolute or exclusive. Many other sources of influence and insight become authoritative in moral deliberation. Historical perspectives, socioeconomic data, scientific data, rational arguments, and an endless variety of other nonbiblical sources are authoritative in the making of particular moral judgments. The real question, then, is the relationship of biblical authority to the authority of nonbiblical sources for Christian ethics. James Barr has helpfully suggested that the whole notion of authority is relational.

[Authority] is a relational or hierarchic concept; it tries to order and grade the various powers, or sources of ideas, that may influence us. . . . The notion of authority defines the priority of one such force over another. . . . Authority is used in an attempt to relate or to grade the forces bearing upon Christian belief and action. ''Authority'' . . . thus defines relation. (It) defines i) the relation between the Bible and ourselves, so that the Bible may be seen as something binding upon us, something to which we have to submit ourselves; and ii) the relation between the Bible and other documents or sources of knowledge which might also influence our minds or actions at the same time.[3]

It is well, however, to avoid from the beginning the notion that we can create a hierarchical order of influences on the Christian moral life and locate the position of Scripture in absolute terms within the hierarchy. We have already seen enough of the way in which Scripture functions in Christian ethics to know that this is not possible. We can suggest in advance of our fuller discussion in this chapter that a more multifaceted understanding of biblical authority is needed than has usually been espoused in the church. Most views of biblical authority have been too rigid to allow a dialogic relationship of biblical material with nonbiblical material in moral judgments. Such traditional views have collapsed in the face of developments in modern theology and biblical studies, and this creates a new context in which questions of authority must be raised.

143

Traditional Views of Biblical Authority

Traditionally biblical authority has been associated with the concept of inspiration. This began as early as the fixing of the written Torah during the period following the Babylonian exile. For Jews, the text itself became the locus of divine revelation, and within that text, in all of its segments and details, could be found a divine word and guidance applicable to present and future generations. In the early church, as documents took written form and became influential in the life of the church (letters of Paul, Gospels), the text also came to be regarded as divinely inspired. Using texts such as 2 Tim. 3:16, "All scripture is inspired by God," and 2 Peter 1:21, "Men moved by the Holy Spirit spoke from God," a concept of divine authorship through inspiration developed.

Edward Farley and Peter Hodgson refer to this as the development of a "scripture principle," the view that Scripture is "a unique deposit of divine revelation—a deposit whose special qualities are due to its inspired origins, and which is to be handed down through the ages by an authoritative teaching tradition."[4] Although varied in details some form of this "scripture principle" has characterized both Protestant and Roman Catholic views of biblical authority until after the Enlightenment, when views of inspiration began to erode due to a number of inherent weaknesses and a new spirit of criticism. Although many continue to hold traditional views of inspiration they are in the present the source of considerable controversy, as in the Southern Baptist Convention.

1. In spite of a common traditional appeal to inspiration as the focus of biblical authority there has emerged no consensus in the church on the meaning of inspiration and its applicability to the Bible. Various typologies have attempted to organize this diversity of uses for the notion of inspiration.[5] Such typologies range from absolute inerrancy which declares the actual words of the text to be the direct product of divine communication, to limited notions of inspired infallibility in matters of faith and practice communicated through socially conditioned contexts, to inspiration located in the authors or community that gave us the biblical texts but which regards the texts themselves as human products.

David Kelsey, in his delineation of seven representatives of the ways in which Scripture is construed in modern theology, lists only one use that corresponds to the classic church appeal to Scripture as inspired, B. B. Warfield's construal of Scripture as inspired, inerrant doctrine. A second and third use in Kelsey's list might be viewed as modified views of Scripture as inspired in content. These construe Scripture as the source of distinctive concepts (Hans-Werner Bartsch) or of salvation history (G. Ernest Wright). What all of these discussions make clear is that the nature and locus of inspiration has been difficult if not impossible to define.

2. Inspiration-based concepts of biblical authority tend to invest undue sacral authority in the text of the Bible itself. Christianity then becomes a book-centered religion rather than a God-centered one.[6] This has been a greater danger in Protestant theology than in Roman Catholicism where notions of inspiration have expanded to include church tradition as well. Such a sacralizing of the text tends to reduce the biblical authors and communities to the role of mere conduits and to obscure what we might learn from the Bible about genuine relationship to God.

3. Ironically, views that connect inspiration to authority tend in practice (and in spite of theory) to elevate portions of Scripture to positions of authority that imply they are more inspired than the rest. This has often been the case of the New Testament in relation to the Old, and even of the Gospels within the New Testament. Some of this grows out of commonsense observation. We do not take the admonition against boiling kids in their mother's milk with the same gravity as the Ten Commandments. But if the authority of Scripture is rooted in its inspiration, one is forced to posit a God who was more inspiring on some occasions than on others. Obviously a more multifaceted view of biblical authority results in a less problematic view of the God who addresses us through the text in a dynamic way rather than a God whose inspiration is statically embodied in the text itself.

As the limitations of inspiration models of biblical authority have become more obvious in modern times, there have been other developments which in the opinion of many have caused a permanent collapse of traditional notions of biblical authority.

The Collapse of Biblical Authority

We wish to highlight two separate arenas where challenges to traditional views of the Bible as the deposit of inspired, revelatory content are forcing a modern rethinking of the nature of biblical authority.[7]

145

1. The first challenge comes from the *development of historical-critical methods of biblical study.* Beginning with the Enlightenment, but coming to full fruition in the 19th and 20th centuries, methods of critical study were applied to the Bible. First to develop was text criticism, which sought to establish the most ancient and authentic text from among the divergent readings of the manuscripts and the versions. Of course, this had the effect of relativizing the text. If authority lay inherent in an inspired text, which textual tradition was thus authoritative, or did authority only lie in an original unrecoverable text?

Next came literary criticism, with its concerns for authorship and sources, closely followed by tradition history and its interest in tracing the development of traditions through generations of the biblical communities and their institutions. Such studies made readily apparent that biblical materials were not the product of some momentary activity of divine deposit. They were the result of complex literary and historical development within the life of the biblical communities of faith as they witnessed to their experiences in relation to God. Stories were told and retold, combined and edited, preserved and embellished. Inspiration models focus on the text itself, but critical study shifted some of that focus and attention to the processes behind the text and the communities where those processes unfolded.

More recently the application of secular literary criticism to biblical texts (e.g., structuralism, new genre research on metaphor, semiotics, and linguistic theory) have increased our awareness of the diversity of ways in which biblical narrative and poetry function. The address and meaning of a text is seen less as a quality which resides in the text alone than as a quality that arises out of the reader's encounter with the text.

Finally and most recently, the increased application of social scientific methods of research to the Bible has produced a much greater appreciation for social location as a factor in the original shaping of the text as well as in our own reading and interpretation of biblical texts. Although the Bible is still the story of God's graceful initiative, the actual shaping of the biblical witness to that grace seems more clearly located in and affected by the human communities of biblical times than inspiration views of authority would have suggested.

The result of decades of development of critical methods is that for those open to such study it is no longer possible to maintain a view of Scripture as the collected deposits of eternal revealed truth or doctrine simply waiting to be applied authoritatively to our lives.

2. A second area of challenge to traditional views of biblical authority has come from *liberation and feminist theologies and the hermeneutics appropriate to them.*[8] These theologies, from the perspective of marginalized people, challenged the prevailing modes of Western, white, male biblical interpretation as ideologically biased. They saw clearly that biblical authority does not reside abstractly in texts. It only functions as texts are interpreted and used. When texts are interpreted predominantly from the social locations of the powerful, the rich, the white, and the male culture, then biblical authority is invoked, consciously or unconsciously, to authorize and empower that reigning cultural ideology.

Liberation and feminist theologies are correct in seeing that texts are always interpreted. They do not come to us without being affected by the biases we bring with us as readers, listeners, preachers, or teachers. There are no self-interpreting biblical texts. There are no totally objective methods. Even the claim of objectivity for historical-critical method is a false claim. Female presence and female images in the Bible remained invisible to "objective" scholarship, because women were treated as invisible in the church which produced the scholars. The biblical concern for the poor and the oppressed was often spiritualized because of the cultural biases of comfortable, middle-class societies whose institutions supported the scholars. The call of liberation and feminist theologies is for an advocacy stance which clearly identifies, and thus can critically reflect upon, one's own sociopolitical and theological commitments. Their own advocacy stance on behalf of the poor, the oppressed, and the marginalized is not an abandonment of critical reflection, but a refusal to let the inevitable biases of every interpreter remain hidden and unexamined, thus allowing biblical authority to function in behalf of those hidden biases.

In liberation hermeneutics, particularly crystallized in the influential work of Juan Luis Segundo,[9] biblical authority could be reclaimed out of captivity to oppressive social contexts by a hermeneutics of suspicion. One approaches the biblical text suspicious of the social lenses through which it has been read. This leads to a hermeneutics of retrieval. When the prevailing biblical understandings are shown to be in the service of oppressive sociopolitical interests, then a new reading of the biblical texts is possible, a recovery of central liberation themes

147

showing a divine bias toward the poor and the oppressed which is central to major portions of the biblical tradition. These themes are already present in the texts but obscured by the hermeneutics of oppression.

Feminist biblical scholars[10] took the hermeneutics of suspicion one step further to the evidence of oppressive bias within the biblical texts themselves. The biblical communities were patriarchal in character and the telling of the biblical faith story reflects that character in no small measure. Feminist biblical scholars have begun a long overdue process of recovering women's roles in the biblical story,[11] but this task of retrieval is not one of recovering a central biblical concern for sexual oppression similar to the biblical concerns for political and economic oppression. Women have not only been pushed to the margins in the interpretation of the biblical story, but all too often are relegated to the margins in the biblical story itself.

Thus, a feminist hermeneutics cannot simply be one of retrieval, but must move beyond that to one of reconstruction and reclamation. Feminist scholarship does not seek merely to retell the biblical story, but to add something new in the retelling. Alongside recovery of women's part in shaping the biblical tradition comes a new claim to liberating elements of the tradition applied specifically to the oppression of women in ways the biblical communities could hardly have imagined.

It is clear that for those who grant any legitimacy to the liberation and feminist critique the traditional notion of biblical authority as a deposit of timeless revealed truth cannot be sustained. Biblical interpretation becomes more dialogic. The content of biblical tradition is critiqued by the experience of God in our own times and communities (*praxis*). The content of Scripture is shown to have its own culturally conditioned biases, and the way in which it traditionally has been read has been conditioned by social and cultural location. Text and tradition must be subjected to critical reflection growing in part out of our experience of God's ongoing activity in our own lives and times.

The above-described critique has led some, such as Farley and Hodgson, to reject the very notion of scriptural canon: "In our judgment continued use of the concept of canon, however modified, is not helpful and should be abandoned."[12] This, by no means unusual, statement is primarily a reaction to the notion of canon as fixed authoritative content for Christian faith and ethics. Although skeptical about the notion of canon herself, Elisabeth Schüssler Fiorenza suggests the need for a move from viewing the Bible as timeless archetype to seeing it as prototype, "an open-ended paradigm that sets experiences in motion and invites transformations." [13] We will explore dimensions of this suggestion later in the chapter.

Biblical Authority: Focus and Locus

If we have indeed suffered the collapse of biblical authority as it has often been understood, then how are we to understand it? A beginning response suggests that questions of biblical authority properly focus not on the Bible itself (qualities inherent in the book) but on the *presence and activity of God.* By the same token, questions of biblical authority are not properly located in the realm of intellectual assessment of all great world literature but are instead located in the *church* which alone of the world's institutions claims a special relationship to the Christian Bible. [14]

1. All those who have located the authority of the Bible in its character as an inspired book share in common the view that the Bible is somehow directly from God in a way that other writings are not. James Barr points out that this view of inspiration tends to locate the importance of the Bible in its origins. [15] Because the Bible came into being as a result of the direct inspiration of God it is to be regarded as the central authority for faith and life in the church.

In spite of the collapse described earlier, this viewpoint is still widespread in the church, and the implications for Christian ethics are far-reaching. Since the Bible constitutes the only document inspired of God, the tendency is to make the Bible a self-sufficient authority for Christian moral judgments. God's will is revealed in the Scripture, and its contents can then be used prescriptively to determine what we should do. This position allows little flexibility in the way we regard the various materials of the Bible. Since the whole Scripture is inspired, it is equally authoritative, and this tends to imply that we use all biblical materials in the same manner when consulting it for ethical resources, although in fact this is seldom the case. In sum, the stress on inspiration makes the authority of the Bible inherent in the Bible itself, its origins and character. As Sallie McFague decries, the Christian faith has often become a "book religion"—as seen most clearly in Protestantism's *sola scriptura*—although it is evident in the book Christianity worships

149

that it is the transformative power of God's love, not a text, that is the focus of Christian faith.[16]

Earlier we referred to the gospel claim that Jesus "spoke with authority." The authority of Jesus (*exousia*) was a speaking "out of his being" that evoked power out of the being of his hearers. The point here is that the Bible is, as a book, not the authority. It does not say "these documents speak with authority"; it says "Jesus spoke with authority." Discussions of the Bible as authority need to be clear that it is not the Bible's own authority as a book, but the mediated authority of testimony from those who experienced the power of Jesus' words. *Through* the Scriptures Jesus might yet speak with authority, but that does not substitute the Bible for Jesus. In fact, both Jesus and the Bible point to God, in whom we live and move and have our being, as the final source where both Jesus' power and our own rests.

It is our contention, then, that the question of biblical authority is not properly focused in the inherent character of the Bible itself. The question is more fruitfully focused on God who is active in the world and whose will is disclosed to persons in and through that activity. Here exegesis and ethics find a significant common ground. Both seek to discern the disclosure of God's will for the people of faith. Exegesis strives to interpret the biblical record of God's self-disclosure to the communities of Israel and the early church in such a way that it illumines the church's understanding of God's activity and the revealing of the divine will for the present-day Christian community. Christian ethics, faced with questions of how Christians are to understand and conduct themselves in a complex and changing world, seeks to read the signs of God's activity and to discern the divine will for the present, and in so doing calls on the resources of the historic Christian faith, including in primary position the Scriptures and their history of interpretation in the church. In a sense exegesis moves from the historic witness to the present witness while Christian ethics begins with a present demand to be and do, and draws on the historic witness to meet that demand. But both activities are the necessary activities of the same community, the church. As such, it is a travesty that the work of biblical study and of ethics have been so often compartmentalized from one another in the life of the church.

Theologically, the problem with locating biblical authority in the concept of inspiration is the narrow view of God which results. It is as if God ceased to be active after the closing of the canon. The tendency is to speak as if God's disclosure of the divine will is limited to the distant past, and as if it is only in the written record of that past that God's presence and will can be known. A strict view of inspiration leaves no room for the ongoing activity of God and the possibility that God might be revealed through sources other than the Bible.

At stake here is the freedom of God.[17] It has always been the tendency of the religious community to attempt to limit and control the graceful activity of the God who says "I will be merciful to whom I will be merciful" (Exod. 33:19, cf. also Rom. 9:15). This dynamic can already be seen in the biblical communities themselves. When the prophet of the exile announces Cyrus as God's Messiah, the instrument of God's deliverance (Isa. 45:1), the people reject the notion because for them Cyrus was not a proper source of God's grace; this in turn calls forth the prophet's rebuke (Isa. 45:9-13).

God was not only active in relationship to the biblical communities. God has continued to make the divine will known to the church in all succeeding ages, and is still present, disclosing the divine will for the church and the world. The job of exegesis and ethics is to aid the church in discerning that will. This wider understanding of God's activity greatly opens the range of possibilities for theological and ethical sources of insight. The history of the church and its understandings of the faith, secular ideologies, the course of contemporary events, data from nontheological disciplines—all these and many more become possible avenues through which God may confront us or inspire us with knowledge of the divine will for all creation.

There is, however, a danger here as well. In stressing the universal activity of God there is a risk of completely relativizing the Bible. There are those who regard the Bible as just one among many expressions of religious experience in the human community. All are to be regarded as authoritative in the same sense. This view takes seriously the ongoing activity of God, but does not take seriously the uniqueness of the Bible's witness to that God. This uniqueness is not inherent in the Bible as one piece amidst the corpus of the world's literature. It appears only when the location for the shaping of moral character and conduct is the church. It is the faith community that claims a special place for the Bible as part of the confession of its own identity.

2. The Bible is the church's book.[18] It has no special status outside the faith community. In chapter 7 we have already indicated the seriousness we attach to the church as the context for the Christian moral

life. Here we need but briefly indicate that the church is therefore the necessary context in which an appeal to or role for biblical authority in Christian ethics must be assessed.

We have earlier argued that the nature of Christian ethics is as community ethics (chapter 2). Here we assert that authority ascribed to Christian Scripture is community authority. The Bible as a book does not in itself assert authority. Biblical authority is enacted by the Church as it uses the Bible for preaching, teaching, liturgy, and guidance in its life and mission. The canon of Scripture originated not because of inherent qualities in the literature itself, but because of what that literature evoked in the life of the biblical communities. The formal declaration of canonicity in synagogue and church took place as the recognition of authority already generated by the *use* of those books in the communities of faith.

The important work of David Kelsey[19] is representative of recent work which focuses biblical authority in terms of the Bible's function in the life of the church rather than its inherent character as a revelatory document. By focusing on *uses* of Scripture he assumes an ecclesial location as necessary for understanding appeals to the Bible. It is the church that is the user, although in a variety of ways. Kelsey asserts that the Bible cannot itself (even rigorously studied) determine the basic character of Christian faith or settle disputes over its character. Church communities, bodies, and traditions must come to a certain commonality of perspective (what Kelsey calls "imaginative construal") before normative appeals can be made to the Bible in matters of theology or ethics.[20] Farley and Hodgson summarize the work of Kelsey in terms that are consistent with our position on the church as the necessary location for an appropriate understanding of biblical authority. "Kelsey develops an explicitly functional understanding of scripture. Scripture, he says, has authority to the extent that it functions in the church to shape new human identities and transform individual and communal life. It can be understood theologically to function this way because it is God who is active in scripture—not God 'saying' or 'revealing' (the classic images), but God 'shaping identity,' 'using' the uses of scripture toward a specific end: the actualization of God's eschatological rule."[21]

Biblical Authority and Christian Ethics: Some Proposals

1. Biblical authority in ethical matters should be viewed in terms of primacy rather than self-sufficiency. By this we mean that among all

of the possible sources of ethical insight and influence the Bible stands out as primary because of its function in the church, but it is by no means totally adequate as the sole source for shaping Christian character and conduct. The authority of the Bible is a necessary factor in the Christian moral life, but it is not self-sufficient. James Gustafson writes, "An authority can be unique without being exclusive. The Bible has such a status. . . . Thus, for Christian ethics its authority is inescapable without being absolute."[22]

For those seeking to do *Christian* ethics the Bible does have a special significance not shared by other sources of ethical insight. The Bible cannot be totally relativized as simply one among many sources of ethical insight.

First of all, it is the document which establishes the particular identity of the historic community called the church. The Bible is the record of the origins of the church and of the faith tradition it bears. It is the only witness to the person and work of Jesus Christ who stands as the focusing center for the Christian faith and for the Christian moral life. It is more than just a matter of origins, however, since it is also the church's experience that the Bible continues to be a source of empowerment to new being in every generation. That this has taken different forms and emphases does not negate the importance of the consistent testimony to the Bible as a source of such authority (*exousia*). Christian ethics is free to choose among the many sources of ethical wisdom available, but it is not free to ignore the Bible unless it wishes to end the continuity of historic identity in which the church stands.

Secondly, not only does the Bible serve to establish the historic identity of the church, but it provides a chief influence in shaping the perception and action of the church in current moral issues. Through the liturgy, proclamation, and teaching of the church the Bible influences the way in which the Christian community discerns God's will in the world and acts on it. The Bible is already present and functioning to shape Christian moral agency in the life of the church. Although the range and diversity of such uses of Scripture is great, the Bible's functioning influence is almost never wholly absent in any Christian congregation. As such, the Bible influences the ability of the community of faith and its members to find God's active will in nonbiblical sources of moral authority as well. Only as the church comes to know God in its own historic traditions can the work of discerning the divine activity in the present be completed.

Thus, the Bible's unique relationship to the church makes it the *constant* source to which the church refers in the shaping of moral character and in the making of moral decisions. For Christians no other sources of moral wisdom can claim these characteristics. The primacy of the Bible as an authority for Christian ethics indicates its position as the single *necessary* reference point. It is to be taken seriously in *all* ethical reflection within the church.

2. Although the Bible may be the primary authority it is not a sufficiently broad base of authority for Christian ethics in the modern church. While a necessary source, the Bible must be in constant dialog with the many other sources of knowledge and insight through which God might be disclosed. As mentioned in chapter 1, such nonbiblical sources are necessary simply for data in understanding the issues of modern times and our lives in such times. Many issues could not be foreseen at all in the biblical communities, while others have form, complexity, and context that were not anticipated.

Biblical authority may, however, function to help us claim the authority of nonbiblical sources. It is from the Bible that we have drawn models of the transforming power of encounter with God. As we come to understand the images, symbols, and metaphors used to describe that encounter in the biblical communities, we become sensitized to the possibilities for such encounters with God and their transforming power in our own world. It is our knowledge of God mediated through Scripture which helps us to discern God acting in the present. Since our God is radically free, divine presence and action will not be limited to official religious tradition or institutions. Further, the models for understanding, describing, and proclaiming that divine activity may not be the models of the Bible or of church tradition. The Bible authorizes our efforts to couple biblical insight with insight drawn from our own time and place to create models appropriate to proclaim God's "new thing" (Isa. 42:9) in continuity with God's graceful presence in our past.[23]

It is precisely the Bible itself which anticipates and makes this point. It has become clear that in the growth of the biblical material Israel and the early church did not hesitate to draw on sources already in existence outside their communities of faith if those materials served to communicate more clearly their understanding of the relationship to God and the divine will for the people of God. Many elements of Israelite law and covenant seem to rely on well-known international legal traditions. Wisdom literature is now widely understood as a secular genre characteristic of royal courts in the ancient Near East which Israel borrowed and used to its own purposes. The author of the Gospel of John used a whole range of philosophic categories current in the Hellenistic world of his day to present his unique witness to the life of Jesus. The list could easily be extended. It is sufficient to say that the Bible itself makes clear that the sources of theological and ethical insight are not narrowly limited to those materials that arise only from within the community of faith itself. The community is constantly "finding" God in its wider world and appropriating materials from that world to express faith.

This has continued to be true throughout the history of the church. St. Augustine's theology and ethics were profoundly influenced by neoplatonism, and St. Thomas Aquinas utilized the "pagan" philosophy of Aristotle. It is no less true for our present day. The church cannot do ethics on the basis of the Bible alone. Within the church itself we are dependent on a long history of biblical interpretation and its related moral and theological tradition. Outside the church we must take account of the sociopolitical context in which ethical issues arise; we must heed the voices helping us to understand the cultural context in which the church seeks to shape moral character and discharge its mission to the world; we must avail ourselves of knowledge for understanding, and secular categories for communicating the church's moral concerns. There are far more nonbiblical sources available to the church in its exercise of ethical judgment than we could list here.

The task of the church, then, is to bring its unique resources based in the Scripture into dialog with the many nonbiblical sources of ethical insight. The Bible remains primary in its authority for this process, because it is the key to distinguishing Christian ethics from ethics done in some secular mode.

3. The authority of the Bible for Christian ethics rests as much in its modeling of process as in its mediation of content. The Bible is composed of the collected testimony of persons and communities to the transforming and redemptive activity of God. To be called by the text to the remembrance of this testimony is not for the sake of the ancient events in themselves. That is the interest of the historian of antiquity. We are called by the text to remember for the sake of our own redemption, to enable us to discern the redemptive activity of God in the events of our lives.

155

McFague suggests that the sharp divisions between Scripture, tradition, and experience disappear when understood as a process of "witness to experiences of the salvific power of God." These form a continuum, a "sedimented interpretation," in which we see the redemptive power of God modeled in images, metaphors, and concepts appropriate to mediate that redemptive power anew in each age.[24] Authority resides not in the book but in the transformative encounter with God which the Bible mediates. Our encounter is in a long line of previous encounters with God's redemptive power.

> What constitutes this book [the Bible] are a number . . . of experiences of persons and communities witnessing to the transforming power of God in their lives, interpreted in terms not of some past time but of their own time. If we wish to take Scripture seriously and see it as normative, we should take it on its own terms as a model of how theology should be done, rather than as the authority dictating the terms in which it is done. . . . It is not so much an interpretation that one looks for in the Bible as a process, not so much a content as a form.[25]

To focus on process as well as content does not mean the abandonment of the notion of canon as some have suggested. It does mean that we must understand canon in a different way than the traditional conception of a definitive collection of timeless, divinely revealed truths. Taken in this way, it has been clear for generations that not all of the Bible can be taken with equal seriousness. This has led to the common practice of selecting a canon within the canon by those who nevertheless attempt to maintain a traditional position which regards the whole of the Bible as divinely inspired. The problem is not in the existence of the canon—that is a given of our historic tradition—but in our conception and use of it. Those who wish to reopen the canon seem to suggest that God's redemptive presence is legitimized in non-biblical sources only by canonization. Recent biblical work on the concept of canon has altered our understanding of the canon's conceptualization and function.[26] It has become clear that the focus should be as much on process as on product. The canon itself is testimony to a process of "adaptability to life"[27] and not to successive deposits of unalterable, revealed truth. The canon functions not in isolation from our own experience of God but precisely in the process of letting our own story be intersected by the biblical story and reflecting critically and acting faithfully in the church out of those intersections. The end result toward which we should strive is a deabsolutized canon which allows for the honoring of ancient witness to the degree that it reveals to us the basic truths of our faith while at the same time honoring the power and authority of our own experience of God.[28] We shall have more to say on the role of the canon in the next chapter.

Attention to biblical authority as it mediates a process does not mean there is no continuity of biblical content to be claimed. McFague finds it necessary to speak of "the paradigmatic content of demonstrable continuities" from the Bible.[29] Our identity as the church is obviously shaped by images, concepts, and metaphors that are part of the Bible's content and not just its witness to a process. But these cannot be regarded as revelatory deposits functioning as divinely sanctioned doctrine. The content must be constantly tested by the process. Which stories and images continue to manifest the redeeming power of God? Some matters of content are reassessed by the church, e.g., the biblical acceptance of slavery, Paul's admonition for women to keep silent in the church. Some matters of content are reasserted, e.g., God's preferential option for the poor and the oppressed. Some matters of content remain central although our interactions with them may change, e.g., the gospel story of the life, death, and resurrection of Jesus.

4. Finally, we would suggest that any view of biblical authority adequate for Christian ethics must be cognizant of the diversity within the biblical tradition.[30] Different types of biblical material must be appropriated in different ways (a matter to be fully discussed in the next chapter). The problem with most discussions of biblical authority is that they seem to imply a monolithic view of the Bible and its use. There is no single way in which the Bible is authoritative in ethical matters. For example, a clear and consistent moral imperative within much of the biblical witness, such as the imperative to identify with and care for the poor, carries a definite authority in ethical discussions of poverty within the modern church. On the other hand, the biblical witness concerning attitudes toward marriage and sexuality is more diverse. There is no one biblical perspective, and yet the biblical materials still carry authority in that they help set the necessary framework for the church's discussion of ethical issues in this area. The point to be made here is that the Bible is functioning authoritatively in different ways with different meanings in these examples.

We suggest that biblical authority operates differently depending on

157

the nature of the biblical materials that speak to a given issue. Further, we wish to argue that such a multifaceted view of biblical authority is necessary if the totality of the Bible's resources is to be made available to Christian ethics. It is a narrow definition of authority, implying a prescriptive use of inspired materials, that has led to a narrowing of the biblical resources available to Christian ethics so that only passages explicitly addressing moral matters are often used.

Our treatment of biblical authority as primary is intended to allow for a more flexible and functional view of biblical authority, and at the same time to stress the necessary biblical frame of reference within which ethical inquiry must take place if it is to be Christian. It remains next to discuss the actual processes involved in making available and appropriating biblical resources for the Christian moral life.

9

MAKING BIBLICAL RESOURCES AVAILABLE

In spite of general agreement that the Bible is an important resource for the church in ethical issues, the fact is that in practice its role is often an insignificant one. Christian ethicists often acknowledge the Bible in chapters on biblical foundations, but its influence is meager within the pages of discussion that follow. Biblical scholars concerned with textual, historical, and literary issues often betray little interest in how biblical materials might be claimed as a resource in the lives of communities which still view those texts as Scripture. It seems ironic that in a time when critical scholarship has clarified so much in our understanding of the Scriptures that the Bible actually seems less available as a resource for the Christian moral life than in previous generations.[1] One can only speculate on the reasons for this. Perhaps the explosion of biblical knowledge has made the Bible seem complex and formidable. On the other hand, it may be that modern life with its emphasis on immediate gratification has made church people less willing to undertake the disciplined study of the Bible which might unlock its resources. The seeming urgency of ethical issues may stand in tension with the longer term nurturing of Christians in their own biblical inheritance so that the insights of those ancient communities might inform the decisions of the present.

This chapter is intended to suggest how the Bible might be made available as a resource for Christian ethics. Initially its concern is with two matters that seem largely ignored both by scholars and those in the local parish.

First, too little attention has been paid to the distinctive character of the Bible as the source of moral insight and guidance. The Bible is often consulted as if its unique character requires no special understanding. The results of such consultation are usually disappointing. Without understanding its nature the Bible may seem obscure, contradictory, and irrelevant.

Those dealing with an ethical issue may spend enormous amounts of energy investigating the sociopolitical factors of a given situation. Great attention is paid to characterizing and evaluating different types of data, and the tendency is often to stress the uniqueness of each situation. This makes it all the more interesting that if the Bible is consulted at all, it is somehow expected to speak directly to the issue as if it were a compendium of disembodied material having no character or context of its own. Our thesis is that to understand the character of the biblical witness is to crucially affect its use.

Second, even less attention has been given to a disciplined method for the study and use of the Bible. This is especially true in the local church where even the pastor may not be equipped to do basic exegesis of a biblical text. Many Christian ethicists concerned for method also display a lack of basic exegetical tools. The fault lies partly in the guild of biblical scholarship where critical study of the Bible has been defined in such a technical sense that it has become the province of the professional alone. A seminary faculty member once told us that since exegesis of the Old Testament required the ability to read Hebrew he had ceased to teach exegetical method to seminarians. But the fault must also lie with a generation in the churches that is one of the least knowledgeable about Scripture in the recent history of the church. It is possible to be an active church member for an entire lifetime and still have no systematic knowledge of the Bible.[2] In the face of such monumental indifference it is little wonder that exegesis is becoming the sole possession of the scholarly guild.

We believe that if the church is to recover the Bible as an ethical resource, it can and must develop a capacity for disciplined reflection on the Scripture. In short, it must learn to do its own basic exegesis.

The Character of the Biblical Witness

It is not necessary to discuss the unique character of the Bible at length. Whole volumes have been written on this. It is important, however, to note several aspects of Scripture which are crucial and often overlooked in the use of the Bible for ethics.

1. Most of those who have turned to the Bible for moral guidance have overlooked the *immense variety* of biblical literature which might be pertinent to ethical concerns.[3] Since Western Christian ethics has most often been issue-oriented, the tendency has been to consult the Bible narrowly concerning a particular issue. Sometimes this has been broadened to explore the biblical material on a key concept or ideal such as justice. The result is that the Bible's applicability to ethical issues has often been limited to those portions of Scripture which address ethical concerns directly. Passages of moral exhortation have been the most consulted. Greatest interest has focused on law codes (especially the Ten Commandments), prophetic oracles, the moral teachings of Jesus, and those epistles which address particular moral concerns in the early church.

In reality the Bible has a much greater range of resources for ethical insight than has usually been utilized. Many materials do not directly address issues that are important or even existent for us, but they witness to the efforts of the biblical communities in concrete historical circumstances to discover and live according to the will of God, and this forms the linchpin for the shaping of moral identity and faithful decisions in any age. Narrative accounts, historical events, wisdom sayings, parables, eschatological material, theological reflection, and liturgical material—all of these may yield as much ethical insight as passages that explicitly address ethical issues and sometimes with greater force.[4]

The story of Jacob wrestling with the night visitor (Gen. 32:22ff.) is an example. On the surface it may not seem to speak to ethical concerns, yet it does. Jacob has to this point lived a completely self-serving life, a life of cheating and deception. As a consequence, he is alienated from his brother Esau, who has vowed to kill him. He is forced to live in Haran, far from the promised land, and although he prospers there in material wealth, there comes a time when Jacob must risk the journey back to reunion with his separated brother. On the banks of the Jabbok River, Jacob spends the night alone. He knows

161

that on the next day he will meet his brother, and he does not know what fate awaits him. Unexpectedly, a man leaps upon him in the night, and they struggle until dawn. This is no ordinary visitor, but Jacob, still attempting to control his own destiny in his own interests, demands a blessing from this adversary. Instead, he is humbled; his thigh is thrown painfully out of joint by a mere touch, and he is given a new name. No longer will he be called Jacob, the name of his own self-interest. He is to be named Israel, a name which points to a role beyond himself as the ancestor of a whole people and the bearer of God's promise; a name which means "one who strives with God." Contrary to his lifelong belief, destiny was not in his control but in God's. As he limps from that place, Jacob names it Peniel ("face of God") because there he saw God "face to face" (32:30). Jacob is a changed man. He is now prepared for the meeting with his brother on the following day. Esau, whom Jacob expected to encounter as an enemy intent on killing him, is truly his brother, and Esau embraces Jacob joyfully. With new understanding Jacob says, "Truly, to see your face is like seeing the face of God" (33:10). The conquest of his self-sufficiency, the finding of his new identity, and even the inflicted pain which causes him to limp away, form the preconditions to genuine reconciliation with his brother Esau.

Seen fully this text becomes one of profound significance for ethical issues involving conflict and alienation, both personal and social (e.g., racism, war, sexism). It suggests that many we regard as enemies are really brothers and sisters, and that the path to reconciliation lies through those dark nights when God encounters us in the form of human struggle. By risking such struggle and painful injury we can hear our true name and be enabled to see the face of God in that of our alienated brother or sister.[5]

Or again, the eucharistic texts of the New Testament take on new ethical significance when bread has become not simply a symbol of Christian community in Christ, but also a symbol of division in the world between those who have bread and those who must die for lack of it. A renewed exploration of the brokenness of the bread and of Christ's body in our broken world has deep moral implications for the church's response to global hunger and poverty. But a narrow definition of ethical resources in the Bible would not have included eucharistic texts.

A narrow selection of biblical material seems to have its origin in a focus on decision making as the sole subject of ethics. Since many ethical decisions we must make are not directly addressed in the Scriptures, it must indeed seem rather limited as an ethical resource. We are suggesting that one key to making the Bible available as an ethical resource is to see in its variety a wealth of insight into the biblical values and norms that shape the life and commitment of the community of faith itself as well as the decisions such communities make.

2. In unlocking the biblical witness as a resource it is crucial that the *form and context* of a passage be given as much attention as its content. The character of the Bible is such that its materials generally speak in a very concrete form out of a particular context in the life of the biblical communities. The Bible is not given to generalized, universal address. Thus, it is a travesty for church people and scholars to pick and choose from the Scripture as if its content could be directly applicable apart from a serious consideration of form and context.

The sole focus on content has led to numerous distortions. There are those who abstract the content of great themes such as covenant, justice, and the kingdom of God as if these were given no concrete reality in the Bible, and as if these themes could be appropriated apart from the struggles to understand them in a particular manner in a particular situation. Even the same content may take on different meaning in different contexts. For example, the story of Adam and Eve in Genesis 2–3 is one of human freedom and the responsibility of the man and the woman to bear the consequences of their decision. In 1 Tim. 2:13-15 the story is used to suggest a subordinate, sinful status for women. These are differences in meaning for the same content that can only be understood in terms of the radically different social location and community behind each text. The Genesis text received its final shape around the time of the Davidic kingdom with its new emphasis on the role and risks of human responsibility, while 1 Timothy reflects an early church struggling in the context of attitudes and practices in the Greco-Roman world.

Biblical scholarship in this century has particularly advanced our understanding of the importance of form and context. Form criticism, from its beginnings in the 19th century, has developed a broadly accepted stress on observing and identifying the genre (form) by which many texts are structured. These established patterns often provide clues to the setting in life (*Sitz im Leben*) which gave rise to traditions and texts. This can lead to radically changed understandings. For example, the Psalms were long regarded by most church people as the poetry of pious individuals. It is now clear, and reflected in most church curriculum and study material, that the Psalms primarily come out of Israel's corporate worship and reflect the community's basic faith understandings, rather than that of an individual poet.

More recently, important new ground has been broken in applying methods of sociological research to the biblical texts in an effort to better understand the social contexts out of which those texts come. The result has been a heightened sense of the importance of social location both in the origins of a text and in its trajectory of interpretation and reinterpretation down to the present.[6] For example, the work of Norman Gottwald and others has placed a new stress on the emergence of Israelite community as a unique egalitarian social structure in the ancient world.[7] Research on the gospel of John now stresses the conflict between the early church and the synagogue as the necessary context for understanding its unique emphases.[8]

Related to these developments is a renewed interest in the community base for the development and preservation of biblical tradition. It is the community of faith, Israel or the early church, that has judged these traditions, as passed on in these texts, to be worthy of preservation for future generations.[9] We shall have more to say on this in our discussion of the canon. Here we may simply say that attention to the community context can make us sensitive to models for our own community response even when the content of an issue is dissimilar. For example, beyond the prophetic indictments against various forms of idolatry and social injustice lies a very concrete understanding of the covenant nature to which the community is called. We may not face the content of the prophets' concern for Baalism or royal privilege, but the form of their speaking betrays the underlying covenant understanding even when it is not mentioned directly. And our understanding of the prophets' social context makes clear the demand of God's word for those who oppose privilege and injustice and champion equity and justice amidst the prevailing patterns of any social setting. Attention to form and context allows us to move beyond the content of opposing the Baals to the question of what it means to be a prophet and a just community. We sometimes look beyond the content of a passage on a particular issue to patterns of response by the faithful community in many concrete situations, including our own.

3. In both the Old and the New Testaments *doing is intimately tied to being.* Those with ethical concerns most often approach the Bible asking, "What shall we do?" The Bible resolutely tells us that what we do is dependent on who we are called to be. We are called to be the faithful community of the people of God. It is out of this identity that we are to decide and act. The tendency is to seek help in deciding an ethical issue without attending to the summons into relationship with God which comes through the community of faith.

The Bible is clear that to know God's will is to do it. These are elements that simply cannot be separated from one another, and the presupposition of both is relationship to God through the faith community. "He has showed you, O [mortal], what is good; and what does the Lord require of you but to do justice, and to love kindness, and to walk humbly with your God?" (Micah 6:8). Here relationship to God is made inseparable with the doing of justice. When Jesus characterizes the great commandment as love of God and love of neighbor he is implying this dual reality in the life of faith, that relationship to God is the corollary of service to the neighbor. "Be doers of the word, and not hearers only," says the author of James (1:22) in a similar vein. This should not send us off in a frenzy of mindless activity even in the best of causes. It should tell us that discerning God's will and doing it are necessarily related. Such discernment comes only through the identity-shaping influence of the faith community.

The biblical materials were preserved by the community of faith for a particular purpose. The Bible spoke the Word anew in each generation, calling men and women into the relationship of faith. Those who ignore this dimension do not find in the Bible a very helpful source of ethical insight. Some study the Bible only as a historical document of the church's roots, and hence find it irrelevant to the present. Others ask it to make decisions for them and are disillusioned when it often fails to do that.

The Bible itself tells us we cannot separate being and doing. Thus, if the Bible is to be a resource for the moral life we must give up an exclusive focus on the ethics of doing. We must ask, "Who are we to be?" as well as "What are we to do?" Of course, our deciding and acting can be informed by the Scripture, but not apart from its role in forming the basic identity and character of those (individually and corporately) who do the deciding and acting from within the relationship of faith. We shall return to these matters at later points.

We have traced three elements in the character of the biblical witness that are important in approaching the Bible as an ethical resource: the immense variety in biblical literature, the importance of form and social context, and the intimate relation of being and doing. Now we must turn our attention to more concrete methods for unlocking the resources of particular texts.

The Importance of Exegesis

If the Bible is to serve as an ethical resource there must be some disciplined method for understanding and explaining the meaning of biblical texts. In most churches the Bible is consulted on a haphazard basis. If the text consulted seems understandable on the surface it may be used and have some influence. If the message of a text is not immediately apparent it will be dismissed or perhaps not even discovered in the first place. The Bible is the complex record of the biblical communities in their relationship to God over a period of more than 1500 years. As such, the Bible could not be expected to be a self-interpreting document. Yet church people invest little systematic effort at understanding its message. If the Bible is to be made available to ethical concerns then persons in the churches must learn the fundamentals of exegesis.

Exegesis, according to the *American Heritage Dictionary*, is "a critical explanation or analysis; especially interpretation of Scriptures." It is derived from two Greek words, *ex* meaning "out" and *hegeisthai* meaning "to lead, or guide." It is the word commonly used in biblical studies to indicate the process of critically explaining a text, drawing out its meaning. The tools and techniques of exegesis have been developed extensively. But exegesis is a word rarely found in the vocabulary of persons in the local parish, and the process it represents is usually absent as well.

Somehow the idea has gotten abroad that exegesis is a task so complex that it is to be reserved for the specialist, the biblical scholar, or more academically inclined pastors. There are even many pastors who suggest that the explication of biblical texts is a task beyond their skills. They want books and articles to perform this task for them, thereby telling them what to preach and teach. Yet one of the fundamentals of the Reformation was the right of the whole church, clergy and lay, to interpret Scripture. It would be ironic if, in our time, the interpretation of Scripture became the province of only those few in the scholarly guild of biblical studies. As it is today, church people are seldom expected to enter into the process of disciplined reflection that exegesis requires. They are not asked to master the resources of their own faith tradition.

But it is our contention here that a mastery of basic exegetical skills is possible for any serious inquirer. We also contend that such mastery is necessary if biblical resources are to be available to the church in facing the ethical challenges of this day.[10] We can now proceed to discuss various aspects of basic exegesis.

The first task of exegesis is to *examine the text.* For the average church member this cannot be done in the original language, so one must rely on translations. Fortunately, many excellent translations are available. The Revised Standard Version, The Jerusalem Bible, The New English Bible, The New American Bible, and The New International Version are but a few that might be used with profit.[11] When congregations are working on biblical materials it is helpful to have several different translations present for comparison.

When translations are compared several things might happen. If the translation of a text varies radically from one version to another, one should assume that serious translation problems exist, and translators have exercised differing judgments. This would certainly mean that one must be cautious in using a single translation of that text as a strong basis for some ethical stance. One might have to consult commentaries or other helps to make a judgment on which translation seems more probable. In any case, the caution flag should be raised.

If the translations differ, but not in ways that change the substance of the passage, then the group working on the text is simply enriched by a wider variety of possibilities for expressing and making a passage communicate in translation. One of these may seem clearer and more illuminating than another and might then become the basic text for moving on to discuss its implications for the life of faith.

Translations may differ on some key word or phrase. This may then focus study effort into a particular channel in an effort to illumine some key concept. For example, in the commandment "You shall not kill" some translations have said "You shall not murder." Does this verse refer to all taking of life, including war and self-defense, or does it refer to the narrower range of offenses implied by using the word murder? Further inquiry would be needed, and the translation comparison would indicate the direction of that inquiry.

The by-product of careful attention to the text is that even brief experience with the use of differing translations teaches the dangers of absolutizing any one biblical translation. Groups learn immediately that the Bible is not a manual of moral information to be mechanically applied. Even to discover what the text says requires disciplined, reflective judgment. Hopefully this learning will carry over into discovering what the text means.

Once the text itself has been investigated, the exegete turns to a careful and critical discovery of the meaning of the text. If the Bible is truly to become available as a resource for the Christian moral life, its passages must be understood as thoroughly as possible, both in the literary form by which they communicate with us and in the concrete historical circumstances which produced them. Since we wrote earlier on the importance of form and context in understanding the Bible, we need not argue the point here. We can turn directly to the manner in which exegesis operates.

It is usually best to begin by examining the *literary style and organization* of a passage. Exegesis might be understood as a process of seeking answers to the particular questions raised by a given text. What type of literature is represented by the text? Where does the emphasis fall as it is organized? Is there a logical stylistic structure to the passage? Is the passage part of a larger piece of material? How does it relate to that larger literary context (e.g., is it the climactic point of the whole piece)? Can anything be said about authorship? Are there direct literary parallels to the passage (e.g., a gospel story or teaching might appear in three or four retellings)? Does the emphasis change among these parallels?

Closely related to literary questions are *questions of form or genre.* Many times the formal structure of a passage is of a distinct type that in itself tells us something about the meaning of the text and its use. Examples might be prayers, oracles of judgment, parables, or visions. Without knowing the specific context of a passage we would begin to know something about it by being told it was one of these distinct genres. Many such genres have been distinguished in the Old and New Testaments. The exegete must ask if the passage falls into any distinct formal category that allows it to be classed with a particular genre. If so, how does this affect our understanding of the passage's use in the biblical communities? How does it affect the way in which the passage speaks its message?

In raising *questions of historical context* about a passage we are seeking to understand the life experiences of Israel or the early church which lie behind the text. There are often two levels of historical context with which the exegete must be concerned. The first is the concrete historical experience itself as witnessed to directly by the text. For example, there is the central experience of the resurrection. Secondly, there is the historical context to which this witness was intended to speak. Although there was only one resurrection, each Gospel directs its witness to a different period and set of circumstances in the life of the early church.

To take an Old Testament example, Isaiah 40–55 constantly uses the language of exodus, God's deliverance of Israel out of bondage in Egypt. We therefore need to understand the experience of the exodus event as fully as possible. But the prophet is writing during the Babylonian exile, and we are also called to an understanding of the tragedy of that experience. Then we can see that the prophet has taken the experience of the exodus and, by placing it in the context of his own exilic experience, has transformed it into the hope of a new exodus. In making the Bible available for Christian ethics it is crucial that we see how a passage functioned in its own historic circumstances. The Bible can only come alive to our ethical concerns if we understand how it was alive for the communities of faith where it originated.

Finally, we may raise *theological questions* to the text. In light of its literary and historical contexts what is the theological message of the passage? What are its main theological motifs? What are the larger theological themes to which this passage relates? Are there key words or concepts that point to theological underpinnings which go beyond this passage? What was the theological importance of this passage to the biblical community of its time?

It is important to note that persons doing exegesis in the local church are not without helpful tools. There are many excellent commentaries, Bible dictionaries, Bible atlases, concordances, handbooks of biblical theology, and introductions to biblical literature.[12] One should, however, avoid consulting these too quickly. Before using these tools one should carefully examine the passage under consideration and determine what the significant questions are which must be addressed. Then, reflecting on the text, one should begin to form initial judgments on the literary, historical, and theological dimensions of the text. At this point one consults the available tools for assistance in reaching the fullest understanding of the passage.

Having examined a passage in its immediate context, the Christian exegete must also take note of the full range of a passage and its themes in the entire canon. The church considers both the Old and New Testaments as Scripture; therefore, a boundary for exegesis cannot be drawn between them. Specific passages or their related themes must be seen in their complete development in the whole canon. We shall return to the importance of the canon in detail in the next section. Let it suffice at this point to indicate that the indispensable tool for this effort is a concordance. A concordance lists key words alphabetically and records every instance where that word appears in a biblical passage. Every serious student of the Bible, whether scholar, clergy, or laity, should practice the use of a concordance. Not to do so is to look at a biblical text with blinders on, thinking that what one sees immediately at hand is all there is to see.

Those who define the task of exegesis narrowly as the descriptive task of the objective historian would conclude the discussion of exegetical method at this point.[13] The text and its original meaning have been described as fully as possible. For the church this is not enough. Exegesis in the church must go beyond mere description to reflect on how the words of the biblical text become the Word of God which addresses God's people anew in our time. The church's exegete must ask how a passage, fully and critically understood, lays its claim on the contemporary community of faith. What insight or guidance is given there for the church in its current struggles to be the faithful people of God?

In this final step the Bible becomes fully available as a resource for the church's ethical concerns. The Bible's application to ethical issues is not mechanistic; it is dialogic. One pole of the dialog is the situation out of which our current moral concerns grow. The other pole is a full understanding of the biblical witness as we recover it through disciplined, exegetical reflection. Only as the biblical voices become fully audible can the dialog take place. The relationship between the Bible and ethical concerns then becomes a dynamic one in which there are many options whereby the Scripture might influence the Christian moral life. Without careful exegesis the biblical witness is not fully heard, and the contemporary pole of the dialog becomes a monolog confirming its prejudgments by picking and choosing from Scriptures that have not been allowed to speak with their own voice.

This call to develop the capacity for exegesis in the local church is not an attempt to impose a narrow method. There is room for considerable variety in exegetical style. It is a call for the church to engage in disciplined reflection on its own scriptural resources. Only through such disciplined and systematic understanding of the biblical materials can the Bible properly function as a source of moral insight in the church.

The Canon as a Framework of Control

We have suggested that the task of exegesis is not completed until a text and its themes have been considered within the full range of the Christian canon. This has not been a customary viewpoint. Under the widespread influence of the critical method the tendency has been to analytically dismantle passages. Seldom has the theological meaning of the whole been given much attention. This is particularly true with respect to large bodies of biblical material. For example, is it not important that the oracles of an eighth-century prophet named Isaiah and the oracles of an anonymous sixth-century exilic prophet are preserved together in the same biblical book? Are not the different Gospel portraits to be read in relation to one another? Even more importantly, does the concept of the canon not imply that we are to read the New Testament in light of the Old Testament and vice versa?

Recently, attention to redaction criticism (the critical understanding of influences shaping whole biblical books or literary traditions) has brought some new interest to this area. At the same time there has been renewed interest in the meaning of the canon. Brevard Childs has been one of the prominent voices in arguing that "the canon of the Christian church is the most appropriate context from which to do Biblical Theology."[14] We believe he is right, and that the wider framework of the canon is of particular importance in appropriating biblical materials for Christian ethics.

The concept of the canon (and the word itself) are not familiar to many church people. Basically the word "canon" is used in the Christian tradition to refer to that collection of books judged by the church to be authoritative for Christian life and doctrine. The word itself seems

171

to come from a Semitic root meaning "rod" and derivatively "a measure." Thus, the biblical canon is a theological measure in the ongoing tradition of the church.

A lively recent discussion has developed around the nature of the canon and its role. Some voices have argued that canonization is but the final stage in the tradition-building process and is not to be valued more highly than any discernible stage in that process. For some, canon is even to be seen as but a stage in the process that reinterprets traditions from biblical times to the present, and should not be given any special authority (i.e., as Scripture).[15] These positions are difficult to translate into a usable understanding for the church, which claims the whole of the Bible as Scripture, since one can focus on the claims of any level of the tradition (pre- or post-canon) without being obligated to measure its theological or ethical claims against the whole of Scripture.

Brevard Childs has reemphasized the importance of the canon and claimed the final form of the canonical text as the *only* normative basis for biblical theology (therefore also ethics).[16] On the one hand this is a welcome corrective to reductionist exegesis which seems to reflect only on various discernible levels in the development of texts and seldom on the whole. Nevertheless, Child's exclusive focus on the *final* form of the text seems unnecessarily restrictive.[17]

James Sanders seems to occupy a somewhat mediating position.[18] He stresses the importance of the process whereby communities received and adapted tradition until it achieved its final fixed form. This process and the discernible evidence in levels of the text can, for Sanders, be the proper focus of theological interpretation, but he also stresses the need to set that reflection in the context of the final canonical form which the tradition took.

The canon exists as a reality in the churches which still claim that the whole of scripture is foundational for their faith. At least for those who wish to impact the life of the church and its moral influence in the modern world, the options cannot be limited to a rigid, dogmatic view of the canon, on the one hand, or a total devaluing of the canon on the other. Childs and Sanders have led the way to a renewed interest in questions of how the canon is to be understood in the life of the church.

Several basic observations on the *nature of the Christian canon* must be made.

1. The clear understanding of the church is that the Christian canon

is composed of both Old and New Testaments. Both together form the Scripture of the Christian church. Many in the church have tended to separate the two testaments. At best the Old Testament has been regarded as second-class Scripture. Exclusive focus on the New Testament has truncated the traditional witness of the church that the whole Scripture is the Word of God. This leaves the New Testament cut off from much of its rootage and impossible to be fully understood. From the point of view of the church's ethical concerns, it vastly narrows the range of available resources and creates a false and narrow context for understanding the rest. Many noted works in Christian ethics deal with biblical foundations by treating only the New Testament.[19] Concern for the canon as the total framework for our biblical reflection acts as a corrective to this arbitrary narrowing of resources.

Here we might note that, although for Christians Jesus Christ is the focusing center for faith and ethics, there is no single understanding of his life and work that can give a simple, monolithic standard of moral judgment. Indeed, it is increasingly clear that to understand Jesus requires not only the diverse witnesses of the New Testament to his life and work, but also the rich heritage of the Old Testament which provided foundation and content for Jesus' own understanding and proclamation of the good news that God had acted to redeem the world. The church has preserved the canon, not as mere historical documentation, but as necessary to the full understanding of its faith centered in Jesus Christ.

2. The Christian canon should not be regarded as books which the church chose and granted authority. The church has always stressed that the complex process of the formation of the canon represented only the recognition by the church of authority from God already established in the life of the church. Such authority resides not in the texts themselves but in the experience of the biblical communities with those texts. The canon is composed of texts which testify to the God who had called the community into new being. These texts, then, themselves continue to mediate this divine power to new being. "The concept of canon was an attempt to *acknowledge* the divine authority of its writings and collections. . . . In speaking of canon the church testified that the authority of its Scriptures stemmed from God, not from human sanction."[20] This perspective provides a safeguard against the notion that the church, having made the canon, can therefore redo

173

it, leaving out those portions which some regard as outdated or irrelevant. In the principle of the canon the church acknowledges all of the Old and New Testament as possessing the authority of God's Word. In matters of ethics this means that we are not free to disregard the totality of Scripture as in some way authoritative for the Christian moral life.

3. The canon developed in the context of actual faith communities. Therefore, it reflects all the gifts *and* failures of those communities. For example, the New Testament contains, not only witness to the ethic of coequal discipleship rooted in the ministry of Jesus, but also the household codes (*Haustafeln*) of Colossians 3 and Ephesians 5, in which that ethic was subverted due to pressure toward cultural acceptability (e.g., advising slaves to submit to masters and wives to husbands).[21]

A canon which reflects the realities of actual community experience with God is necessarily pluralistic.[22] The canon does not speak in a single voice. This is both a witness to the variety of experience with God and a corrective to warn us against absolutizing any selection of the voices through which Scripture speaks. That the biblical communities themselves can be seen judging and reinterpreting and measuring the tradition against their own experience of God can be read as a support for similar activity on our part.

This will, of course, necessitate attention to every level of witness preserved within the text as well as to the final form as the ultimate shape given to the text by the biblical communities. *The canon is a record, not only of a destination but a record of the journey as well.*

4. The canon is the source of life and death, liberation and oppression, hope and despair. Critical exegesis has always tended to equate the clear analytical understanding of a text with our ability to appropriate that text as meaningful. But in some instances, our clear understanding of a text becomes the source of problems and impediments to our theological appropriation. For example, the clearer we have become about the patriarchal structures of biblical communities, the more difficult it has become for women in the church to claim the traditions of these communities as meaningful.[23] To claim that the word of God speaks to us through the Scripture is not to claim the cultural character of the biblical communities as automatically normative. It seems clear that the word of God is sometimes communicated to us in

spite of the social and political bias, the narrow vision, and the participation in the brokenness of sin which we see in the biblical communities themselves alongside their witness to God's grace. Indeed, to recognize this is sometimes to allow us to hear the word of God more clearly.[24]

5. The canon is also the possession of the modern church. Thus, it is appropriate that it be received and interpreted only in conversation with our own experience of a living God and the demands of that God for faithfulness in our time. The goal is a canon in truthful dialog with our own experience of faith, especially in terms of the particularities of our own social location for faith experience. The conversation will be as diverse as the canon itself, and to the degree that we can receive that diverse witness we will be enriched with new eyes and new ears for our own receiving of the biblical word. The dynamic relationship of canon and contemporary faith experience is therefore two-way. As we come to see the pluralism of the canon's own witness, we become more attentive and receptive to the diversity of modern witness to what God is doing to bring liberation and reconciliation in our own time.

The questions of canon and its role seem especially crucial for a revitalized use of the Bible in Christian ethics. As we suggested in chapter 8, the goal toward which we should strive is a deabsolutized canon which allows for the honoring of ancient witness to the degree that it reveals to us the basic truths of our faith while at the same time honoring the power and authority of our own experience of God alongside that of the biblical communities.[25] Only such a goal can do justice to the notion of a living God who speaks to us through a living word.

How do we understand the *functioning of the canon* as a context for our appropriation of biblical resources? In our earlier discussion of biblical authority we stressed that the authority of Scripture is not absolute. Other factors enter into moral judgment. Here we would particularly wish to stress that in the immense variety of biblical materials, our own subjective judgments are bound to play a role in the selection of scriptural resources. In fact, our dialogic understanding of the process of appropriating Scripture would require it. But the principle of the canon insures that our subjective ethical dispositions be tested out on the broadest possible scriptural framework. We are forced to take seriously those scriptural materials that disagree with our judgments as much as those which agree. Our subjectivity is not replaced

175

by some objective scriptural standard. The Bible is not such a monolithic document. Our subjectivity is to operate in the framework of control provided by the whole canon. Let us see how the canon might function in that way.

The importance of the canon in the Christian tradition means that any person who seeks to do exegesis within and for the church must do it in the context of the total canon. We have already stated that this means a passage cannot be understood only in its own immediate context. The understanding gained in study and reflection on any given passage must be brought into conversation with the full range of materials in the Christian canon, Old and New Testaments. The interpreter must first ask if that passage is explicitly referred to in any other place in the Bible. If so, how does the tradition function there? Is it similar or different from the initial text? If the passage is not referred to explicitly, are there places in the Old or New Testament where similar language is used? Or are there places where similar concepts and subject matter are taken up?[26] When the full range of pertinent material is before us we can then seek the dynamic relationships between materials within the Bible itself. A passage seen by itself might appear quite different in meaning and significance when seen alongside a much wider range of related biblical material.

Implications for Christian ethics are obvious. One cannot with integrity enter dialog with the Scripture over ethical issues if the biblical warrants appealed to are narrow selections that have not been tested against the totality of the biblical witness. Of course, to do exegesis in the context of the canon runs the risk of discovering tensions and contradictions in the biblical material rather than a uniform moral witness. One can no longer cite only that pole of the tension most compatible with a position reached on other grounds. The canon often forces those who come to the Bible for moral guidance to face these tensions directly as a part of the moral struggle. We suggest that often these tensions prove to be present in the contemporary ethical situation and need to be faced there as well.

●　　●　　●

At this point it might be helpful to interrupt our discussion and briefly demonstrate with a particular text having ethical implications how a broader canonical context can change our understanding of a passage.

Matthew 26:6-13 (see also Mark 14:3-9; John 12:1-8) tells of an incident in which a woman approaches Jesus and pours a jar of expensive ointment on his head. The disciples are scandalized by such waste and complain that money for the ointment could better have been given to the poor. Jesus intervenes by saying, "Why do you trouble the woman? For she has done a beautiful thing to me. For you always have the poor with you, but you will not always have me." He goes on to treat the anointing as a foreshadowing of his preparation for burial.

Jesus' statement, "For you always have the poor with you," has been a constant nemesis to those in the church who have tried to arouse the conscience of Christians to the harsh realities of poverty in our society and elsewhere in the world. Those who have defined the gospel solely in terms of individual and "internal" salvation use this text to justify a total lack of concern for the victims of poverty and the establishment of a just social order. They maintain that this text proclaims the futility of seeking to relieve the condition of the poor and focuses attention instead on the person of Jesus. To them this means the elevation of spiritual needs over material needs.

Indeed, if our exegesis is limited narrowly to this text we might well come to this point of view. Jesus *does* rebuke the disciples in their desire to give to the poor. He *does* turn attention to his own person. But does Jesus intend that we should not be concerned with the material needs of those who suffer? Is attention to Jesus' own person a turning to "spiritual" matters? When we move to a wider canonical context our understanding of this passage begins to alter.

The first move is naturally to the wider description of Jesus' ministry in the Gospels. From the very beginning Jesus identified his ministry with the poor and the oppressed. In Luke 4:16-19, at the inauguration of his public ministry, Jesus preaches at Nazareth and chooses as his text Isa. 61:1-2:

> The Spirit of the Lord is upon me, because he has anointed me to preach good news to the poor. He has sent me to proclaim release to the captives and recovering of sight to the blind, to set at liberty those who are oppressed, to proclaim the acceptable year of the Lord.

Jesus associated himself with the poor and with society's outcasts and was criticized for it (Matt. 11:19; Luke 7:34). In his preaching, Jesus

177

spoke with concern for the poor and indicated that they were especially blessed by God (Luke 6:20-21). Perhaps most striking is the passage on the great judgment in Matt. 25:31-46:

> I was hungry and you gave me food, I was thirsty and you gave me drink, I was a stranger and you welcomed me, I was naked and you clothed me, I was sick and you visited me, I was in prison and you came to me.

Jesus makes clear that his very person is identified with the poor and the needy to the extent that acceptance of him is equated with ministering to their needs. "Truly, I say to you, as you did it to one of the least of these my brethren, you did it to me" (Matt. 25:40).

In light of the strong witness elsewhere in the Gospels to Jesus' concern with the material needs of the poor, we surely cannot understand Jesus' statement in Matt. 26:11 to be a repudiation of his own ministry. Jesus is focusing attention in this passage on his own passion, but would not be urging that we ignore the needs of the poor and needy.

Moving more widely in the canon we find in Deut. 15:7-11 a text with a statement so similar to that of Jesus that it raises the probability that Jesus is directly referring to it. This passage is a part of the law, the Torah, which was central to the faith of Jesus and the Jews of his time. The passage is making clear that concern for the poor is obligatory in the community of faith.

> There will be no poor among you . . . if only you will obey the voice of the Lord your God. . . . If there is among you a poor man, one of your brethren, in any of your towns within your land which the Lord your God gives you, you shall not harden your heart or shut your hand against your poor brother, but you shall open your hand to him and lend him sufficient for his need. . . . You shall give to him freely, and your heart shall not be grudging. . . . *For the poor will never cease out of the land;* therefore, I command you, You shall open wide your hand to your brother, to the needy and to the poor. . . .

This passage suggests that if the demands of the covenant were fully embodied there would be no poverty, but since Israel, like all human communities, is a "stiff-necked people," some of its inhabitants will inevitably be poor. Therefore, God's people are commanded to care for them. This task is part of what it means to be the people of God; it is not an optional activity.

This greatly alters our consideration of Matt. 26:6-13. Jesus is responding not to the disciples' desire to give to the poor, but to their rebuke of the woman. He is reminding them that the existence of the poor is a constant judgment against the whole covenant community. The woman is not to be self-righteously singled out; the poor are a corporate responsibility. By calling attention to the constant presence of the poor Jesus is not urging us to forget their needs. He is directly referring to God's command that we care for the poor, and their constant presence is an indictment pointing to our failure as the covenant community. It is because they are always present that we do have a responsibility. Jesus then goes on to use the woman's gift to focus attention on his own passion, his own ultimate involvement in human suffering.

A wider canonical context completely alters our view of this passage. If we had searched more broadly we would have found even more texts relating the people of God to the welfare of the poor (the prophets, Paul). Far from allowing anyone to narrowly interpret Matthew 26:6-13 as elevating spiritual over material needs, an exegesis in the context of the whole Scripture overwhelms us with the power of the moral imperative regarding the poor and needy.

● ● ●

It might now be suggested that in using the Bible as a resource for Christian ethics the *canon acts as a framework of control* in several important ways.

1. The canon serves to stress the crucial role of the community of faith in appropriating biblical resources. The canon grew out of the life experience of Israel and the early church in discerning the will of God. The church's recognition of the whole canon as authoritative implies the continuity of those communities. Thus, the canon means that the church is the appropriate context within which the Bible is made available to the modern ethical concerns of the faith community. It cannot be interpreted with integrity by individuals in isolation from the wider community of faith.

2. The canon also reminds us of the ongoing activity of God. When we must relate to the whole sweep of Scripture, we see God revealed

in ever-new ways within the Bible itself. Although every portion speaks with authority of God's presence as it was apprehended in a particular time and place, it is clear that no one word is the final word concerning God's self-revelation. The Scripture points beyond itself to the reality of God. Faith understands that same God as active in our present. Thus, the canon encourages a dialogic use of Scripture, not to discover God enshrined in the past, but to assist us in discerning God's activity and will in our own day.

3. As a corollary to the previous point, the canon helps prevent the absolutizing of the biblical text. The biblical words are not to be worshiped as such (a practice sometimes called bibliolatry). Exegesis in the context of the canon shows the sweep and variety within the Scripture and guards against the absolutizing of any one expression within the Bible. It teaches that the nature of the biblical word is dynamic and not static, thereby suggesting that in ethical matters we cannot seek to apply it mechanically.

4. The canon helps prevent the selecting of texts for ethical use based on the predisposition of the selector. The canon's stress on the wholeness of Scripture means that moral judgments cannot be based on marshaling only those texts that bolster a position already reached on other grounds. Even when it presents us with difficult tensions and contradictions, attention to the canon requires that the totality of the biblical witness be weighed in reaching moral judgments. To pick out some portions as relevant and to reject others is to create one's own canon. Ethical statements based on such a limited canon are more often than not misleading. To do Christian ethics is to enter dialog with the whole of the Christian canon recognized as Scripture throughout the history of the church.

5. Finally, emphasis on the canon helps avoid critical reductionism. The tendency in critically analyzing biblical texts is to focus on the parts and to fail to see their relationships in the whole. Concern for the canon constantly calls the critic back to the dynamic interrelationship of the whole Scripture. This does not mean a repudiation of critical methods, it simply implies a constant concern to move beyond criticism to discover the address of the Word, and this can never be done by simply looking at the critical results of examining a single text or even a single book. In seeking moral guidance this broader framework is essential.

If the Bible is made available through understanding its character, and through careful exegesis of its passages in the context of the whole canon, then it can become a rich resource for the Christian moral life. We turn to a discussion of ways in which the Bible can act as such a resource.

The Bible as a Resource for the Moral Life

One of the mistakes often made in discussing the relation of the Bible to Christian ethics is to suggest a single, multipurpose model for how Scripture is to be used, such as moral law, moral ideal, or moral analogy.[27] As the previous discussion suggests, this ignores the multifaceted nature of biblical resources. It also suggests a monolithic character for ethical concerns in the church. We wish to suggest that there are several ways in which the Bible might appropriately function as a resource for Christian moral life.

1. The Bible acts as a shaper of Christian identity. It is the prime source of the self-conscious identity of the community of faith, and thus, of those individuals who choose to identify themselves with the church and its faith tradition. The Bible is the witness of Israel and the early church to their struggles to be the faithful community of the people of God. It tells of their response to God's revealing of the divine self in their concrete life experience. In recognizing this witness as authoritative the church has established the self-understanding of those biblical communities as the normative guide for the church's attempt to be the faithful community in our own time. It is in relation to the Bible that moral agency becomes distinctively Christian. For those concerned with Christian ethics this means that the Bible is a primary source for those basic virtues, values, and visions which give Christians a particular identity which they share with the wider community of the church. In facing ethical issues this use of the Bible informs the perspective Christians bring to the issue. In simple terms, this use of the Bible refers to the shaping of the decision maker as well as the decision, character as well as conduct.

If the Bible acts to shape basic identity, it should be apparent that this is not a function which can be left until a moral dilemma presents itself for decision. This use of the Bible requires the long-term nurturing of the community of faith by those responsible for ordering its life. If the distinctive virtues, values, and visions of the church have not already been internalized from study and reflection on the biblical resources, then it will not be possible to draw upon them meaningfully

181

in the midst of moral and ethical crisis. The starting place for this function is not a defining ethical issue but the Bible itself. It is to be studied for its own basic witness to the shape of Christian moral character, as well as studied for its practical application to some particular moral issue.

In this function it should also be clear that the entire canon acts as a resource. The Scripture in its entirety acts to mold moral character in the individual and in the community. Thus, stories are as ethically important as commandments; psalms are as influential as teachings. The basic character of the church is shaped by reflecting on the whole range of experience recorded in the Scripture. Ethical significance is not limited to texts that explicitly address moral concerns.

For example, the Gospels are filled with stories that tell of Jesus' associations with those considered to be outcasts and sinners by others in the society of his time. Completely apart from any explicit instruction, the witness of these stories shapes the kind of community the church is called to be: inclusive, accepting, renewing. The person who brings these attitudes to ethical situations dealing with poverty or criminal justice will find her or his decisions transformed.

Or again, those whose nurture in the biblical tradition has shown them the love songs of the Song of Songs as well as the more somber opinions of Paul on marriage will approach questions of sexual ethics with a sense of the possibilities for fullness as well as the dangers inherent in human sexuality.

Basic attitudes such as the Hebrew affirmation of creation as good or the Pauline conviction on the universality of the gospel have become fundamental to the perspective the church brings to ethical concerns. But these attitudes do not stay strong and sharp apart from their nurture at the wellsprings of the Bible itself. Thought of in this way, the ongoing study of the Bible and reflection on its wisdom in the church is an essential element in the church's moral life.

2. The Bible can act as the giver of moral imperatives. Here we are speaking of those areas in which the Bible speaks to us by means of direct moral address indicating an ethical stand which is not optional to those who are the people of God. Many ethicists and church leaders, in their desire to counter the use of the Bible as a prescriptive moral code, have tended to limit the function of the Bible to the setting of ideals or as a resource for moral dialog. This glosses over the fact that the Bible sometimes acts, with a clear consensus, as the source of

direct moral imperative which is intended as basic to the identity of the Christian moral agent, individual or community. Both Old and New Testaments consistently affirm Jesus' summary of the greatest commandment, "You shall love the Lord your God with all your heart, and with all your soul, and with all your mind . . . and you shall love your neighbor as yourself" (Matt. 22:37-39). Thus, it is required of those who would love God that they put the welfare of their neighbor on a par with their own. This imperative profoundly affects any approach to ethical problems.

With such moral imperatives there is no need to wait for a specific issue to arise. The imperative is to be internalized as such. The church's stand in these matters is firmly established in the biblical material, although it must be stressed that considerable latitude will no doubt remain in regard to strategy and implementation of that stand. It should be obvious that such moral imperatives are closely related to our previous function of the Bible as the shaper of Christian identity. Indeed, our distinction here is an artificial one. The moral imperatives made clear in the biblical witness are to be internalized as part of the basic identity of the community of faith. We have separated them only because we were speaking previously about the shaping of values and attitudes, and here more directly about the identification of a particular moral stand.

A more extended example may be helpful at this point. In light of the world food crisis and the tragedy of global hunger the church has wrestled with its response to this complex area of ethical concerns. Examination of the biblical materials shows a clear and unambiguous word on the relation of the community of faith to hunger and poverty. In the Old Testament God especially loves and cares for the poor (Pss. 10:12; 12:5; Isa. 25:4; 29:19). God does not accept their condition but promises to deliver them (Ps. 132:15; Prov. 15:15). Because God has identified with the poor, so too the community of faith is called to special concern for these persons. The rights of the poor are established in the law codes. Poverty is a judgment on the community's distribution of resources, and concern for the poor cannot, therefore, be left to voluntary benevolence. The prophets become the strong advocates of the poor and the oppressed, and urge this as the concern of the whole covenant community.

In the New Testament, as we have already noted, Jesus radically identifies with the poor and the oppressed,[28] and he commands his followers to take up this concern as essential to discipleship (Matt. 25). The early church in Jerusalem shared all material resources in order to provide for the needy (Acts 2:44-45). Numerous references in the Epistles indicate that identification with and concern for the poor remained a central imperative for the early church (2 Cor. 8:9; 9:9; Heb. 13:16; James 2:1-7).

The witness of both Old and New Testaments makes clear that concern for those forced to live a marginal existence in hunger and poverty is not an optional activity for the people of God. Nor is it only a minor requirement to be dealt with in token charities. Identification with these persons is at the heart of what it means to the community of faith. A clear moral imperative is established here for those who would be the church.

A final word of caution is necessary. The church must constantly guard against those who would declare moral imperatives in areas where the biblical witness does not warrant this.[29] The history of the church is filled with examples of those who endowed some limited portion of Scripture with absolute moral authority. Careful exegesis in the context of the entire canon is a safeguard. When a moral concern is expressed in biblical materials that range from law codes to teaching narratives to parables to epistles, then its demand is necessarily stronger than a concern expressed in a more limited context. Only those concerns consistently identified throughout the Scripture as moral imperatives necessary to the authentic self-understanding of God's people can be claimed as necessary marks of faith on biblical grounds.

3. The Bible can provide theological perspectives which focus the church's response to ethical issues. Even when basic identity and imperatives are clear within the church, its response to ethical concerns can be crippled by narrowness of theological perspective. In its diversity the Bible provides a complete range of theological viewpoints, no one of which can be called *the* biblical theology, but all of which might be made available as appropriate contexts for ethical response in a given set of circumstances. The appropriateness of any theological perspective offered in the biblical material must be judged on the basis of the moral situation with constant attention that it does not distort the basic biblical self-understanding of the church.

This use of the Bible can best be illustrated by focusing further on the issue of hunger and poverty. If the biblical imperatives concerning the poor and the hungry are clear, it has been less clear how those imperatives are to be acted upon in the life of the church. Much will depend on the theological perspectives which focus our response. A dominant biblical theological model in the Old Testament is salvation history. The focus is on God's actions in history to redeem Israel. The central event, of course, is the crossing of the sea and the deliverance out of bondage in Egypt. This exodus event becomes paradigmatic for Israel's life and faith. Stress is placed on the situations of distress in which the community constantly finds itself, and on the community's inability to deliver itself. Although God may judge the people, the community can ultimately put trust and hope in the assurance of God's deliverance. This is an extremely appropriate model for theologies founded in the suffering and oppression of the world's poor and hungry, and has been heavily used by the liberation theologies. Deliverance, redemption, and salvation, effected by God's intervention against the world's hostile forces, provide the basis for hope in seemingly hopeless situations.

For a response to global hunger and poverty on the part of U.S. middle-class churches this may be a much less appropriate theological framework. Too often when these churches have used the salvation history themes they appear to place themselves primarily in the immodest role of God's agents bringing deliverance and salvation. The crisis focus of the salvation history perspective tends to stress rescuer responses from those who are not themselves among the dispossessed. Thus, our aid and charity approaches to concern for hunger and poverty appear patronizing and self-congratulatory, and seldom address the larger systemic issues.

Alternative theological perspectives might transform this inadequate ethical response. For example, if we turned to other literature of the Old Testament, we would find a stress on God as creator as well as deliverer. Out of this grows an emphasis on preserving and enriching life within the created order and a focus on the importance of human freedom and human moral responsibility in this task. Such a theological perspective would discourage sole reliance on the rescuer mentality and impel us to work for the establishment of a more just and harmonious economic and political order. Causes would be treated rather than symptoms alone. We would also be forced to place greater importance on our own role as bringers of life or death in the human order by the decisions we make and the systems we support. Our role in patterns that have created the suffering of world poverty and hunger

185

would be exposed, and the church could be called to repentance for its participation.

In this use of the Bible a particular action is not dictated, but a variety of possible frameworks for action are presented. It is important not to absolutize any of these. The richness of the Bible as an ethical resource lies partly in the constant critique and corrective that a variety of theological perspectives provide in relation to one another. Our choice of biblical foundations ought to be made as carefully as our choice of ethical strategies.

4. The Bible can act as a resource for decision making on particular issues when a clear moral imperative is not already internalized within the community. What are we to do in a given moral situation? We have left this use until last because this has often been the entire focus of discussions on the relationship between the Bible and Christian ethics.

This use of the Bible starts with the issue that calls for decision. One comes to the Bible with an agenda already set. Here the use of the Bible becomes truly dialogic. The biblical material is placed into dialog with all of those factors defining an issue in a concrete situation in the life of the church. The amount of resource material one finds in the Bible will vary. For some issues there may be places in the Scripture where that same issue is directly addressed. Material pertinent to the issue at hand may be implied in stories of biblical people and events. There may be a variety of materials and perspectives on a given question. Biblical principles such as justice may apply to the given issue. When the issue is such that it is not directly addressed or even implied at all (e.g., organ transplants), then one may be forced to rely solely on the biblical witness to general values and attitudes that might inform contemporary deciding.

It is important to exhaust the full range of the biblical canon in seeking resources for decision making. Then the resultant biblical material may function in several different ways.

An investigation of biblical resources may reveal a polarity of positions. Responsible moral judgment cannot absolutize one or the other of these poles but must struggle for decision within the tension established in the biblical witness. For example, the Bible teaches that one is to obey God rather than human authorities when human demands seem in conflict with God's will (see the stories of Daniel), but it also teaches obedience to civil authorities as these offices are ordained by God (Romans 13). One can only responsibly reach ethical decisions in this area by taking both poles of this tension seriously. The Bible then serves to identify the creative tension in which decision making must take place. The tension may be an unequal one. Christians in revolutionary situations have had to struggle with the question of violence. The overwhelming witness of the Scripture is against violence as a normal means to moral ends. Jesus' restraint of Peter in Gethsemane in favor of willingly going to his own death has often been cited as an example. But the Bible also witnesses to God's wrath against the wicked, and those in the biblical communities are sometimes called upon to stand physically against evil. Those who must struggle with this question must take account of the preponderant emphasis on one pole of this tension, and carefully weigh the biblical witness to circumstances under which the other pole might be enjoined. A final decision can only be one taken in the risk of faith within the tension of the biblical witness.

A careful search of biblical materials may uncover a whole range of options or perspectives. In the area of sexual ethics, for example, one must reckon with the widest divergence of material. Genesis 1 and 2 affirm the created goodness and harmony of the male–female relationship. Proverbs warns of the dangerous snares of sexual enticement. Sexual attraction to one's wife is in keeping with wisdom, but the lure of the harlot is folly. The Song of Songs is a book of love songs extolling the joys of love and sexual relationship. It does not speak of marriage or societal norms. Paul in 1 Corinthians 7 seems to regard marriage as better than unbridled passion, but recommends celibacy as the best course. First Timothy 2:12ff. regards women as subordinate as a result of being the first transgressor, and implies that the value of sexual relationship is only in childbearing for the redemption of the woman. Certainly no single view of human sexuality shows through here, and it would be sheer folly to declare one of these as *the* biblical view. Those who approach the Bible for guidance on questions of sexual ethics must take all of these viewpoints into account. It will be especially important to investigate the way in which each is responding to the context of its own time. The biblical materials then become resources for helping to clarify the options and priorities in our own concrete situation.

Finally, the ethical issue at hand may simply not be addressed by the biblical material. Issues such as organ transplants, genetic experimentation, and abortion are all issues which deal with biological data not known or in any way dealt with in the biblical material. Yet even here the Bible may play a role in decision making. An investigation of biblical resources may serve to set the boundaries within which moral inquiry takes place. Surely the biblical stress on the sanctity of human life and on the quality of human existence form boundaries within which these issues must be decided even if the specific issues themselves are not mentioned. This moral framework already begins to limit the decisions that might be taken.

In using the Bible as a resource for decision making it is important to emphasize that the Bible can never take the burden of decision off the decision maker. Biblical material may provide a focus in the process of decision making, but biblical claims will never be *completely* sufficient as the basis for moral decision. As noted earlier, they must function dialogically with other, nonbiblical sources of moral insight. Our previous discussion of biblical authority noted that in this more relational use of Scripture, insights from the biblical material function as the primary source for Christian ethical reflection but are not self-sufficient.

Finally, we must say one last word on the matter of control in using the Bible for decision making. We have noted that fundamental to the Scripture is the insight that being is inseparable from doing. The basic control, when the church attempts to decide what it should do, is its own understanding of what it has been called to be. The biblically based identity of the church as the people of God forms the constant reference point for any ethical decision on a particular issue. To use another term we introduced earlier, the church's decisions must be consistent with its vision. A decision that violates that basic identity and vision is suspect even though it might be claiming biblical warrants. In fact, the church has often tended to place the cart before the horse by deciding immediately on ethical issues without taking adequate measure of the biblical resources available to assist in decision making. Making decisions apart from the formation of basic Christian character is hollow and meaningless. The Bible must relate to both these realities if it is to be truly available as a resource for the Christian moral life.

10

SUMMARY AND CHALLENGE

Our discussion of Scripture and the moral life has developed around two themes: community and moral agency. It has done so from within a twofold consensus: (1) Christian ethics is not synonymous with biblical ethics; (2) the Bible is nonetheless formative and normative for Christian ethics. The first task in this concluding chapter is to offer a summary. The second is to draw the implications and challenges. Our summary will touch only on those points which most directly link Bible and ethics. The purpose is only to *highlight* the relationship of Scripture and ethics, rather than distill the results of the entire discussion of the moral life.

Moral Agency

Biblical materials promote moral agency and address the major dimensions of the Christian moral life. It is an unrelenting assumption of biblical materials that we are morally responsible for the world of which we are a part, and that this responsibility is learned in the communities to which we belong. In the biblical view of things, we ourselves are "unfinished" agents in an "unfinished" world. We are coparticipants with God in a dynamic history that evokes our responsibility for the condition of creation itself. A certain power is invested in us for the ordering of life. The Bible assumes this and in so doing promotes moral agency as a uniquely human quality. To be human is, biblically speaking, to be morally responsible, with and before God.

189

Biblical materials themselves address virtually all the dimensions of moral agency. By this we mean that the Bible addresses character formation and decision making and action. It addresses both our "being" *and* our "doing." It is concerned with moral virtue, and with moral value, obligation, and vision as well.

Character formation is the learning and internalizing of a way of life formative of our own moral identity. It is our moral "being," the expression of who we are. The process is sometimes referred to as conscience formation, but that is too narrow a notion. Conscience is character only as an ethical compass functioning in the face of a particular choice, usually a dilemma. Conscience is vital, but character is considerably more than conscience. Character includes our basic moral perception—how we see and understand things—as well as our fundamental dispositions, intentions, and motives. Character includes our moral capacities as well as our active moral traits.

The vital link with Scripture is that for Christians biblical materials help form character. They shape our moral identity and can do so at the deepest levels of our being. Consider this hypothetical example. A person is drawn to the figure of Jesus, from whom she both consciously and unconsciously takes the clues for her own way of being and doing. She has a certain portrait of Jesus which she has internalized. His life is centered in God in utter trust and he has apparently little anxiety about his place and power in society. Rather, he identifies with the outcasts and befriends the excluded. He manifests a gentleness toward nature but an impatience with human pretense. He shows the full range of human emotions but stays by his course with resolve.

We do not ask whether this person's portrait of Jesus is accurate. Rather we speculate about how her perceptions, dispositions, intentions, and motives might be affected by it. Her general way of seeing might be influenced by the moral sensitivities which search out those often invisible to many in society—the outcast, the ill, the poor. She might acquire an awareness that is attuned to human suffering and an ability to empathize with people in pain. She might acquire certain dispositions, such as an underlying hopefulness about improvement of the human lot, an appreciation for nonhuman life in the world of nature, and an impatience with people's claims to high and enduring achievement. There may be particular intentions as well: to seek nonviolent resolution to conflict; to champion the causes of the oppressed; to seek the reign of God before all else.

190

What presented this compelling portrait? It was likely a collage of biblical materials: the healing and feeding narratives in Jesus' ministry; the parable of the Good Samaritan and the cycle of the lost sheep, coin, and son; the teachings on the mountain; the echoes of the prophets; the announcement of Jesus' ministry in Luke 4; the events of Passion Week; or other accounts. We list these simply to register the possibility that a set of biblical materials has portrayed a paradigmatic figure who became for this person a chief source for her way of looking at the world and responding to it. The presentation of Jesus helped define what was real for her; it generated a certain set of moral priorities she made her own; it disposed her to act and react in patterns that set her on one course instead of another. Her motives, attitudes, and intentions flowed from what she felt was in keeping with the good life she saw enfleshed in Jesus.

The Bible can and ought to be a force in molding perspectives, dispositions, and intentions. It will always interact with many other forces, but that does not diminish the fact that Scripture can nurture a basic orientation and generate particular attitudes and intentions. In a word, the Bible can help form moral character.

But what biblical materials can do so? It is not evasive to say all of them. The whole panorama of materials is engaged—the narrative accounts, the law, the prophets and the psalms, letters of instruction, exhortation, and encouragement, theological ruminations, and devotional elements. There really is no major type of biblical material which cannot play a significant role in the complex phenomenon we call moral development. Thus, one of the pitfalls in the use of Scripture in ethics is what can be termed "genre reductionism." "Genre reductionism" is the selection, whether deliberate or not, of only certain kinds of biblical materials as those materials which are pertinent to ethics. Thus materials of direct moral exhortation, such as prophetic oracles, the Ten Commandments, the Sermon on the Mount, or Paul's admonitions, are chosen, but the historical narratives, psalms, parables, miracle stories, and apocalyptic visions are not. The complex nature of character formation argues against such selectivity for Christian ethics. For that reason we have emphasized the important role of the canon as a framework of reference and control.

Of course different materials may work in different ways. The theological discourses of Paul or the author of Job, for example, might be the source of certain reasoned convictions and beliefs, thus influencing character via what the person regards as propositionally true. The apocalyptic visions might stimulate one to see the world differently—some things come alive with meanings not discerned before those strange images illumined them for us. The piety of the devotional materials might generate within us certain attitudes of mystery, humility, and reverence that carry over into our moral habits. (The nature psalms, for example, might move us toward a different response to the environment.) At no point can we say on principle which biblical materials belong to those affecting the development of moral character, and which do not. Thus Christian ethics, while it must seek to decipher what effects the different kinds of materials have, must not succumb to genre reductionism.

Decision making and action are the other major arenas addressed by the biblical materials. Biblical materials influence decisions in many ways. We have already mentioned the influence on character as the "architect" of so many of our choices. In addition, biblical materials have been formative of long moral traditions which supply content and which provide an orientation for us as we deliberate particular issues. Biblical materials never make the decisions themselves—we must do that. Too, the biblical moral traditions themselves are both pluralistic in content and open to change, so we must make choices within and beyond them. They nonetheless supply a strong point of reference and a morally rich world to draw from. They may, for example, offer images, examples, and analogies for our own moral imagination. They may supply the norms or standards by which to measure our choices, or be the source for helping to establish the boundaries of morally permissible behavior. They may help locate the burden of proof (what the normal bearing will be on some issue, and what kind of case constitutes a morally justified exception). In any case, the biblical materials provide a rich and varied fund for decision making, even if they can never supply all the crucial elements, such as the sociohistorical analysis and empirical studies we emphasized earlier.

We add that the biblical materials themselves make action imperative. Nothing is quite so consistently emphasized in Scripture as the *embodiment* of faith—the very test of the presence of faith is in the moral expression of it.

We have used other terms, beyond character formation and decision making, to describe the moral life, chiefly virtue, value, obligation, and vision. Each of these uncovers a different aspect of the moral life, and the biblical materials address all four of them. Any version of Christian ethics which omits any of them is a truncated one, and any use of Scripture in ethics which leaves out any of them is a diminished one.

Christian ethics certainly emphasizes virtue. Biblical materials are properly used in worship and education to foster the prized qualities of gentleness, kindness, perseverance, courage, humility, righteous anger, and others. Scripture gives constant attention to matters of virtue to the kinds of persons we are and are to be.

Christian ethics is equally concerned with engendering the good society, which is to say that it is concerned with values, or moral goods realized in society. Both the Jewish concern for social righteousness and the Greek emphasis on structures which nurture sound character emphasize the importance of values in Christian ethics. The biblical materials themselves give rise to many values for the Christian moral life. Justice, love, equality, and peace (*shalôm*) are prominent among them.

Moral obligation and the ground rules for life together have been an enduring preoccupation of Christian ethics. The basic moral requirements for living together at all, and the moral boundaries within which we live our lives, is an ongoing concern of Christian ethics. So, too, are obligations which arise from the character of particular relationships (e.g., parent/child, friend/friend, friend/enemy, employer/employee, citizen/ruler). Biblical materials are filled with the language of obligation, both in the most basic and general sense (respect for persons, truth-telling) and with reference to particular relationships (social roles and community tasks). Clearly, discussions of obligation in Christian ethics draw consistently on biblical materials, just as do discussions of virtue and value.

We gave "moral vision" a special location on the chart used in chapter 3, bridging both character and decision making, and setting the broad terms on which the moral life is understood and lived. Here we emphasize Scripture's role in supplying much, though never all, of the substance of moral vision. We may be moved and shaped by great narratives, great figures, sublime speeches, poems and oracles, and impelling protagonists and antagonists in the dramas of life, death, and moral choice. Here is the materials of hope and despair, agony and ecstasy, suffering and joy. Here is the simple and everyday, the great and mysterious. Here are all the textures of life itself in its deepest and

193

widest dimensions, and the relationship of such life to God. When people immerse themselves in the worlds of the Bible, they are given the furnishings of a moral "cosmos." It is not a settled thing, either within Scripture itself or in our own lives. It is dynamic in both contexts, and part of our ongoing experience. But this moral world is indispensable to "seeing," to discerning meaning and direction. "Without the great revelations, epics and philosophies as part of our natural vision," Allen Bloom writes, "there is nothing to see out there, and eventually little left inside. The Bible is not the only means to furnish a mind, but without a book of similar gravity, read with the gravity of a potential believer, it will remain unfurnished."[1] For Christian ethics, much of the vision of a moral world, and much of its furnishing, is supplied by Scripture.

The Bible, then, addresses and promotes virtue, value, obligation, and vision in the Christian moral life. It names and helps form virtues and values, encourages and specifies obligations, and fosters and renews moral vision. Any use of Scripture in ethics which fastens on only one or two of these is an inadequate use, just as any reduction of Christian ethics to an ethics of virtue, value, duty, or vision only, is inadequate to the plural dimensions of the moral life.

Community

Biblical materials locate the moral life and moral agency primarily within the life of the faith community. The Bible is a book of a people. In fact, it arises as Scripture precisely because of the experience of divine power as the power of "peoplehood." The biblical materials are testimony from ancestors who could not deny their collective experience of God. There is little surprise, then, that steady use of the Bible in Christian ethics ultimately locates the moral life within the context of a community and its checkered history. The moral life is understood from the beginning as a part of community faithfulness toward God, as seen in the way of life of the community. "Morality" is of little interest in isolation and is viewed instead as a crucial part of community faithfulness. The moral life is placed near the center of Christian faith itself, as the practical expression of community faith.

Differently said, the Bible has become the charter resource for the Christian ethic as a *koinōnia* ethic, a community-creating ethic rooted in a compelling experience of God. The use of Scripture in the community is to help form Christians as those who learn the story of Israel and of Jesus well enough to experience the world from within those stories, and to act in keeping with that experience, as members of the community of faith. The Bible aids in the crafting of a good and just life learned as part of the community's own ongoing life.

To view the Bible as the charter resource for the moral life is to accord it very high authority. It is to assert that what is morally significant for our lives can be collectively discerned with the aid of these writings. The claim is not that the Bible provides all that is necessary for an ethic, but that the Bible is a faithful and reliable guide for what it means to be a people of God who seek to walk in "the Way." The authority is not in Scripture's comprehensiveness but in its sufficiency as a mediator of the real presence of God in the moral life.

We have noted in some detail the community's roles in the moral life: as a community of moral identity formation, as a bearer of moral tradition, as a community of moral deliberation and of action. Scripture plays an essential role in each of these. The first uses Scripture in the complex and never-ending task of character formation. Moral traditions in the church also aid moral development, and they begin with and always include that canonical part of the tradition we call "Scripture." Moral traditions are also a steady source for the content of an ethic and supply a framework of accountability for the moral life. Here, too, Scripture supplies content and framework. The deliberative process itself uses Scripture in the ways we've discussed in conjunction with decision making. A moral issue itself might be addressed directly by biblical materials, but it is just as important that biblical materials remind decision makers who they are and the context of faith in which they make decisions. Finally, and to underscore what was said earlier, action is an implicit imperative of Scripture. The origins of Christian ethics are in the Hebrew insistence on the social embodiment of faith in the one God as this is made visible in a way of life. Scripture is itself the witness to this, and a prod to its continuation.

In summary, biblical materials understand Christian ethics as community ethics. The moral life is a critical dimension of the community's life of faith and the community itself acts as both moral agent and creator of moral agents. The community has formed and preserved the canon of Scripture, claimed these biblical traditions as authoritative, and continues to provide the context within which each generation appropriates the biblical resources for the Christian life. The biblical materials themselves assume and promote moral agency as a distinctive quality of being human in relationship to God and address the major dimensions of the moral life itself.

Implications for the Life of the Church

The important relationship between the Bible and Christian ethics described in the preceding discussion has implications for the church, both in its gathered life and in its scattered life.

1. The various functions of the church as a gathered community are not always considered primary arenas for the church's ethical life. In a commonly held view, ethics refers to the church's dealing with issues in the world. Elements of church life, such as preaching, liturgy, Christian education, and congregational nurture, are often understood to address personal faith and congregational community. These are considered essential to the life of the church, but are not considered moral or ethical matters. Ethical concerns are then held separate and considered optional, available to those in the congregation who are more "socially concerned." The moral witness of the church in the world becomes an interest group.

On the other hand, there is a widespread view among some of those involved in the response of the church to ethical issues that the reading and study of the Bible, which takes place largely in the gathered life of the church, is only a kind of distant background to the church's moral life in the world. An inner city pastor, who is a longtime friend of one of the authors, once blurted, "I don't have time to be reading the Bible. People are starving out there!" The urgency of moral issues may sometimes contribute to a view that the work of claiming our biblical resources is a low priority. In this view Bible reading and response to issues in the world become an "either-or" matter.

To be sure, there are occasions when ethical issues find their way into the internal life of the church. An occasional "prophetic sermon" is preached. The liturgy may include a powerful sending forth to service and action. The Christian education program may include a series on topical issues of the day. But the fundamental dynamic in all of these activities is that ethics is located "out there." These occasional activities seem to function as pep talks encouraging us to get back out there where ethics is done.

196

Although the views just described still have currency, the late 70s and early 80s have seen the increased attention to voices in the church that suggest a wider view of the Christian moral life and a more central role for the Bible in Christian ethics. For example, the U.S. Roman Catholic bishops have issued lengthy pastoral letters on peace and on economic issues.[2] Although analyzing the issues themselves in helpful ways, these pastoral documents have been distinguished by their call for the whole life of the church to reflect and prepare for the tasks of peacemaking and the pursuit of economic justice. Not coincidentally, these documents take their starting point from a serious assessment and appropriation of biblical foundations that inform response to these challenging issues. An additional example is the experience and witness of base Christian communities in Central and South America.[3] While deeply involved in Christian response to the patterns of poverty and oppression in their own social contexts, these communities bear constant witness to the importance of grounding and preparing for that task in the worship and Bible study of the gathered community. It is neither an optional nor extraneous activity, but a central part of the way in which the community of faith understands and equips itself for its mission in the world.

In keeping with the witness of these examples we believe that a clear understanding of the Bible's role in the Christian moral life means that *the gathered life of the church is as fundamentally ethical in nature as the scattered life of the church.* In the shaping of moral agency the Bible has its greatest influence on the Christian moral life, and in the internal life of the gathered community many of the clearest opportunities for the development of moral agency occur.

The internal life of congregations has too often become an end in itself. To see the activities of the gathered community as the development of moral agents called to responsible life as agents of God's reconciling work in a broken world would provide purpose to many congregations that have turned in upon themselves, and unity to congregations whose social witness is seen as an optional interest for only some of their members. Preaching, liturgy, Christian education, and congregational nurture all become activities crucial to the moral life, and it is the Bible that provides the foundation and resources for them all. It is only in relation to the biblical witness that these activities serve to establish anew the basic identity of the church as the faithful community of the people of God. Each of these elements in the gathered

197

life of the church would serve to communicate basic virtues, values, obligations, and visions which transcend the interests of individual persons and congregations. To draw out the moral dimensions of the church's internal life would heighten awareness of membership in the whole body of those whose character and conduct are shaped by a common biblical faith.

To unite biblical resources with ethical concerns in the gathered life of the church is to take up the long-range task of development and nurture. The church's moral responsibility is not limited to the immediate response to crisis issues. If basic biblical understandings are not incorporated by Christians before a moral and ethical crisis arises, then biblical resources are unlikely to play any significant role.

If the church wishes to relate its biblical heritage to its ethical concerns, every aspect of its life must be seen as a part of this task. Worship is crucial because it is the continual medium for those basic symbols, stories, images, rituals, and traditions, founded in the biblical tradition, that carry the meaning of the faith and serve to form Christian character. Worship has a direct impact upon the "seeing" so central to the Christian moral life.

Current debates in the churches over the use of inclusive language in worship serve to illustrate this matter. If the language for God and for humanity in the liturgy makes exclusive use of masculine pronouns, vocabulary, and images, then it is simply a fact of our modern society that many women will feel, and be, excluded from what is happening in the worship service. But what is less often seen is that this issue is not confined to the sanctuary. Insensitivity to inclusiveness in our liturgies contributes to insensitivity to inclusiveness in our societies. The virtues, values, obligations, and visions which shape us may not include the influence of important biblical themes such as creation (male and female) in the image of God (Gen. 1:27), or oneness (male and female) in Jesus Christ (Gal. 3:28), if the liturgy week after week does not reflect the influence of such themes.

Worship and ethics are inevitably joined. Yet few worship experiences are planned using these serious shaping questions: What are the moral influences consciously or unconsciously present in the way we now conduct worship? What, in planning the worship experience, would contribute to the appropriate shaping of Christian character and conduct? What, as best we can judge, will be the outcome for Christian moral development of worship planned in this particular manner, and conducted with these particular materials? These ought not be the only questions in the planning of worship, of course. The meaning of worship is more than its meaning for the moral life. But it cannot be less. Thus, the worship life of the congregation ought in part to be governed in a deliberate manner by the considerations central to the Christian moral life.

The task of Christian education is equally crucial. It is obvious that in children's education we are directly contributing to the shaping of moral character, and to moral agency overall. Nevertheless, the use of Bible stories with children seldom makes explicit in curriculum or teaching the ethical dimensions of the biblical traditions. It has even been thought in some influential Christian education circles that children ought to be protected from Bible stories that expose them to important moral dilemmas (like the struggle for freedom from tyranny between God and Pharaoh in Exodus).[4] Greater consciousness of the role the Bible plays in shaping us as moral agents should result in new sensitivity to the foundations laid in educating our children.

Unfortunately there are still many churches where Christian education is limited to children, with little of any serious nature offered for adults. Apparently Christian education is not seen as serving any serious purpose for adults, and yet study and reflection on our biblical and theological resources is fundamental for equipping church people for their role as moral agents. Ironically, it is often those most anxious to make the church "relevant" who ignore this basic need for long-term reflection on and grounding in the church's own moral resources. Even when adult education is a regular part of congregational programs, ethics concerns are relegated to topical, issue-defined courses. An important implication of our work is to see that there are moral influences which flow from all occasions for reflection on our faith in the educational life of the church. In particular, Bible study has as much potential for the moral life as an issue course. Indeed, liberation theologies with their roots in social praxis might be opened to North American middle-class churches as much by study of the book of Exodus with attention to its liberation themes as by the selection and discussion of a particular socioeconomic issue. We must avoid patterns of adult education that separate Bible reading and reflection on moral issues as if they are separate interest groups. The resources of our historic faith and the consideration of the church's witness in the world

199

belong together—in the education program and in the Christian moral life.

2. It is the church's life as a scattered community encountering the world that has usually been regarded as the primary locus for Christian ethical concern. The need for moral decision and action arises as issues present themselves from the wider social context and demand Christian response. Many in the church have labored to undertake this response seriously. Yet, Christians sometimes fail to bring with them any self-conscious understanding of their own identity as the church when they tackle ethical questions. Many who are deeply concerned with moral matters nevertheless show little awareness of particular resources within their own faith traditions, particularly the Bible.

Our understanding of the Bible's relationship to Christian character and conduct implies that *the scattered life of the church is as fundamentally biblical as the gathered life of the church.* It is in the Bible that what is commonly called "Christian social action" finds its roots. The church interacts with society on ethical issues, not out of some pious "do-goodism" or out of a vague humanism, but out of a biblical calling to work as agents of confrontation, witness, and reconciliation in a broken world. The church's ethical involvement finds an adequate rationale only as it relates to biblical understandings of God's will.

The results of relating biblical understandings to ethical concerns is nowhere seen more clearly than in some of the powerful theologies of liberation of Latin America, Africa, and Asia. On the one hand, these theologies grow out of the involvement of the church in the actual struggles and sufferings of persons in need of liberation. They are founded in the church's practical engagement. On the other hand, they have drawn deeply on biblical understandings in their seeking after God's will in these situations. Christian conduct is grounded in and empowered by the biblical witness.

These theologies of liberation indicate that the positioning of the church in the midst of moral struggles enables the biblical word to be fully heard and its implications to be fully appropriated. Inability to hear God's word is often the failure of the church rightly to situate itself in the brokenness of the world it is sent to reconcile. Only in such a context is it really possible to discover the full moral address of Scripture. For example, the Bible's radical imperative to identify with and care for the dispossessed cannot really be understood by a middle-class suburban congregation apart from the effort and risk to become involved with the hungry, the poor, or the oppressed. When the church is truly scattered in the world and shares its brokenness, it is impelled back to its basic biblical foundation to see with new eyes. A new climate for the reception of God's word is created and a new vision is born. In turn, a new urgency is brought to the work of the gathered community in equipping the church for its moral task. The gathered community and the scattered community can now be seen as complementary in relation to the Christian moral life. Neither can function with integrity apart from the other, and in the biblical witness their unity is found.

In practical terms this means that those in the church who are concerned with ethical issues must take worship, study, and reflection seriously as essential to the empowerment of the church's moral witness. It means that decisions and actions cannot be taken hastily apart from some clear assessment of the particular resources that the church might bring to an issue. This does not mean that the church is rendered incapable of timely response. It simply suggests that those who are involved with ethical issues in the wider social context must also be concerned and involved with the long-term task of shaping moral virtues, values, obligations, and vision in the church, so that Christians might stand ready for meaningful and timely response.

This more holistic understanding of Bible and Christian ethics in the life of the church can lead to a greater sense of unity in the church's purpose in the world. For example, another task for which the church is sent into the world is evangelism, the church's witness to a particular faith perspective. Ethical activists and those concerned with evangelism have often stood in separate camps within the church. The understanding of the Christian moral life we have developed in the preceding chapters makes clear that this is a false division. If Christian moral activity is properly rooted in biblical faith then the church is constantly witnessing to that particular faith as it is at work in the world. Moral involvement and evangelical witness become joined. The church's witness to the meaning of its own faith is then properly joined to its concern for reconciliation in a broken world, and both are grounded in the biblical witness. Salvation becomes a term that encompasses both issues of belief and issues of ethical concern for the fullness of human life.

In our time moral issues confront us with unabating frequency and growing complexity. For the church, sent into the world as one of

God's agents of hope and reconciliation, such times are filled with challenge. It is our conviction that the ancient testimony of Scripture still speaks a central word to the modern faith community. The Bible's multifaceted role in shaping our character as moral agents and in framing our moral decisions and actions make it imperative that we continuously reflect on its testimony in conversation with the wisdom of our own time. We believe that there are many signs in our time that connections between ancient biblical witness and contemporary moral challenge are being creatively and fruitfully made. Our hope has been to deepen the understanding of the relationship between the Bible and Christian ethics so that effort might be continued and extended in the life of the church for the sake of the world.

NOTES

Preface

1. The literature is considerable. For a sampling, see Thomas W. Ogletree, *The Use of the Bible in Christian Ethics* (Philadelphia: Fortress, 1983); Allen Verhey, *The Great Reversal: Ethics and the New Testament* (Grand Rapids: Eerdmans, 1984); Charles Curran and Richard McCormick, eds., *Readings in Moral Theology, No. 4: The Use of Scripture in Moral Theology* (New York: Paulist Press, 1984); Letty M. Russell, ed., *Feminist Interpretation of the Bible* (Philadelphia: Westminster, 1985); William C. Spohn, s.j., *What Are They Saying about Scripture and Ethics?* (New York: Paulist Press, 1983).

Chapter 1: Consensus and Questions

1. "New Life: The Promise and Risk of Genetic Engineering," *The New York Times*, 8 June 1987.
2. "Farmers to Face Patent Fees to Use Gene-Altered Animals," *The New York Times*, 6 Feb. 1988.
3. See Jonathan Schell, *The Fate of the Earth* (New York: Avon Books, 1982). Schell's is a descriptive account of the plausible consequences of a nuclear holocaust. His description effectively communicates the fact that humans for the first time have sufficient destructive power to be "uncreators." For a philosophical discussion of the impact of heightened human power on inherited moral categories, and an effort to reconstruct more viable ones, see the important volume by Hans Jonas, *The Imperative of Responsibility* (Chicago: The University of Chicago Press, 1984).
4. An interesting presentation of how this loyalty to a faith community rather than a civic one appeared to non-Christian Romans of the first centuries c.e. (Common Era) is Robert L. Wilken's *The Christians as The Romans Saw Them* (New Haven: Yale University Press, 1984).
5. The classic account of the Bible questioning us and formulating the religious and moral world is Karl Barth's *The Word of God and the Word of Man* (New York: Harper & Row, 1957). For an extensive discussion of the Great Commandment itself, see Gene Outka's *Agape: An Ethical Analysis* (New Haven and London: Yale University Press, 1972).

Chapter 2: Christian Ethics as Community Ethics

1. Many of us are so accustomed to the currency of this mechanistic/individualistic view in democratic capitalism and in 19th-century Anglo-American liberalism that we hardly realize what an exception it is, even in the history of the West. As the remainder of this chapter seeks to show, the mechanistic/individualistic model accords with neither the Greek nor the Hebrew legacies in Christian ethics. Certainly Stoicism, which strongly influenced Christian ethics in the initial centuries, maintained a relational view of human, and even cosmic, existence. Aristotle, of almost incalculable influence in Christian ethics, recognized mutuality as the very bond of the civil order. The Bible itself mirrors from one angle and then another the core Hebrew metaphor of "covenant" as the character of the relationship of the people to Yahweh and to one another; indeed, in some versions, to all creation (e.g., the Noachic covenant). All of these and other formative strands in Christian ethics either assume or explicitly state the relational character of existence. The moral life is part of this. The classic treatment of the origins and development of Christian ethics and the social forms of the Christian community remains that of Ernst Troeltsch, *The Social Teaching of the Christian Churches, Volumes I and II*, intro. by H. Richard Niebuhr, trans. Olive Wyon (Chicago: University of Chicago Press, Phoenix Edition, 1981). Yet even Troeltsch, under the sway of Enlightenment individualism and 19th-century Protestant liberalism, projects back onto Jesus and the early church an individualism which isn't present in the texts or the ethos of those communities. For a discussion of "individualism and commitment" in U.S. society, chiefly white middle-class circles, see the significant study by Robert N. Bellah, Richard Madsen, Wm. M. Sullivan, Ann Swidler, and Steven M. Tipton, *Habits of the Heart: Individualism and Commitment in American Life* (Berkeley, Los Angeles, London: University of California Press, 1985).

2. Joyce Hollyday, "Rest for the Weary," *Sojourners*, 17/1 (January 1988):20.

3. Moral philosophy is extremely important to Christian ethics and our veiled polemic here does not intend to deny that. The disagreement we raise is significant, however. The broad stream of moral philosophy that has flowed from the Enlightenment has carried as its core notions those of individualism and universalism. What can be known for sure (epistemology) and what can be done about it (ethics) are to be discovered by autonomous and rational individuals shorn of their attachments to traditions and other parochial influences, including religious ones. All that truly counts in the quest for morality is what individuals have in common as rational beings in quest of the good and their duty to it. The outcome should be truth that holds for all and likewise morality that is categorically applicable. This is what modern moral philosophy has been in quest of—a nonprovincial rational and moral autonomy (universalism) held to by biographically and historically unencumbered individuals (individualism). The nature of Christian ethics as intrinsically a community ethic of a particular people of God embedded in a particular history is at odds with moral philosophy here, despite the richness of much of the latter. A volume which draws together many strands of ethical theory in modern moral philosophy and has been widely used in Christian ethics is William K. Frankena, *Ethics* (Englewood Cliffs, N.J.: Prentice-Hall, Inc., 1963). A more recent influential volume commanding considerable discussion is John Rawls, *A Theory of*

Justice (Cambridge, Mass.: Harvard University Press, 1971). Any thorough exploration of the Enlightenment quest in ethics must go back to Immanuel Kant, *Groundwork of the Metaphysic of Morals,* available in many editions.

4. Wayne Meeks, *The Moral World of the First Christians* (Philadelphia: Westminster, 1986), p. 125.
5. Meeks, *The Moral World of the First Christians,* p. 12. We have also drawn from Meeks' discussion of Paul writing to the Thessalonians.
6. While this way of describing the Christian moral life is appropriate to many traditions in Christian ethics, it draws here especially on the influence of Stanley Hauerwas' writings, specifically *A Community of Character* (Notre Dame: University of Notre Dame Press, 1981). We have been influenced as well by George A. Lindbeck's *The Nature of Doctrine: Religion and Theology in a Postliberal Age* (Philadelphia: Westminster, 1984).
7. See the discussion, "Jesus as Sage: Challenge to Conventional Wisdom," in Marcus J. Borg, *Jesus: A New Vision* (New York: Harper & Row, 1987), pp. 96-124.
8. The text of the *Didache* is available in Jan L. Womer, ed., *Morality and Ethics in Early Christianity* (Philadelphia: Fortress, 1987), pp. 30-33.
9. Ferdinand Lassalle, *Franz von Sickingen,* trans. Daniel DeLeon (New York: New York Labor News, 1910), p. 63, as cited in an unpublished paper, "Christian Soldiers in the Nuclear Age," by John Todd Stewart, cover page. The content is unchanged from the source but we have paraphrased the text at points for reasons of style. The discussion of goal-oriented life and its relationship to means deserves far more attention than we give it here. One of the most helpful discussions is found in Dorothy Emmet's distinction between "teleology A" and "teleology B." See her book, *The Moral Prism* (New York: Macmillan, 1979), pp. 6ff. Teleology B accords well with biblical perspectives and the presentation we make here.
10. It should be noted in passing that what is described here is a common characteristic of religious communities. Religions typically provide not only explanations on a grand, even "cosmic," scale about the meaning of life, most of them also indicate the manner of life which is in keeping with such explanations. That is, they not only offer meaning but a "way" for embodying that meaning. Thus, *hodos* in early Christianity (the Greek word for "way"), *halakah* in Judaism, *shar'ia* in Islam, and *tao* in Chinese religion, to cite a few examples. Characteristically the leader is a sage who teaches a way of life or a path which is in sharp tension with the conventional wisdom of the age. Lao Tzu did so in sixth-century B.C.E. China, the Buddha did so in fifth-century B.C.E. India, Moses taught a way which broke sharply from Egypt's, and Jesus challenged the conventional wisdom of his time. Students who wish to trace the meaning of "way" in Jewish and Christian Scriptures can consult the *Theological Dictionary of the New Testament,* ed. Gerhard Kittel and Gerhard Friedrich, trans. Geoffrey W. Bromiley (Grand Rapids: Eerdmans, 1957), vol. 5. See the entry by Wilhelm Michaelis, *hodos.*
11. See the fascinating discussion in Meeks, *The Moral World of the First Christians,* especially chap. 2, "The Great Traditions: Greece and Rome," pp. 40ff. and the equally fascinating accounts in Robert L. Wilken, *The Christians as the Romans Saw Them* (New Haven and London: Yale University Press, 1984), especially chap. 4, "Galen: The Curiosity of a Philosopher," pp. 68ff.
12. See Wilken, *The Christians as the Romans Saw Them.*
13. From Porphyry's *Vita Plotini,* ibid., pp. 132-133.

14. This discussion of philosophy and early Christianity is indebted to that of Wilken, *The Christians as the Romans Saw Them,* pp. 77-83. On atheism and the conflict of religious visions see Wilken's "Epilogue," pp. 197-205.
15. See Shaye J. D. Cohen, *From the Maccabees to the Mishnah* (Philadelphia: Westminster, 1986).
16. See Raymond E. Brown, *The Churches the Apostles Left Behind* (New York: Paulist Press, 1984).
17. Rabbi Irving Greenberg, in his fascinating essay, "The Third Great Cycle of Jewish History," describes the first cycle as biblical Judaism, the second as rabbinic Judaism, and the third as the Judaism which arises from the events of the Holocaust and the founding of the State of Israel. The three are markedly different from one another in their situations, institutions, practices, and self-understanding. Yet throughout all the discontinuities there continues the basic imperative of the social embodiment of faith. Greenberg writes: "The ultimate message of the infinite has been turned over to a flesh and blood people to deliver to others and to incarnate in its own life. While Jewish sociology and Jewish theology are not identical, they are profoundly inter-related" ("The Third Great Cycle of Jewish History," *Perspectives,* n.d., p. 1).
18. It is difficult to exaggerate the difference for Christian ethics made by Constantine and the new social arrangements for the church which followed him. One of the most succinct and pointed discussions of this is chap. 7, "The Constantinian Sources of Western Social Ethics," in John Howard Yoder, *The Priestly Kingdom: Social Ethics as Gospel* (Notre Dame: University of Notre Dame Press, 1984), pp. 135-150.
19. See the discussion by Bruce Birch, "The Covenant at Sinai: Response to God's Freedom," in *Social Themes of the Christian Year,* ed. Dieter Hessel (Philadelphia: The Geneva Press, 1983), pp. 142-148.
20. See the discussion in Bruce C. Birch and Larry L. Rasmussen, *The Predicament of the Prosperous* (Philadelphia: Westminster, 1978), especially chap. 4, "Deliverance," pp. 80-98.
21. See the important work of James Cone, *God of the Oppressed* (New York: Seabury Press, 1975).
22. Excellent treatments of the process and its substance are found in relatively brief compass in: Walter Brueggemann, *The Prophetic Imagination* (Philadelphia: Fortress, 1978); Bruce C. Birch, *What Does the Lord Require? The Old Testament Call to Social Witness* (Philadelphia: Westminster, 1985); and in extensive detail in Paul Hanson, *The People Called: The Growth of Community in the Bible* (New York: Harper and Row, 1986); and in Norman Gottwald, *The Tribes of Yahweh* (Maryknoll, N.Y.: Orbis Books, 1979). Elisabeth Schüssler Fiorenza's *In Memory of Her* (New York: Crossroad Books, 1984) is an important treatment of New Testament materials and interpretation. Paul Hanson's volume, in addition to examining the process we describe here, is the most thorough investigation known to us of all aspects of the theme of "community" in the Old and New Testaments.
23. See the discussion of Walter Brueggemann in *The Prophetic Imagination,* especially chaps. 1 and 2, together with Bruce C. Birch, *What Does the Lord Require?,* chaps. 3 and 4.
24. This discussion draws heavily from Larry Rasmussen, "Creation, Church, and Christian Responsibility," in *Tending the Garden: Essays on the Gospel and the*

Earth, ed. Wesley Granberg-Michaelson (Grand Rapids: Eerdmans, 1987), pp. 124-125.

25. C. H. Dodd, *The Founder of Christianity* (New York: Macmillan, 1970), p. 90.
26. Ibid., p. 102.
27. Borg, *Jesus: A New Vision*, Preface, n.p. We are grateful to Borg for the reference to Dodd, cited above. We also mention the important work of E. P. Sanders, *Jesus and Judaism* (Philadelphia: Fortress, 1985).
28. Paul Lehmann, especially in his *Ethics in a Christian Context* (New York: Harper and Row, 1963), is the theologian who most has provided the impetus to view the whole of Christian ethics from its orientation in *koinōnia*.
29. Meeks, *The Moral World of the First Christians*, p. 94.
30. For discussion of the development of the canon, see the first part of James Kugel and Rowan A. Greer, *Early Biblical Interpretation* (Philadelphia: Westminster, 1986).
31. Ibid., p. 93.
32. Ibid., p. 94.
33. The terms and distinctions are those of Wayne Meeks, *The Moral World of the First Christians*, p. 96.

Chapter 3: Charting the Moral Life

1. Among other places, the etymology of these terms is insightfully discussed in Paul Lehmann's *Ethics in a Christian Context* (New York: Harper and Row, 1963), pp. 23-25. A helpful volume which explains basic terms in philosophical ethics is: Paul W. Taylor, *Principles of Ethics: An Introduction* (Encino, Calif.: Dickinson, 1975.)
2. This short description of "agency" draws from the longer treatment by Paul Camenisch in his chapter in Charles E. Strain, *Prophetic Visions and Economic Reality* (Grand Rapids: Eerdmans, 1988). No page citation, since at the time of this writing the book had not yet been published.
3. Recounted by George Will in "The Wilde Wild West," *The Washington Post*, 1 Aug. 1982.
4. Aristotle, in the *Nicomachean Ethics*, II.i.4-5, trans. H. Rackam, Loeb Classical Library, vol. 19 (Cambridge: Harvard University Press, 1926, Reprint 1982), p. 73.
5. Plato, *The Republic* (Baltimore: Penguin Books, 1974) 2nd rev. ed., pp. 107-108. The Hebrew Scriptures' "Book of Wisdom" also contains a similarly dramatic passage. The context is very different, however. The presentation is that of the "misguided reasoning" of the "godless" who have made a pact "with Death." Their speech includes this:
   As for the virtuous man who is poor, let us oppress him;
   let us not spare the widow,
   nor respect old age, white-haired with many years.
   Let our strength be the yardstick of virtue,
   since weakness argues its own futility.
   Let us lie in wait for the virtuous man, since he annoys us
   and opposes our way of life,
   reproaches us for our breaches of the law

and accuses us of playing false to our upbringing.
He claims to have knowledge of God,
and calls himself a son of the Lord.
Before us he stands, a reproof to our way of thinking,
the very sight of him weighs our spirits down;
his way of life is not like other men's,
the paths he treads are unfamiliar.
In his opinion we are counterfeit;
he holds aloof from our doings as though from filth;
he proclaims the final end of the virtuous as happy
and boasts of having God for his father.
Let us see if what he says is true,
let us observe what kind of end he himself will have.
If the virtuous man is God's son, God will take his part
and rescue him from the clutches of his enemies.
Let us test him with cruelty and with torture,
and thus explore this gentleness of his
and put his endurance to the proof,
Let us condemn him to a shameful death
since he will be looked after—we have his word for it.
(Wis. 2:10-20 JB)

6. The discussion does not imply there were no significant differences between Plato and Aristotle. There were, and they have great meaning for Christian ethics. Plato was the source for religious ethics in an idealistic mode. He regarded "true reality" to exist on another plane, together with its unchanging moral content. For Christian ethics this approach meant relating eternity to time and an abiding moral order to the flux and flow of history. Aristotle's approach, by way of contrast, was a "naturalistic" one. He saw a *telos*, or goal, for every species and contended that by studying the world around us, we could discern its patterns, including the moral patterns appropriate to human behavior. Later Christian ethics would draw again and again on "idealistic" and "naturalistic" approaches to ethics. The point in the discussion above, however, is that Plato and Aristotle share the classic concern for virtue which was part of classical culture.

7. This is manifestly the case for Christian "situation ethics." There is one norm, love, and the decision-at-hand. Rules-of-thumb exist for making decisions, but little or no attention is given to the formation of the decision maker herself or himself. Joseph Fletcher's *Situation Ethics* (Philadelphia: Westminster, 1966) is usually considered *the* statement of Christian situation ethics.

8. Martin Luther, *Lectures on Romans*, trans. and ed. Wilhelm Pauck, and published as vol. 15 of *Library of Christian Classics* (Philadelphia: Westminster, 1961), p. 4.

9. The quotations here are from Gerhard O. Forde's discussion of Luther in "The Exodus from Virtue to Grace: Justification by Faith Today," *Interpretation* 34 (January 1980):37. We should add that *Interpretation*, a quarterly journal, specializes in the treatment of biblical materials, often including the way they address moral issues.

10. The 20th-century ethicist who has remade Luther's point with even more power and nuance than Luther is Reinhold Niebuhr. See his magnum opus, *The Nature*

and Destiny of Man (New York: Charles Scribner's Sons, 1941, 1943), especially vol 1, chap. 7, "Man as Sinner," and vol. 2, chap. 4, "Wisdom, Grace, and Power." Niebuhr explores even more insightfully than Luther our capacities for self-deception and evil in the guise of good, but at the same time he avoids Luther's propensity to relativize ethical choices in the face of God's overwhelming judgment and mercy. See vol. 1, pp. 219-227.

11. Cited by Vicki Kemper, with Larry Engel, "A Prophet's Vision and Grace: The Life of Dom Helder Camara," in *Sojourners* 12 (December 1987):14. The poem is from Dom Helder Camara, *A Thousand Reasons for Living* (Philadelphia: Fortress, 1981), p. 71.

12. Langdon Gilkey, *Shantung Compound* (New York: Harper & Row, 1966), ix. Gilkey's account is a firsthand one even though the book was published some 20 years after his experience of Shantung Compound. He used journals kept during those years and checked his account with others who had lived there.

13. Ibid., p. 99.

14. Ibid., p. 109.

15. Ibid.

16. Ibid., p. 110.

17. Ibid.

18. Ibid. The outcome of the parcel distribution episode was as follows: After indecision by the Americans, the matter reverted to the Japanese authorities. They took the matter to authorities in Tokyo who decided that each internee was to receive one parcel each and the remaining parcels would be sent to other camps. The whole episode ended with stinging humor. As the mountain of goods was sorted, it was discovered that included were two hundred pairs of boots sent by the *South African* Red Cross. There were two South Africans in the camp at the time. They posted the following notice: "Due to the precedent that has been set, the South African community is laying claim to all 200 of the boots donated by their Red Cross. We shall wear each pair for three days to signal our right to what is our own property, and then shall be glad to lend some out when not in use to any non-South Africans who request our generous help" (ibid., p. 113).

19. Niebuhr, *The Nature and Destiny of Man*, vol. 2, p. 244.

20. Ibid., p. 247.

21. Ibid., p. 248.

22. One of the benefits of Thomas Ogletree's *The Use of the Bible in Christian Ethics* (Philadelphia: Fortress, 1983) is his organization and discussion of ethical theory at the outset of the book. What we here call "teleological" ethics he calls "consequentialist" ethics. The reader is referred to his work for a discussion of the biblical materials in light of this stream in ethics. Ogletree gives equal space to "deontological" ethics, which we discuss as "obligation" in the moral life, and to "perfectionist" ethics, which we have named "virtue" and character. They, too, are part of the schema taken to the discussion of biblical materials. The chapter in which these are presented, "Preunderstandings of the Moral Life," pp. 15-47, has the additional benefit of uncovering the human reality which gives rise to these ethical theories. The chapter notes, as well as the selected bibliography, provide guidance for further study.

23. A fuller discussion of this, and the inadequacies of both value ethics and obligation

ethics for Christian ethics, is part of Charles L. Kammer III's *Ethics and Liberation: An Introduction* (Maryknoll: Orbis Books, 1988). See especially chaps. 5 and 6. The discussion in Ogletree, cited in the previous note, is pertinent as well.

24. Tom L. Beauchamp and James F. Childress, *Principles of Biomedical Ethics* (New York: Oxford University Press, 1979), p. 29.

25. Without question the author who has formulated the most thorough and consistent ethic of moral obligation, and has had the greatest influence in modern Christian ethics in this direction, is Immanuel Kant. His most important writings are: *Groundwork of the Metaphysic of Morals*, trans. H. J. Paton (New York: Harper and Row, 1964); *Critique of Practical Reason*, trans. Lewis White Beck (Indianapolis: Bobbs-Merrill, 1956); *Religion within the Limits of Reason Alone*, trans. T. M. Greene and H. H. Hudson (New York: Harper and Row, 1960). An important volume in moral philosophy which combines teleological and deontological theories is William David Ross, *The Right and the Good* (London: Oxford University Press, 1930). The Christian ethicist of the 20th century who has most consistently developed a Christian ethic of moral obligation is Paul Ramsey. His writings are many, but in this connection see *Deeds and Rules in Christian Ethics* (Edinburgh: Oliver and Boyd, 1965).

26. As mentioned in an earlier note, Kant is the philosopher who has most thoroughly developed ethics as the ethics of obligation and who has most influenced modern Christian ethics in this way. He does it on the basis of respect for persons. As a moral minimum, other persons must never be abased as mere means to my subjective ends. More expansively, love itself means making the welfare of others my own. Love, then, is not a feeling so much as practical benevolent treatment. See especially Kant's *Groundwork of the Metaphysic of Morals*. Paul Ramsey's *The Patient as Person* develops these notions for medical ethics (New Haven: Yale University Press, 1970).

27. We are again indebted to Kammer's good discussion in *Ethics and Liberation: An Introduction*.

28. Cited by Beauchamp and Childress, *Principles of Biomedical Ethics*, preface, vii.

29. "Pat Robertson vs. the Facts," *The New York Times*, 10 Oct. 1987.

30. From a paper by Roy Branson, "Apocalyptic and the Moral Imagination," proceedings from a conference on "Bioethics: Old Models and New," held at Loma Linda University, November 1986, pp. 1-2.

31. Many examples could be cited, but the most thorough recent effort to conceive Christian ethics in a nonanthropocentric way is James M. Gustafson's *Ethics from a Theocentric Perspective* (Chicago: University of Chicago Press). Volume 1 was published in 1981, volume 2 in 1984.

32. The pathfinding essays in the revision of Christian ethics are those of Beverly Wildung Harrison, *Making the Connections: Essays in Feminist Social Ethics*, ed. Carol S. Robb (Boston: Beacon Press, 1985). The work is carried on in Barbara Hilkert Andolsen, Christine E. Gudorf, and Mary Pellauer, eds., *Women's Conscience, Women's Consciousness: A Reader in Feminist Ethics* (Minneapolis: Winston Press, 1985). The volume acknowledges Harrison's work and is dedicated to her.

33. Jeremy Rifkin, *Declaration of a Heretic* (Boston, London, Melbourne, and Henley: Routledge and Kegan Paul, 1985), p. 99.

34. The practitioner of moral philosophy and theological ethics who underscored the

way key metaphors in our moral vision affected the moral life as a whole is Richard Niebuhr, especially in *The Responsible Self: An Essay in Christian Moral Philosophy* (New York: Harper and Row, 1963). Work has been carried on by many others; considering our example of the physicians, a particularly noteworthy representative is William F. May, *The Physician's Covenant: Images of the Healer in Medical Ethics* (Philadelphia: Westminster, 1983). See also Philip S. Keane, s.s., *Christian Ethics and Imagination* (New York: Paulist Press, 1984).

35. The suggestion of television's "bible" as a way to explain the role of moral vision is from May, *The Physician's Covenant*, pp. 17-19.

36. Donald Capps' *Deadly Sins and Saving Virtues* (Philadelphia: Fortress Press, 1987) has three sections, "The Deadly Sins," "The Saving Virtues," and "The Saving Graces." Capps discusses these using the stages of the life cycle developed by Erik Erikson in *Childhood and Society*, 2nd rev. ed. (New York: W. W. Norton & Co., 1963). As he does so, he draws from narratives about biblical figures in order to illustrate the sins, virtues, and graces, and their dynamics.

37. The image is taken from the title of Dorothy Emmet's book, *The Moral Prism* (New York: St. Martin's Press, 1979). The use of the image here is not out of keeping with her own. But her own work uses it far more extensively. We highly recommend the volume as one which superbly treats aspects of the moral life which our volume does not.

38. The chapter, "Radical Reformation Ethics in Ecumenical Perspective," especially the subsection, "A Detour Concerning Logic," in John Yoder's *The Priestly Kingdom* (Notre Dame: University of Notre Dame Press, 1984), pp. 113-116, has been especially helpful here.

39. Students who wish to explore this should see: Alexander Schmemann, *For the Life of the World: Sacraments and Orthodoxy* (New York: St. Vladimir's Press, 1973); Paulos Gregorios, *The Human Presence: An Orthodox View of Nature* (Geneva: World Council of Churches, 1978); Stanley S. Harakas, *Toward Transfigured Life* (Minneapolis: Light and Life Publishing Co., 1983).

40. Examples include: Gustavo Gutierrez, *A Theology of Liberation* (Maryknoll: Orbis, 1971); James H. Cone, *God of the Oppressed* (New York: Seabury, 1975); Robert McAfee Brown, *Theology in a New Key* (Philadelphia: Westminster Press, 1978); Karen Lebacqz, *Justice in an Unjust World* (Minneapolis: Augsburg, 1987).

41. An intriguing example from early Christian ethics (2nd century) is that of Clement of Alexandria and his attempt to reconcile the Christian way of life with the aristocratic Hellenism of his day. See his writings, "The Instructor," "The Stromata," and "The Rich Man's Salvation," in vol. II of *The Ante-Nicene Fathers* (New York: Charles Scribner's Sons, 1926).

42. Tom F. Driver, *Christ in a Changing World: Toward an Ethical Christology* (New York: Crossroads, 1981), p. x.

Chapter 4: The Elements of Character Formation

1. As reported by William F. Buckley in "The Higher Laws of Charles Colson," *New York Daily News*, 27 Nov. 1987.

2. James Q. Wilson, "The Rediscovery of Character: Private Virtue and Public Policy," *The Public Interest* 81 (Fall 1985):3.

3. In Christian ethics, the work of Stanley Hauerwas on the relationship of character

and community is important. Here we are drawing from his discussion in *A Community of Character* (Notre Dame: University of Notre Dame Press, 1981), especially Part One.

4. Ronald F. Thiemann, "The Scholarly Vocation: Its Future Challenges and Threats," *Theological Education*, 24/1(Autumn 1987):96.

5. Martin Buber, *I and Thou*, trans. Ronald Gregor Smith (New York: Charles Scribner's Sons, 2nd ed., 1958).

6. Ibid., p. 4.

7. Ibid., p. 18.

8. Ibid., p. 11.

9. For a treatment of biblical materials on this theme, see chap. 5, "Wisdom and Creation," in our book, *The Predicament of the Prosperous* (Philadelphia: Westminster, 1978), pp. 98-125.

10. Buber, *I and Thou*, p. 11.

11. We do not use the distinction of "personal ethics" from "social ethics" as arenas of Christian ethics. All ethics are personal *and* social and cannot be separated. In fact, one of the tasks of Christian ethics is to show their intimacy. Nonetheless, there is a limited truth in the distinction. Some morality is "personal" in that an individual exercises considerable control over the choices made. But we are better served to distinguish "simple" and "complex" morality, or use the terms Sheldon Wolin did in comments about President Carter. He judged Carter rather good on "the clean virtues": honesty, self-control, personal decency, fidelity, compassion, etc. "Clean" virtues are those over which a person has considerable individual control. I can choose whether to lie, drink, swear, or smoke, and the consequences of my choices generally fall and stay within the range of my power. Something like "simple" or "clean" virtues comprise the content of "personal ethics," if that term is to be used at all. Much of life is bound up with "dirty virtues," however. (Wolin does not mean "vices"; he means "virtues.") These are virtues which necessarily involve many lives simultaneously. They cannot be exercised apart from a complex social interaction. They invariably entail conflict among group interests and usually involve political compromise. They involve actions which become part of a social mix over which no one of the individual actors has control. "Freedom," "justice," and "equality" all partake of this kind of virtue and value. Wolin's discussion is from the *New York Review of Books*, as reported by Martin Marty in *CSCM Yearbook IV* (Valparaiso, Ind: Center for the Study of Campus Ministry, 1981), p. 85. We add that the distinction "personal" from "social" in Christian ethics has usually participated in the assumption this volume rejects, namely, that the individual exists prior to, and apart from, society. On "dirty virtues" and the implications of complex social interaction for ethics, see the classic in Christian ethics, Reinhold Niebuhr's *Moral Man and Immoral Society* (New York: Charles Scribner's Sons, 1932).

12. The work of Lawrence Kohlberg has been a starting point and reference for much recent discussion of moral development. His most significant writings include two major collections of essays: *Essays on Moral Development, Volume One: The Philosophy of Moral Development* (San Francisco: Harper & Row, 1981) and *Essays on Moral Development, Volume Two: The Psychology of Moral Development* (San Francisco: Harper & Row, 1983). Kohlberg's theory is one of universal stages of moral development, each next stage dependent on the successful negotiation of the former one. The most significant revision of Kohlberg to date is

Carol Gilligan, *In a Different Voice: Psychological Theory and Women's Development* (Cambridge: Harvard University Press, 1982). It is likely, in our judgment, that future studies in "stage theory" will show that the assumed stages of development are far more susceptible to cultural influences and configurations than originally recognized by Kohlberg or in the important work of Jean Piaget and Erik Erikson. Erikson's *Childhood and Society,* 2nd rev. ed. (New York: W. W. Norton & Co., 1963) outlines the stages of the life cycle many have used in development theory. Donald Capps' volume, *Deadly Sins and Saving Virtues* (Philadelphia: Fortress, 1987) uses Erikson's schema and draws on biblical materials for illustrative examples relevant to current pastoral care. In any event, current discussions of moral development in Christian ethics draw heavily from these and other writers in cognitive and developmental psychology. A full integration of theories of moral development and materials and methods from Christian traditions remains to be done.

13. Developmental literature continues to underscore the importance of childhood influences. A delightful recollection of moral substance learned in early childhood is provided by Robert L. Fulghum in a feature we cite in full, "All I Ever Really Need to Know I Learned in Kindergarten."

"Most of what I really need to know about how to live, and what to do, and how to be, I learned in kindergarten. Wisdom was not at the top of the graduate school mountain, but there in the sandbox at nursery school.

"These are the things I learned: Share everything. Play fair. Don't hit people. Put things back where you found them. Clean up your own mess. Don't take things that aren't yours. Say you're sorry when you hurt somebody. Wash your hands before you eat. Flush. Warm cookies and cold milk are good for you. Live a balanced life. Learn some and think some and draw and paint and sing and dance and play and work every day some.

"Take a nap every afternoon. When you go out into the world, watch for traffic. Hold hands and stick together. Be aware of wonder. Remember the little seed in the plastic cup. The roots go down and the plant goes up and nobody really knows how or why, but we are all like that.

"Goldfish and hamsters and white mice and even the little seed in the plastic cup—they all die. So do we.

"And then remember the book about Dick and Jane and the first word you learned, the biggest word of all: LOOK. Everything you need to know is in there somewhere. The Golden Rule and love and basic sanitation. Ecology and politics and sane living.

"Think of what a better world it would be if we all—the whole world—had cookies and milk about 3 o'clock every afternoon and then lay down with our blankets for a nap. Or if we had a basic policy in our nation and other nations to always put things back where we found them and cleaned up our own messes. And it is still true, no matter how old you are, when you go out into the world, it is best to hold hands and stick together" (cited from *Kansas City Times,* 17 Sept. 1976).

14. Clifford Geertz describes worldview and ethos extensively as the elements of culture. See *The Interpretation of Cultures: Selected Essays* (New York: Basic Books, 1973). See also the important discussion of the social construction of reality in Peter Berger's *The Sacred Canopy* (Garden City, N.Y.: Doubleday, 1967). We

have taken our discussion of these two dimensions of the social world from Marc Borg's chapter, "The Social World of Jesus," in his *Jesus: A New Vision* (New York: Harper and Row, 1987), pp. 79-96. Borg draws upon Geertz and Berger as well as others whom we have also used here and elsewhere in this book.

15. These comments on language are far too spare a report of consensus among otherwise widely varied social theories. Of special significance in Christian ethics is the social role of language. This has been most fruitfully pursued by feminist theologians and ethicists. In systematic theology, see Sallie McFague's work, especially *Models of God: Theology for an Ecological, Nuclear Age* (Philadelphia: Fortress, 1987); in social ethics, see Beverly Wildung Harrison's *Making the Connections: Essays in Feminist Social Ethics,* ed. Carol S. Robb (Boston: Beacon Press, 1985), especially the essay, "Sexism and the Language of Christian Ethics," pp. 22-41, from which our brief comments are taken, including the quotation cited here (p. 23).

16. Jerome S. Bruner, *Child's Talk: Learning to Use Language* (New York: Norton and Co., 1983).

17. The physical act of blushing is a nice example of nonverbal communication which illustrates moral formation. Animals don't blush, but humans do. The human infant doesn't, however. Blushing depends on the internalization of social rules and expectations. Many of these are "moral" in nature, reflecting notions of right and wrong, good and bad, proper and improper behavior. That this remains social in character, even when internalized, is clear: we never blush in private, only among others. Morality is "between" us, even when it is also deep inside us.

18. A compact and helpful discussion can be found in *The Westminster Dictionary of Christian Ethics,* ed. James Childress and John Macquarrie, 2nd ed. (Philadelphia: Westminster, 1986). The entry is "Character," by Richard Bondi, pp. 82-84. The discussion also refers the reader to other relevant entires, such as "Act," "Action," "Agent," "Habit," "Vice," "Virtue." *The Westminster Dictionary of Christian Ethics* is a volume students of ethics should become acquainted with. An excellent multivolume work also ranging widely in subjects of basic moral concepts and theory is *The Encyclopedia of Bioethics,* ed. Warren Reich (New York: Free Press; London: Collier MacMillan, 1978).

19. The notes on etymology are taken from *On Language,* the column by William Safire, "Character Issue," *The New York Times Sunday Magazine,* 22 Nov. 1987.

20. James Gaffney, "Values, Victims and Visions," *Commonweal* 15 (Aug. 1986): 426-429.

21. Ibid., p. 426.

22. Ibid.

23. Ibid.

24. Abraham Heschel, *Who Is Man?* (Palo Alto, Calif.: Stanford University Press, 1965), p. 11.

25. See "Leading Psychologist Expands the Boundaries," *The New York Times,* 20 Oct. 1987.

26. One report of several studies supporting this conclusion is supplied by Daniel Goleman, "Personality: Major Traits Found Stable through Life," *The New York Times,* 9 June 1987. James' comment is cited from this article.

27. Marcus Borg's comment is appropriate here, and important " . . . [t]he term 'faith' has undergone a subtle but decisive shift in meaning in the modern period. For

many people, faith now means 'believing in the existence of God.' In earlier times, it didn't take 'faith' to believe *that* God existed—almost everybody took that for granted. Rather, 'faith' had to do with one's *relationship* to God—whether one *trusted* in God. The difference between faith as 'belief in something that may or may not exist,' and faith as 'trusting in God' is enormous. The first is a 'matter of the head,' the second a 'matter of the heart'; the first can leave one unchanged, the second intrinsically brings change" (Marcus J. Borg, *Jesus: A New Vision* [New York: Harper & Row, 1987], p. 35, note). We add that the close connection of faith and ethics as a way of life assumes the meaning of faith in the second sense, as delineated by Borg. We also add that our discussion includes faith in the first sense, but not simply "believing in the existence of God." Rather, a set of beliefs which, in the context of a basic trust, order our experience and provide substance for our basic perception of our world. Thus we modify Borg, yet share with him an emphasis on faith as trust, as the most fundamental meaning.

28. Martin Luther, *Luther's Large Catechism* (Minneapolis: Augsburg, 1935), p. 44.
29. Gaffney, "Values, Victims and Visions," p. 426.
30. The article on Bruner cited above includes his comment about the physicists he conversed with when he was a visiting scholar at Princeton's Institute for Advanced Studies. One of them claimed physics "was 5 percent observation and 95 percent speculation." They meant that their models largely determined what was looked for, what was found, and how it was interpreted. Important work for religious studies in this area has been done by Ian Barbour; see his volume *Myths, Models, and Paradigms: A Comparative Study in Science and Religion* (New York: Harper & Row, 1987).
31. This discussion of character elements, as well as moral knowledge and its relation to our experience, is very fruitfully explored in the fine work of Daniel Maguire. See especially *The Moral Choice* (Minneapolis: Winston Press, 1978). One of the chapters addresses itself specifically to the meaning of motive and moral style.
32. As reported by Janis Johnson in "Two Educators, Legislator, Explore Moral Choices and Public Service," *The Washington Post*, 18 Feb. 1977. Readers may wish to consult the article on "Conscience" in *The Westminster Dictionary of Christian Ethics*, cited above, and/or the volume by C. Ellis Nelson, ed., *Conscience: Theological and Psychological Perspectives* (New York: Newman Press, 1973).
33. John Ehrlichmann, "What I Have Learned," *Parade*, 26 Sept. 1982, p. 7.
34. Cited by David Halberstam in *The Best and the Brightest* (Greenwich, Conn.: Fawcett Publications, 1972), p. 88. At the same conference in Washington cited in note 32 on conscience, Harlan Cleveland said the following; it supplements Bowles's testimony: "A written code of ethics is never comprehensive enough [to cover the moral choices public servants face]. . . . The level of responsibility in government depends on the moral sensitivity and internalized standards of hundreds of thousands of public and private executives. The more complex things become, the more personal decisions must be . . . . Wise sayings from Aristotle, the Bible, our parents, and so forth may be useful but they are never singularly applicable to each case. They don't provide much guidance on what to do next, such as how to control race riots, solve the Vietnam War or whether to build a new office building."

35. Dirk Johnson, "Coming Home, with AIDS, to a Small Town," *The New York Times*, 2 Nov. 1987.

Chapter 5: Character Formation and Social Structure

1. John Sabini and Maury Silver, *Moralities of Everyday Life* (Oxford, New York, Toronto, Melbourne: Oxford University Press, 1982), p. 57. The diary entries are cited from the volume by E. Cohen, *Human Behavior in the Concentration Camp* (New York: Grosset & Dunlap, 1953).
2. Ibid.
3. Ibid.
4. Ibid.
5. Ibid.
6. Sallie McFague, *Models of God: Theology for an Ecological, Nuclear Age* (Philadelphia: Fortress, 1987), p. 137.
7. "Theodicy" is the name given the theological-moral effort to speak coherently about the reality of evil while also claiming that God is good. See Douglas John Hall, *God and Human Suffering* (Minneapolis: Augsburg, 1986); Dorothee Soelle, *Suffering* (Philadelphia: Fortress, 1973); and James H. Cone, *God of the Oppressed* (New York: Seabury Press, 1975), especially chap. 8, "Divine Liberation and Black Suffering" (pp. 163-194); and chap. 9, "Liberation and the Christian Ethic" (pp. 195-225). The Jewish writer who has deeply influenced many writing in Christian ethics is Elie Wiesel. See his account of his own experience in the concentration camps in Birkenau, Auschwitz, Bune, and Buchenwald, as told in *Night* (New York: Avon Books, 1969); see also his novels, which should be read in chronological order so as to accompany Wiesel's wrestling with the issues of evil and good: *Dawn* (New York: Avon Books, 1970); *The Accident* (New York: Avon Books, 1970); *The Town beyond the Wall* (New York: Avon Books, 1969); *The Gates of the Forest* (New York: Avon Books, 1967); *A Beggar in Jerusalem* (New York: Avon Books, 1971); *The Oath* (New York: Avon Books, 1973); *The Testament* (New York: Summit Books, 1981). The publication dates of the English language editions do not always reflect the order of publication of the French originals. A fine volume in Christian ethics which interprets Wiesel's works and wrestles with the issues of evil, suffering, and the possibilities of affirmation and goodness is Robert McAfee Brown's *Elie Wiesel: Messenger to All Humanity* (Notre Dame and London: University of Notre Dame Press, 1983).
8. Ibid., pp. 55-57.
9. Ibid., p. 56 (emphasis added).
10. Richard L. Rubenstein, *The Cunning of History: Mass Death and the American Future* (New York: Harper & Row, 1975), pp. 4-5.
11. See Hannah Arendt, *Eichmann in Jerusalem: A Report on the Banality of Evil* (New York: Penguin Press, 1977).
12. Sabini and Silver, *Moralities of Everyday Life*, p. 56. This is their reporting of Arendt's findings.
13. Dietrich Bonhoeffer, "After Ten Years," in *Letters and Papers from Prison*, The Enlarged Edition, ed. Eberhard Bethge (New York: Macmillan, 1971), pp. 5-6.
14. Sabini and Silver, *Moralities of Everyday Life*, p. 56.
15. Walter Rauschenbusch, *Christianizing the Social Order* (New York: Macmillan,

1912), p. 127. Rauschenbusch's insight was made in different words by Justice Louis Brandeis in the 1930s. He wrote: "Our government is the potent, the omnipresent teacher. For good or ill, it teaches the whole people by its example. Crime is contagious. If the Government becomes the lawbreaker, it breeds contempt for law, it invites every man to become a law unto himself, it invites anarchy." This is cited in the Congressional Iran-Contra report, which adds: "The Iran-Contra affair [of the Reagan Administration] resulted from a failure to heed this message." From: "The Law and the Devil," *The New York Times*, 19 Nov. 1987. Readers should know that Rauschenbusch himself is a key figure in the Social Gospel movement of Protestantism in the United States in the first three decades of this century. His volume, *A Theology for the Social Gospel*, is one of the important books in the history of Christian ethics. Among other issues, it takes structural evil seriously.

It should also be noted that our remarks about the power of social structure to channel behavior do not negate the power of character, especially collective character, to alter events and structures. The strength of character shown in the Civil Rights Movement is ample demonstration. *The Boston Globe Magazine*, reporting on the television series about the movement, "Eyes on the Prize," includes this: "If Moses Wright hadn't decided to stand up and testify, or the people of Montgomery hadn't decided to do that themselves [protest discrimination on buses], it wouldn't have happened. Legislation wouldn't have done it. Certainly political leadership never would have done it. The federal government and the Constitution wouldn't have done it. And if you talk about the underclass, the only way the problem will ever be solved is if the individuals within the underclass understand that they have to change it. And that they are no less or more resourced than the poor black folks in the rural South who started this movement" (Ed Siegel, "Let My People Go," *The Boston Globe Magazine*, 18 Jan. 1987, p. 57).

16. "Waldheim Assails 'Slanderers,' Vows Not to Step Down," *The New York Times*, 16 Feb. 1988. We have also drawn information from *The New York Times* of 9 February 1988 ("Inquiry for Austria Declares Waldheim Knew of War Crimes"), 18 February 1988 ("Waldheim Linked to Nazi Roundup"); and from the *Nairobi Daily Nation*, 16 January 1988 ("Austrians Divided over Waldheim's Nazi Issue").

17. See the biography by Robert Edwin Herzstein, *Waldheim: The Missing Years* (New York: Arbor House/William Morrow & Company, 1988). Curiously, Herzstein declares Waldheim "not evil" because he found him to be "well meaning," for the most part. This is a moral judgment which is faulty because Herzstein has reduced ethics to intentions only. Intentions are important, but comprise only part of character; and character comprises only part of ethics—thus our point in this chapter that "good" refers to the convergence of virtue *and* morally right *action*.

18. James Fallows, "The Passionless Presidency," *Atlantic* 243 (May 1979):34-35.

19. Cited by Daniel P. Moynihan in "How Reagan Created the Crash," *The New York Times*, 1 Nov. 1987.

20. These three elements are used as the framework to discuss issues of world hunger in Larry Rasmussen's "The Persistence of Hunger," *Currents in Theology and Mission* 14/4 (Aug. 1987):245-251, and are borrowed from that discussion.

21. John Howard Yoder, *The Priestly Kingdom* (Notre Dame: The University of Notre Dame Press, 1984), p. 5.

22. Walter Wink, *Violence and Nonviolence in South Africa: Jesus' Third Way* (Philadelphia: New Society Publishers, 1987), p. 64.

23. Thomas Merton, "A Letter to Pablo Antonia Cuadra Concerning Giants," *Emblems of a Season of Fury* (New York: New Directions Books, 1961), p. 71. Merton continues later: "We live in an age of bad dreams, in which the scientist and the engineer possess the power to give external form to the phantasms of man's unconscious. The bright weapons that sing in the atmosphere, ready to pulverize the cities of the world, are the dreams of giants without a center. Their mathematical evolutions are hieratic rites devised by Shamans without belief. One is permitted to wish their dreams had been less sordid! But perhaps they are also the emanations of our own subliminal self!" (p. 72).

24. "New Jersey Plan Is Blown Away by Winds of Change," part of a feature series on the making of the Constitution, *The Washington Post*, 15 June 1987.

25. The writings of Reinhold Niebuhr remain the important discussion of human possibilities and limits in history, and the relation of these to human capacities for good and evil. Niebuhr's magnum opus, and one of the great works in Christian ethics in the 20th century, is *The Nature and Destiny of Man* (New York: Charles Scribner's Sons, 1941, 1943).

Chapter 6: Decision Making

1. This volume gives little attention to current social issues in Christian ethics, except occasionally for the purposes of illustration. That is not because we consider them unimportant; rather, they are too important to treat in the space a single volume in ethics allows. Moreover, discussion of current issues is by definition quickly dated. A good source, which is updated every few years, is Paul T. Jersild and Dale A. Johnson, eds., *Moral Issues and Christian Response* (New York: Holt, Rinehart and Winston, 4th ed., 1988). Greenhaven Press, St. Paul, Minn., publishes a running series of pamphlets on moral issues entitled *Opposing Viewpoints*. Like Jersild and Johnson, a spectrum of viewpoints on an issue is assembled. The difference is that the Greenhaven publications are without reference to religious orientation, while Jersild and Johnson are.

2. This is the basic error of "situation ethics." It makes decision king in ethics and neglects both character formation and the structuring of the good society. Yet it has been popular in ethics and many people fail to even think of ethics in any other terms than making moral decisions. (See note 7, p. 208.)

3. See the important essay by John Howard Yoder, "The Hermeneutics of Peoplehood: A Protestant Perspective," in his *The Priestly Kingdom* (Notre Dame: University of Notre Dame Press, 1984), pp. 15-45. This discussion draws upon that essay as well as the introduction, pp. 1-12.

4. Cornel West, *Prophesy Deliverance! An Afro-American Revolutionary Christianity* (Philadelphia: Westminster, 1982), p. 21.

5. See the discussion in Yoder, *The Priestly Kingdom*, p. 26ff.

6. Ibid., pp. 116-122.

7. For an interesting reading of this in the history of culture, see Jaroslav Pelikan, *Jesus Through the Centuries* (New York: Harper & Row, 1985).

8. See note 16, p. 214.

9. From "Leading Psychologist Expands the Boundaries," *The New York Times*, 20 Oct. 1987. The extensive discussion of this is found in Bruner's work, *Actual Minds, Possible Worlds* (Cambridge: Harvard University Press, 1987). A landmark

article along similar lines but in religious studies is that of Stephen Crites, "The Narrative Quality of Experience," *Journal of the American Academy of Religion,* 39/3 (Sept. 1971):291-311.

10. Robert Coles, a psychiatrist who teaches at Harvard University, relates his experience teaching a seminar at the Harvard Business School entitled "The Business World: Moral and Social Inquiry Through Fiction." He used well-known novels as the vehicle for discussing the moral quandaries people in business frequently face. He found that "stories enlivened [the participants'] moral imagination." Stories, he says, "can work their magic on the heart—and help one resist the ever present temptation of the intellect to distance anything and everything from itself through endless generalization. Yes, we used our head in that course. But mostly we sat back and let those stories get to us, prompt us to remember past times and wonder anew about the future. . . . " From Coles, "Gatsby at the B School," *The New York Times Book Review,* 10 Oct. 1987, p. 41.

11. George A. Lindbeck, *The Nature of Doctrine: Religion and Theology in a Post-liberal Age* (Philadelphia: Westminster, 1984), p. 32.

12. The etymological root of "ritual" is the Sanskrit *rita,* signifying "order," and from which we have the words "rite" and "right." Telling a story is a "rite" which seeks the "right" ordering of our experience and provides some guidance for us (the "right" way). We draw here from Nancy J. Duff's use of the work of Ted L. Estess in Duff's excellent Ph.D. dissertation, "Humanization and the Politics of God: The *Koinōnia* Ethics of Paul Lehmann" (Union Theological Seminary, 1987).

13. Lindbeck, *The Nature of Doctrine.*

14. The discussion and quotation here are from Lindbeck. Nancy J. Duff makes insightful use of Lindbeck's work for Christian ethics in her doctoral dissertation, cited above.

15. From Buechner's sermon, "The Annunciation," in his book *The Magnificent Defeat* (New York: Seabury, 1966), pp. 58-59.

16. Ibid., p. 59.

17. See the chapter, "Old Testament Narrative and Moral Address," in *Canon, Theology, and Old Testament Interpretation,* ed. Gene M. Tucker, David L. Petersen, and Robert R. Wilson (Philadelphia: Fortress, 1988).

18. Ibid., p. 55.

19. *The Upside-Down Kingdom* is the title of a book on Jesus by Donald Kraybill (Scottdale, Penn.: Herald Press, 1978).

20. Walter Brueggemann, *The Prophetic Imagination* (Philadelphia: Fortress, 1978), p. 72.

21. This discussion of "the levels of moral discourse" is a simplification and adaptation of Aiken's important and helpful essay by that title in his *Reason and Conduct* (New York: Knopf, 1962), pp. 65ff.

22. These roles and this emphasis on community decision making draw considerably from John Yoder's chapter in *The Priestly Kingdom,* "The Hermeneutics of Peoplehood: A Protestant Perspective," pp. 15-45. Ours is only a skeletal presentation and a considerable adaptation of his, however. We also give different names to some roles and collapse two of Yoder's proposed roles into one.

23. A method very similar to ours is described by Ada Maria Isasi-Diaz and Yolanda Tarango, *Hispanic Women: Prophetic Voice in the Church* (New York: Harper and

Row, 1988), pp. 104-110. The book itself is a report of the experience of Hispanic women doing theological-moral reflection together.

24. See James M. Gustafson, "Moral Discernment in the Christian Life," in *Theology and Christian Ethics* (Philadelphia: Pilgrim Press, 1974), pp. 99-120; and James E. Hug, s.j., "Christian Moral Discernment," in *Tracing the Spirit,* ed. James E. Hug, s.j. (New York: Paulist Press, 1985), pp. 279-305.

25. Cited from the *Encyclopedia of Bioethics,* Warren T. Reich, editor-in-chief (New York: Free Press; London: Collier Macmillan, 1978), p. 439.

26. Ibid., p. 440. Daniel C. Maguire drew this entry to our attention in his review of the *Encyclopedia of Bioethics,* in *Theological Studies* 41/4 (December, 1980):752-763. Maguire's own book, *The Moral Choice* (Minneapolis: Winston Press, 1978), has been helpful to our understanding of relevant moral knowledge and its sources.

27. See p. 107 above.

Chapter 7: The Church and the Moral Life

1. *Economic Justice for All: Pastoral Letter on Catholic Social Teaching and the U.S. Economy* (Washington: United States Catholic Conference, 1986), §129.

2. Ibid., §360.

3. Ibid., §22.

4. The discussion in this chapter relies directly upon work done earlier in the first edition of this book, chap. 4, "The Church as Community Context," pp. 126-141; and in a later chapter by Larry Rasmussen, "Going Public: The Church's Roles," in Charles P. Lutz, ed., *God, Goods, and the Common Good* (Minneapolis: Augsburg, 1987), pp. 29-44.

5. See note 3 above.

6. Recall the discussion of *psychogogia* in chap. 2, p. 23.

7. Cited from Roger L. Shinn, *Tangled World* (New York: Charles Scribner's Sons, 1965), p. 96.

8. Ruben F. W. Nelson, *The Illusions of Urban Man* (Ottawa, Canada: Square One Management Ltd., 1979), p. 48.

9. Bruce Birch, *What Does the Lord Require? The Old Testament Call to Social Witness* (Philadelphia: Westminster, 1985), p. 83.

10. Ibid.

11. The account of the Trocme's and of Le Chambon is preserved in Philip Hallie's *Lest Innocent Blood be Shed* (New York: Harper and Row, 1979.)

12. The task of interpreting Scripture for ethics, and the formulation of a normative ethical stance using Scripture, is complex and the subject of much present debate. Later chapters in this book will take up this discussion. A volume in Christian ethics which presents the issues clearly and illustrates a method for the use of Scripture in the interests of a normative ethic is Lisa Sowle Cahill, *Between the Sexes: Foundations for a Christian Ethics of Sexuality* (Philadelphia: Fortress Press; New York: Paulist Press, 1985). For the important issues of method, see especially chaps. 1 and 2. A normative stand on any given moral issue (Cahill's book is about sexual relationships) can never be settled by reference to Scripture alone. A normative stand on some current matter is the outcome of influences from several sources. Cahill uses four complementary reference points: "the foundational texts of 'scriptures' of the faith community—the Bible; the community's 'tradition' of

faith, theology, and practice; philosophical accounts of essential or ideal humanity ('normative' accounts of the human); and descriptions of what actually is and has been the case in human lives and societies ('descriptive' accounts of the human)" (p. 5). These interact with the more immediate facts of the issue at hand as the community moves to a "normative" stand, i.e., one it recommends in answer to the question, "What ought to be done?" But within this method, and as part of it, the Scriptures cannot be used indiscriminately. That is, attention must be given to how the Bible is rightly to be understood for the issue the community is facing. This is the question of "hermeneutics" and is the subject of Cahill's second chapter, and intimated in our own discussion above. In short, there is both the matter of arriving at a "normative" stand on the moral issue at hand, and the matter of a "normative" reading of Scripture as part of the method used to do so. The normative reading of Scripture interacts with the other reference points in the process of moving to a decision.

13. These paragraphs draw from Alasdair MacIntyre's chapter, "Virtue, Unity of Life and the Concept of a Tradition," in *After Virtue* (Notre Dame: University of Notre Dame Press, 1981), pp. 190-209. The question just cited is from p. 201.

14. John Yoder, *The Priestly Kingdom* (Notre Dame: University of Notre Dame Press, 1984), p. 77.

15. Ibid.

16. An important work in biblical studies which makes this point with great power is Phyllis Trible's *Texts of Terror: Literary-Feminist Readings of Biblical Narratives* (Philadelphia: Fortress, 1984).

17. The relationship of traditions to both the content and framework of an ethic is, of course, not limited to the church as an ongoing community. It pertains to many communities in society, and to the notion of society itself. Justice Felix Frankfurter wrote in a Supreme Court decision of 1940 that "the ultimate foundation of a free society is the binding tie of cohesive sentiment" and that cohesive sentiment "is fostered by all those agencies of the mind and spirit which may serve to gather up the traditions of a people, transmit them from generation to generation and thereby create that continuity of a treasured common life which constitutes a civilization." Cited by Martin E. Marty, "Pluralists Take It on the Chin—Deservedly," in *The New York Times,* 2 April 1988. Much of what we discuss in this chapter would apply to other institutions who find themselves playing similar roles in the moral life. That we do not discuss them does not indicate we think them unimportant in the lives of Christians and others. Our reason is simply that the subject of this chapter is specifically the church in the moral life.

18. H. Richard Niebuhr, et al., *The Purpose of the Church and Its Ministry: Reflections on the Aims of Theological Education* (New York: Harper & Row, 1956), p. 38. The full paragraph reads as follows: "Who, finally, is my neighbor, the companion whom I have been commanded to love as myself? He is the near one and the far one; the one removed from me by distances in time and space, in convictions and loyalties. . . . The neighbor is in past and present and future, yet he is not simply mankind in its totality but rather in its articulation, the community of individuals in community. He is Augustine in the Roman Catholic Church and Socrates in Athens, and the Russian people, and the unborn generations who will bear the consequences of our failures, future persons for whom we are administering the entrusted wealth of nature and other greater common gifts. He is man and angel and animal and inorganic being, all that participates in being."

19. The United Methodist Council of Bishops, *In Defense of Creation: The Nuclear Crisis and a Just Peace* (Nashville: Graded Press, 1986).
20. For a response by Catholics, Protestants, and Jews to the bishops' pastoral letter, see the volume edited by Charles Strain, *Prophetic Visions and Economic Realities* (Grand Rapids: Eerdmans, 1988).
21. As with other discussions in this chapter using the bishops' pastoral letter, this one draws directly from the chapter by Larry Rasmussen in Lutz, *God, Goods, and the Common Good.*
22. We add to this discussion of moral deliberation a note about any analysis which strives to be an ethical analysis. As the community works on moral issues, the following components should be included as essential to ethics: a descriptive component, a critical component, and a normative component. They are all "formal," belonging to the form of ethics as ethics. The moral issues may change, as may their context, but these elements remain the same.

   (1) Ethical analysis has a descriptive component. For any given issue, some kind of empirical case is made or assumed. Descriptive ethical analysis brings it into view. Description answers the question of what facts and interpretations of facts are considered salient. It also uncovers as best it can other dimensions of a moral issue's location. What ideological frameworks are present? What histories are influential? What interests are most powerful for decisions already made or contemplated? Who's making the decisions and by what means? In brief, what is the issue's context?

   Descriptive analysis also pays attention to the presentation of the issue. What moral justification (supporting reasons) is (are) being given by different participants? What actions are they recommending, and why? Which are *not* being considered? Why?

   In a word, good ethical analysis includes a descriptive uncovering of moral reality.

   (2) The second component is one of critical assessment. It follows from the first. What do we make of the moral patterns uncovered, the justifying reasons given, the facts marshaled, the interpretations made? How do they appear in the light of critical reflection? Are the cases made sound ones? Are the specific stands being considered morally worthy?

   (3) The third element is the normative one. In the case of a given moral issue, "normative" means offering a recommended stand and course of action. It also means offering a rationale for these, providing reasons subject to public scrutiny.

   These elements may be given different names. Sometimes description and assessment travel together under the umbrella of "critical ethics" and recommendation is called "constructive ethics." But the work is the same, and ethical analysis means uncovering moral reality, evaluating it, and offering normative proposals. An attentive community of moral deliberation does all three.
23. A helpful discussion both of community and action is found in Frank G. Kirkpatrick's *Community: A Trinity of Models* (Washington, D.C.: Georgetown University Press, 1986). See especially chap. 6, "Religion and the Nature of the Loving Community," pp. 186-220. Recall, too, our discussion in the previous chapter of the pragmatic character of moral truth.
24. See National Conference of Catholic Bishops, *The Challenge of Peace: God's Promise and Our Response* (Washington, D.C.: U. S. Catholic Conference, 1983).

We have used the Roman Catholic bishops' pastoral letters for illustrative purposes. But we have not cited other sources of Catholic moral theology. A convenient and instructive way to follow developments in Catholic ethics is the annual publication of volumes edited by Charles E. Curran and Richard A. McCormick, S.J., entitled *Readings in Moral Theology* (New York: Paulist Press). Materials are organized thematically. The first volume appeared in 1979. McCormick also writes "Notes on Moral Theology" for the journal *Theological Studies*. This is a semi-annual review of literature in Roman Catholic ethics on selected themes.

25. Karl Barth, *Church Dogmatics* IV/2, trans. G. W. Bromiley (Edinburgh: T. & T. Clark, 1958), p. 721.

Chapter 8: The Nature and Role of Biblical Authority

1. It goes without saying that the Bible's normative role has been understood in diverse ways. Useful typologies can be found in David H. Kelsey, *The Uses of Scripture in Recent Theology* (Philadelphia: Fortress, 1975), and Robert Gnuse, *The Authority of the Bible: Theories of Inspiration, Revelation and the Canon of Scripture* (New York: Paulist, 1985).
2. James Gustafson, "Introduction," in H. Richard Niebuhr, *The Responsible Self* (New York: Harper and Row, 1963), p. 22.
3. James Barr, *The Bible in the Modern World* (New York: Harper and Row, 1973), p. 23.
4. Edward Farley and Peter C. Hodgson, "Scripture and Tradition," in *Christian Theology,* ed. Peter C. Hodgson and Robert H. King (Philadelphia: Fortress, 1985), p. 62. See Edward Farley, *Ecclesial Reflection: An Anatomy of Theological Method* (Philadelphia: Fortress, 1982) for a fuller treatment.
5. See Dewey Beegle, *Scripture, Tradition and Infallibility* (Grand Rapids, Mich.: Eerdmans, 1973), pp. 124-125; Robert Gnuse, *The Authority of the Bible,* pp. 20-21; Robert Johnston, *Evangelicals at an Impasse: Biblical Authority in Practice* (Atlanta: John Knox, 1979), pp. 19-34.
6. See such a critique in Sallie McFague, *Models of God: Theology for an Ecological, Nuclear Age* (Philadelphia: Fortress, 1987), p. 43.
7. Farley and Hodgson, "Scripture and Tradition," pp. 72ff., discuss the "collapse of the house of authority."
8. Representative works where biblical hermeneutics have received attention are Juan Luis Segundo, *The Liberation of Theology* (Maryknoll, N.Y.: Orbis, 1976) and Elisabeth Schüssler Fiorenza, *Bread Not Stone* (Boston: Beacon Press, 1984).
9. See Segundo, *The Liberation of Theology.*
10. See especially Elisabeth Schüssler Fiorenza, "A Feminist Biblical Hermeneutics: Biblical Interpretation and Liberation Theology," in *The Challenge of Liberation Theology: A First World Response,* ed. L. Dale Richesin and Brian Mahan (Maryknoll, N.Y.: Orbis, 1981), pp. 91ff.; and *Feminist Interpretation of the Bible,* ed. Letty M. Russell (Philadelphia: Westminster, 1985).
11. See Phyllis A. Bird, "Images of Women in the Old Testament," *Religion and Sexism,* ed. Rosemary Radford Ruether (New York: Simon and Schuster, 1974), pp. 41ff.; and Elisabeth Schüssler Fiorenza, *In Memory of Her: A Feminist Theological Reconstruction of Christian Origins* (New York: Crossroad, 1983).
12. Farley and Hodgson, "Scripture and Tradition," p. 81.

13. Elisabeth Schüssler Fiorenza, "The Will to Choose or Reject: Continuing Our Critical Work," in *Feminist Interpretation of the Bible*, p. 135.

14. A similar claim and many of the points in our discussion would hold true for Judaism, and its relationship to the Hebrew Scriptures which are shared in common with the church.

15. James Barr, *The Bible in the Modern World*, p. 23.

16. Sallie McFague, *Models of God*, p. 43.

17. For a fuller discussion of this concept see Bruce C. Birch, *What Does the Lord Require? The Old Testament Call to Social Witness* (Philadelphia: Westminster, 1985), pp. 52ff., and James A. Wharton, "Theology and Ministry in the Hebrew Scriptures," in *A Biblical Basis for Ministry*, ed. Earl E. Shelp and Ronald Sunderland (Philadelphia: Westminster, 1981), pp. 17ff.

18. An especially helpful book is Phyllis A. Bird, *The Bible as the Church's Book* (Philadelphia: Westminster, 1982).

19. David H. Kelsey, *The Uses of Scripture in Recent Theology*.

20. See David H. Kelsey, "The Bible and Christian Theology," in *Journal of the American Academy of Religion* 48 (1980):400-401.

21. Farley and Hodgson, "Scripture and Tradition," p. 80.

22. James Gustafson, "Introduction," in *The Responsible Self*, p. 22.

23. Sallie McFague, *Models of God*, is an excellent example of constructive theology in this vein.

24. Ibid., p. 42. The phrase "sedimented interpretations" is taken by McFague from Farley and Hodgson, "Scripture and Tradition," p. 85.

25. McFague, *Models of God*, p. 43.

26. See especially James A. Sanders, *From Sacred Story to Sacred Text* (Philadelphia: Fortress, 1987).

27. Ibid., pp. 9ff.

28. I used this sentence in an earlier unpublished response to Elisabeth Schüssler Fiorenza in a panel on feminist hermeneutics, AAR, New York, 1982, and it is quoted in Letty Russell, "Authority and the Challenge of Feminist Interpretation," *Feminist Interpretation of the Bible*, p. 146.

29. McFague, *Models of God*, p. 43.

30. Allen Verhey, *The Great Reversal: Ethics and the New Testament* (Grand Rapids, Mich.: Eerdmans, 1984), pp. 153ff.

Chapter 9: Making Biblical Resources Available

1. See chap. 1 in Birch and Rasmussen, *Bible and Ethics in the Christian Life*, 1st ed. (Minneapolis: Augsburg, 1976), for an extended discussion of the growing gap between the Bible and Christian ethics both in the scholarly guild and in the life of the church. Since 1976 a revived discussion of the relationship between the Bible and Christian ethics has developed especially among ethicists (represented by important works such as Thomas W. Ogletree, *The Use of the Bible in Christian Ethics* [Philadelphia: Fortress, 1983] and Allen Verhey, *The Great Reversal: Ethics and the New Testament* [Grand Rapids: Eerdmans, 1984]). Such a systematic discussion has not yet developed in biblical scholarship or in the life of the church. Developments such as liberation and feminist hermeneutics and the increased attention to social location (see discussion later in this chapter) have important

implications for relating Bible and Christian ethics which are beginning to be addressed (e.g., in almost any of the writings of Walter Brueggemann).

2. See James D. Smart, *The Strange Silence of the Bible in the Church* (Philadelphia: Westminster, 1970) and Elizabeth Achtemeier, *The Old Testament and Proclamation of the Gospel* (Philadelphia: Westminster, 1973). More recently see Bruce C. Birch, "The Role of Memory in Congregational Life," in *The Congregation: Its Power to Form and Transform,* ed. C. Ellis Nelson (Atlanta: John Knox, 1988), 20-42.

3. For a discussion of the theological significance of such variety in the biblical literature see Paul D. Hanson, *The Diversity of Scripture,* Overtures to Biblical Theology (Philadelphia: Fortress, 1982).

4. The neglect and recovery of the significance of Old Testament narrative for the moral life is treated in Bruce C. Birch, "Old Testament Narrative and Moral Address," in *Canon, Theology, and Old Testament Interpretation,* ed. G. M. Tucker, David L. Petersen, and Robert R. Wilson (Philadelphia: Fortress, 1988).

5. A discussion of this image in relation to world resource issues is found in Bruce C. Birch and Larry L. Rasmussen, *The Predicament of the Prosperous* (Philadelphia: Westminster, 1978), pp. 74-75.

6. In her SBL Presidential Address, Elisabeth Schüssler Fiorenza develops a forceful rationale for renewed attention to social location in biblical criticism, "The Ethics of Interpretation: De-Centering Biblical Scholarship," *Journal of Biblical Literature* (1988): 3-17.

7. Norman K. Gottwald, *The Tribes of Yahweh: A Sociology of the Religion of Liberated Israel 1250–1050* B.C.E. (Maryknoll, NY: Orbis Books, 1979); and *The Hebrew Bible: A Socio-Literary Introduction* (Philadelphia: Fortress, 1985).

8. Robert Kysar, *The Fourth Evangelist and His Gospel: An Examination of Contemporary Scholarship* (Minneapolis: Augsburg, 1975).

9. Paul D. Hanson, *The People Called: The Growth of Community in the Bible* (San Francisco: Harper and Row, 1986); and James A. Sanders, *From Sacred Story to Sacred Text* (Philadelphia: Fortress, 1987) have both stressed the crucial role of community.

10. An especially helpful resource is Robin Maas, *Church Bible Study Handbook* (Nashville: Abingdon Press, 1982). This book details methods and tools for adult Bible study in local congregations. Another helpful resource on exegetical processes is John H. Hayes and Carl R. Holladay, *Biblical Exegesis: A Beginner's Handbook,* rev. ed. (Atlanta: John Knox, 1988).

11. An excellent popular treatment of Bible translations and the processes involved is Barry Hoberman, "Translating the Bible," *The Atlantic Monthly* (February 1985), pp. 43-58.

12. Maas, *Church Bible Study Handbook,* includes an excellent bibliography of such tools, pp. 199-208.

13. A classic statement which argues that the task of biblical theology should be limited to the descriptive task of the objective historian is to be found in Krister Stendahl, "Biblical Theology, Contemporary," in *The Interpreter's Dictionary of the Bible,* vol. 1 (Nashville: Abingdon Press, 1962), pp. 418ff.

14. Brevard S. Childs, *Biblical Theology in Crisis* (Philadelphia: Westminster, 1970), p. 99.

15. Hartmut Gese, "Tradition and Biblical Theology"; R. Laurin, "Tradition and

Canon"; and Douglas A. Knight, "Revelation Through Tradition"; all in *Tradition and Theology in the Old Testament,* ed. D. A. Knight (Philadelphia: Fortress, 1977).

16. Brevard S. Childs, *Introduction to the Old Testament as Scripture* (Philadelphia: Fortress, 1979), pp. 76, 83.

17. The phrase itself is problematic. Which textual tradition is the final form? Does this mean Old and New Testaments together as the final canonical context, or can the Old Testament also be studied for its own witness before relating it to the New? See a critique of Childs in Bruce C. Birch, "Tradition, Canon and Biblical Theology," in *Horizons in Biblical Theology* 2 (1980):113-126.

18. James A. Sanders, in *From Sacred Story to Sacred Text,* collects together much of his important work on issues related to the canon and the canonization process.

19. Paul Lehmann, *Ethics in a Christian Context* (New York: Harper and Row, 1963) briefly acknowledges the importance of Old Testament roots (p. 26) and cites the Reformation principle of *tota Scriptura est verbum dei* (The Scripture as a whole is the Word of God, p. 30), but entitles his section on biblical resources "Christian Ethics and New Testament Ethics" (p. 26).

20. Childs, *Biblical Theology in Crisis,* p. 105.

21. Elisabeth Schüssler Fiorenza, "Discipleship and Patriarchy: Early Christian Ethos and Christian Ethics in a Feminist Theological Perspective," in *Proceedings of the Society of Christian Ethics,* 1982.

22. See James A. Sanders, "The Bible as Canon," *The Christian Century* (2 Dec. 1981).

23. See Sharon H. Ringe, "Positive Force for Justice or Benediction to Abuse?" *Engage/Social Action* 11 (July/August 1983):26ff.

24. See Phyllis Trible, *Texts of Terror* (Philadelphia: Fortress, 1984) where a powerful hearing of the Word of God comes out of wrestling with oppressive texts.

25. See note 28, chap. 8.

26. Childs, *Biblical Theology in Crisis,* pp. 195ff. Childs notes a number of negative controls on looking for similarity of subject matter.

27. See James Gustafson, "The Place of Scripture in Christian Ethics: A Methodological Study," *Interpretation* 24 (Oct. 1970):430-455 for a discussion of these models which he also rejects in favor of a more multifaceted model of his own. See also the earlier discussion in chap. 3 where it is stressed that the moral life is not reducible to virtue, value, obligation, or vision *only.* Neither does the Bible relate to only one of these.

28. See pp. 177-178 above.

29. In our opinion the issue of homosexuality as it is being discussed in various church bodies is an example of this. At the most generous count there are seven biblical texts that are claimed to deal with homosexuality, and some of these seem to deal more with violent and lustful behavior or foreign cultic practices than with sexual orientation per se. This makes it clear that homosexuality was, at best, a minor, largely unaddressed concern in the biblical communities. There is no clear and unambiguous moral imperative in Scripture on this matter. Thus, the church's moral decisions on this matter must take into account social and medical data in light of more general biblically based principles, values, and visions.

Chapter 10: Summary and Challenge

1. Allan Bloom, *The Closing of the American Mind: How Higher Education Has Failed Democracy and Impoverished the Souls of Today's Students* (New York: Simon and Schuster, 1987), p. 60.
2. *The Challenge of Peace: God's Promise and our Response. A Pastoral Letter on War and Peace* (Washington: The National Conference of Catholic Bishops, 1983), and *Economic Justice for All: Pastoral Letter on Catholic Social Teaching and the U.S. Economy* (Washington: National Conference of Catholic Bishops, 1986). The United Methodist Council of Bishops followed a similar process in issuing *In Defense of Creation: The Nuclear Crisis and a Just Peace* (Nashville: Graded Press, 1986).
3. See Sergio Torres and John Eagleson, eds., *The Challenge of Basic Christian Communities* (Maryknoll: Orbis Books, 1981).
4. Robin Maas documents this still-common notion and its roots in her unpublished dissertation, "New Foundations for Biblical Education with Children: A Challenge to Goldman," Catholic University of America, 1985. See also her briefer treatment in "Biblical Catechesis and Religious Development: The Goldman Project Twenty Years Later," *Living Light* 22 (January 1986): 124-144.

Bibliography

Achtemeier, Elizabeth. *The Old Testament and Proclamation of the Gospel.* Philadelphia: Westminster, 1973.

Aiken, Henry David. *Reason and Conduct.* New York: Knopf, 1962.

Andolsen, Barbara Hilkert, Christine E. Gudorf, and Mary Pellauer, eds. *Women's Conscience, Women's Consciousness: A Reader in Feminist Ethics.* Minneapolis: Winston Press, 1985.

Arendt, Hannah. *Eichmann in Jerusalem: A Report on the Banality of Evil.* New York: Penguin Press, 1977.

Aristotle. *Nicomachean Ethics.* Loeb Classical Library, vol. 19. Translated by H. Rackham. Cambridge: Harvard University Press, 1982.

Barbour, Ian. *Myths, Models, and Paradigms: A Comparative Study in Science and Religion.* New York: Harper and Row, 1987.

Barr, James. *The Bible in the Modern World.* New York: Harper and Row, 1973.

Barth, Karl. *Church Dogmatics.* Translated by A. T. Mackay, et al. Vol. III, Pt. 4. Edinburgh: T. & T. Clark, 1961.

Barth, Karl. *The Humanity of God.* Translated by Thomas Weiser. Richmond: John Knox, 1963.

Barth, Karl. *The Word of God and the Word of Man.* New York: Harper and Row, 1957.

Barth, Markus, and Verne Fletcher. *Acquittal by Resurrection.* New York: Holt, Rinehart and Winston, 1964.

Beauchamp, Tom, and James F. Childress. *Principles of Biomedical Ethics.* New York; Oxford University Press, 1979.

Beegle, Dewey. *Scripture, Tradition and Infallibility.* Grand Rapids, Mich.: Wm. B. Eerdmans, 1973.

Bellah, Robert N., et. al. *Habits of the Heart: Individualism and Commitment in American Life.* Berkeley, Los Angeles, London: University of California Press, 1985.

Berger, Peter. *The Sacred Canopy.* Garden City, N.Y.: Doubleday, 1967.

Birch, Bruce C. "Old Testament Narrative and Moral Address." In *Canon, Theology, and Old Testament Interpretation,* edited by Gene M. Tucker, David L. Peterson, and Robert R. Wilson, 75-91. Philadelphia: Fortress, 1988.

Birch, Bruce C. "The Role of Memory in Congregational Life." In *The Congregation: Its Power to Form and Transform,* edited by C. Ellis Nelson, 20-42. Atlanta: John Knox, 1988.

Birch, Bruce C. "Tradition, Canon and Biblical Theology." *Horizons in Biblical Theology* 2 (1980): 113-126.

Birch, Bruce C. *What Does the Lord Require?: The Old Testament Call to Social Witness.* Philadelphia: Westminster, 1985.

Birch, Bruce C., and Larry L. Rasmussen. *The Predicament of the Prosperous.* Philadelphia: Westminster, 1978.

Bird, Phyllis A. *The Bible as the Church's Book.* Philadelphia: Westminster, 1982.

Bird, Phyllis A. "Images of Women in the Old Testament." In *Religion and Sexism,* edited by Rosemary Radford Ruether, 41-88. New York: Simon and Schuster, 1974.

Bloom, Allan. *The Closing of the American Mind: How Higher Education Has Failed Democracy and Impoverished the Souls of Today's Students.* New York: Simon and Schuster, 1987.

Bonhoeffer, Dietrich. *Letters and Papers from Prison.* The Enlarged Edition. Edited by Eberhard Bethge. New York: Macmillan, 1971.

Borg, Marcus J. *Jesus: A New Vision.* New York: Harper and Row, 1987.

Branson, Roy. "Apocalyptic and the Moral Imagination." Proceedings from a conference, Bioethics: Old Models and New, Loma Linda University, November 1986.

Brown, Raymond E. *The Churches the Apostles Left Behind.* New York: Paulist Press, 1984.

Brown, Robert McAfee. *Elie Wiesel: Messenger to All Humanity.* Notre Dame and London: University of Notre Dame Press, 1983.

Brown, Robert McAfee. *Theology in a New Key.* Philadelphia: Westminster, 1978.

Brueggemann, Walter. *The Prophetic Imagination.* Philadelphia: Fortress, 1978.

Bruner, Jerome. *Actual Minds, Possible Worlds.* Cambridge, Mass.: Harvard University Press, 1987.

Bruner, Jerome. *Child's Talk: Learning to Use Language.* New York: Norton and Co., 1983.

Buber, Martin. *I and Thou.* 2nd ed. Translated by Ronald Gregor Smith. New York: Charles Scribner's Sons, 1958.

Cahill, Linda Sowle. *Between the Sexes: Foundations for a Christian Ethic of Sexuality.* Philadelphia: Fortress; New York: Paulist Press, 1985.

Capps, Donald. *Deadly Sins and Saving Virtues.* Philadelphia: Fortress, 1987.

Childress, James, and John Macquarrie, eds. *The Westminster Dictionary of Christian Ethics.* Philadelphia: Westminster, 1986.

Childs, Brevard S. *Biblical Theology in Crisis.* Philadelphia: Westminster, 1970.

Childs, Brevard S. *Introduction to the Old Testament as Scripture.* Philadelphia: Fortress, 1979.

Clement of Alexandria. "The Instructor," "The Stromata," "The Rich Man's Salvation." In *The Anti-Nicene Fathers,* vol. II. New York: Charles Scribner's Sons, 1926.

Cohen, E. *Human Behavior in the Concentration Camp.* New York: Grosset & Dunlap, 1953.

Cohen, Shaye J. D. *From the Maccabees to the Mishnah.* Philadelphia: Westminster, 1986.

Cone, James. *God of the Oppressed.* New York: Seabury Press, 1975.

Crites, Stephen. "The Narrative Quality of Experience." *Journal of the American Academy of Religion* 39, no. 3 (September 1971): 291-311.

Curran, Charles E. "Dialogue with the Scriptures: The Role and Function of the Scriptures in Moral Theology." In *Catholic Moral Theology in Dialogue,* 24-64. Notre Dame, Ind.: Fides Publishers, 1972.

Curran, Charles E., and Richard McCormick, eds. *Readings in Moral Theolog.* No. 4, *The Use of Scripture in Moral Theology.* New York: Paulist Press, 1984.

Dodd, C. H. "The Ethics of the New Testament," in *Moral Principles of Action,* edited by Ruth Nanda Anshen, 543-558. New York: Harper and Brothers, 1952.

Dodd, C. H. *The Founder of Christianity.* New York: Macmillan, 1970.

Dodd, C. H. *Gospel and Law.* New York: Columbia University Press, 1951.

Driver, Tom F. *Christ in a Changing World: Toward an Ethical Christology.* New York: Crossroad, 1981.

Duff, Nancy J. "Humanization and the Politics of God: The *Koinōnia* Ethics of Paul Lehmann." Ph.D. diss., Union Theological Seminary, 1987.

Eichrodt, Walther. "The Effect of Piety on Conduct (Old Testament Morality)." In *Theology of the Old Testament,* translated by J. A. Baker, vol. II, 316-379. Philadelphia: Westminster, 1967.

Emmet, Dorothy. *The Moral Prism.* New York: Macmillan, 1979.

Erikson, Erik. *Childhood and Society.* 2nd rev. ed. New York: W. W. Norton & Co., 1963.

Everding, H. Edward, and Dana M. Wilbanks, *Decision Making and the Bible.* Valley Forge, Pa.: Judson Press, 1975.

Everding, H. Edward, and Dana M. Wilbanks. "A Functional Methodology for Relating Biblical Studies and Contemporary Ethics." Unpublished paper for the American Academy of Religion Consultation on the Bible and Ethics, October 1974.

Farley, Edward. *Ecclesial Reflection: An Anatomy of Theological Method.* Philadelphia: Fortress, 1982.

Farley, Edward and Peter C. Hodgson. "Scripture and Tradition." In *Christian Theology,* edited by Peter C. Hodgson and Robert H. King, 61-87. Philadelphia: Fortress, 1985.

Fiorenza, Elisabeth Schüssler. *Bread Not Stone.* Boston: Beacon Press, 1984.

Fiorenza, Elisabeth Schüssler. "Discipleship and Patriarchy: Early Christian Ethos and Christian Ethics in a Feminist Theological Perspective." In *Proceedings of the Society of Christian Ethics* (1982).

Fiorenza, Elisabeth Schüssler. "The Ethics of Interpretation: De-Centering Biblical Scholarship." *Journal of Biblical Literature* 107 (1988):3-17.

Fiorenza, Elisabeth Schüssler. *In Memory of Her.* New York: Crossroad, 1984.

Fletcher, Joseph. *Situation Ethics.* Philadelphia: Westminster, 1966.

Forde, Gerhard O. "The Exodus from Virtue to Grace: Justification by Faith Today." *Interpretation* 34 (January 1980): 32-44.

Frankena, William K. *Ethics.* Englewood Cliffs, N.J.: Prentice-Hall, Inc., 1963.

Furnish, Victor. *The Love Command in the New Testament.* Nashville: Abingdon, 1972.

Furnish, Victor. *Theology and Ethics in Paul.* Nashville: Abingdon, 1968.

Gaffney, James. "Values, Victims and Visions." *Commonweal,* 15 August 1986: 426-429.

Geertz, Clifford. *The Interpretation of Cultures: Selected Essays.* New York: Basic Books, 1983.

Gilkey, Langdon. *Shantung Compound.* New York: Harper and Row, 1966.

Gilligan, Carol. *In a Different Voice: Psychological Theory and Women's Development.* Cambridge, Mass.: Harvard University Press, 1982.

Gnuse, Robert. *The Authority of the Bible: Theories of Inspiration, Revelation and the Canon of Scripture.* New York: Paulist Press, 1985.

Gottwald, Norman. *The Hebrew Bible: A Socio-Literary Introduction.* Philadelphia: Fortress, 1985.

Gottwald, Norman. *The Tribes of Yahweh: A Sociology of the Religion of Liberated Israel 1250–1050* B.C.E. Maryknoll, N.Y.: Orbis, 1979.

Granberg-Michaelson, Wesley, ed. *Tending the Garden: Essays on the Gospel and the Earth.* Grand Rapids, Mich.: Wm. B. Eerdmans, 1987.

231

Gregorios, Paulos. *The Human Presence: An Orthodox View of Nature.* Geneva: World Council of Churches, 1978.

Gustafson, James M. *Can Ethics Be Christian?* Chicago: University of Chicago Press, 1975.

Gustafson, James M. *Christ and the Moral Life.* New York: Harper and Row, 1968.

Gustafson, James M. "Christian Ethics." In *Religion,* edited by Paul Ramsey, 285-354. Englewood Cliffs, N.J.: Prentice-Hall, Inc., 1965.

Gustafson, James M. *The Church as Moral Decision-Maker.* Philadelphia: Pilgrim Press, 1970.

Gustafson, James M. 1981–1984. *Ethics from a Theocentric Perspective.* 2 vols. Chicago: The University of Chicago Press.

Gustafson, James M. Introduction to *The Responsible Self* by H. Richard Niebuhr, 6-41. New York: Harper and Row, 1963.

Gustafson, James M. "The Place of Scripture in Christian Ethics: A Methodological Study," *Interpretation* 24 (October 1970): 430-455.

Gustafson, James M. *Theology and Christian Ethics.* Philadelphia: Pilgrim Press, 1974.

Gutierrez, Gustavo. *A Theology of Liberation.* Maryknoll, N.Y.: Orbis, 1973.

Hall, Douglas John. *God and Human Suffering.* Minneapolis: Augsburg, 1986.

Hallie, Philip. *Lest Innocent Blood Be Shed.* New York: Harper and Row, 1979.

Hanson, Paul D. *The Diversity of Scripture.* Overtures to Biblical Theology. Philadelphia: Fortress, 1982.

Hanson, Paul. *The People Called: The Growth of Community in the Bible.* New York: Harper and Row, 1986.

Harakas, Stanley S. *Toward Transfigured Life.* Minneapolis: Light and Life Publishing Co., 1983.

Haring, Bernard. 1961–1966. *The Law of Christ.* 3 vols. Westminster, Md.: The Newman Press.

Harned, David Bailey. *Faith and Virtue.* Philadelphia: Pilgrim Press, 1973.

Harrison, Beverly Wildung. *Making the Connection: Essays in Feminist Social Ethics.* Edited by Carol S. Robb. Boston: Beacon Press, 1985.

Hauerwas, Stanley. *A Community of Character.* Notre Dame, Ind.: University of Notre Dame Press, 1981.

Hauerwas, Stanley. *Character and the Christian Life: A Study in Theological Ethics.* San Antonio: Trinity University Press, 1975.

Hayes, John H., and Carl R. Holladay. *Biblical Exegesis: A Beginner's Handbook.* Revised Edition. Atlanta: John Knox, 1988.

Hempel, J. "Ethics in the Old Testament." In *Interpreter's Dictionary of the Bible,* vol. II, 153-161. Nashville: Abingdon, 1962.

Hempel, J. *Das Ethos des Alten Testaments.* Berlin: A. Topelmann, 1938.

Henry, Carl F. H. *Christian Personal Ethics.* Grand Rapids, Mich.: Wm. B. Eerdmans, 1957.

Heschel, Abraham. *Who Is Man?* Palo Alto, Calif.: Stanford University Press, 1965.

Hessel, Dieter, ed. *Social Themes of the Christian Year.* Philadelphia: The Geneva Press, 1983.

Hoberman, Barry. "Translating the Bible." *The Atlantic Monthly* (February 1985): 43-58.

Hollyday, Joyce. "Rest for the Weary." *Sojourners* 17, no. 1 (January 1988): 15-20.

Houlden, J. L. *Ethics and the New Testament.* Baltimore: Penguin Books, 1973.

Hug, James E., ed. *Tracing the Spirit.* New York: Paulist Press, 1985.

Isazi-Diaz, Ada Maria, and Yolanda Tarango. *Hispanic Women: Prophetic Voice in the Church.* New York: Harper and Row, 1988.

Jersild, Paul T. and Dale A. Johnson. *Moral Issues and Christian Response.* New York: Holt, Rinehart and Winston, 1988.

Johnston, Robert. *Evangelicals at an Impasse: Biblical Authority in Practice.* Richmond: John Knox, 1979.

Jonas, Hans. *The Imperative of Responsibility.* Chicago: The University of Chicago Press, 1984.

Kammer, Charles L. III. *Ethics and Liberation: An Introduction.* Maryknoll, N.Y.: Orbis, 1988.

Kant, Immanuel. *Critique of Practical Reason.* Translated by Lewis White Beck. Indianapolis: The Bobbs-Merrill Co., Inc., 1956.

Kant, Immanuel. *Groundwork of the Metaphysics of Morals.* Translated by H. J. Paton. New York: Harper and Row, 1964.

Kant, Immanuel. *Religion within the Limits of Reason Alone.* Translated by T. M. Greene and H. H. Hudson. New York: Harper and Row, 1960.

Keane, Philip S., s.s. *Christian Ethics & Imagination.* New York: Paulist Press, 1984.

Keck, Leander E. "On the Ethos of Early Christians." *Journal of the American Academy of Religion* 42, no. 3 (September 1974): 435-452.

Keck, Leander E., and Sellers, James E. "Theological Ethics in an American Crisis: A Case Study," *Interpretation* 24 (October 1970): 456-481.

Kelsey, David H. "The Bible and Christian Theology." *Journal of the American Academy of Religion* 48 (1980): 385-402.

Kelsey, David H. *Uses of Scripture in Recent Theology.* Philadelphia: Fortress, 1975.

Kemper, Vicki, with Larry Engel. A Prophet's Vision and Grace: The Life of Dom Helder Camara." *Sojourners* (December 1987): 12-15.

Kirkpatrick, Frank G. *Community: A Trinity of Models.* Washington, D.C.: Georgetown University Press, 1986.

Kittel, Gerhard and Gerhard Friedrich, eds. 1964–1976. *Theological*

Dictionary of the New Testament. 10 vols. Translated by Geoffrey W. Bromiley. Grand Rapids, Mich.: Wm. B. Eerdmans.

Knight, Douglas A., ed. *Tradition and Theology in the Old Testament.* Philadelphia: Fortress, 1977.

Knox, John. *The Ethics of Jesus in the Teaching of the Church.* Nashville: Abingdon, 1961.

Kohlberg, Lawrence. *Essays on Moral Development.* Volume One, *The Philosophy of Moral Development.* San Francisco: Harper & Row, 1981.

Kohlberg, Lawrence. *Essays on Moral Development.* Volume Two, *The Psychology of Moral Development.* San Francisco: Harper & Row, 1983.

Kraybill, Donald. *The Upside-Down Kingdom.* Scottdale, Pa.: Herald Press, 1978.

Kugel, James, and Rowan A. Greer. *Early Biblical Interpretation.* Philadelphia: Westminster, 1986.

Kysar, Robert. *The Fourth Evangelist and His Gospel: An Examination of Contemporary Scholarship.* Minneapolis: Augsburg, 1975.

Lebacqz, Karen. *Justice in an Unjust World.* Minneapolis: Augsburg, 1987.

Lehmann, Paul. *Ethics in a Christian Context.* New York: Harper and Row, 1963.

Lindbeck, George A. *The Nature of Doctrine: Religion and Theology in a Postliberal Age.* Philadelphia: Westminster, 1984.

Long, Edward LeRoy, Jr. *A Survey of Christian Ethics.* New York: Oxford University Press, 1967.

Long, Edward LeRoy, Jr. "The Use of the Bible in Christian Ethics: A Look at Basic Options," *Interpretation* 19 (April 1965):149-162.

Luther, Martin. *Lectures on Romans.* Library of Christian Classics, vol. XV, translated and edited by Wilhelm Pauck. Philadelphia: Westminster, 1961.

Luther, Martin. *Luther's Large Catechism.* Minneapolis: Augsburg, 1935.

Lutz, Charles P. *God, Goods, and the Common Good.* Minneapolis: Augsburg, 1987.

Maas, Robin. "Biblical Catechesis and Religious Development: The Goldman Project Twenty Years Later." *Living Light* 22 (January 1986):124-144.

Maas, Robin. *Church Bible Study Handbook.* Nashville: Abingdon, 1982.

Maas. Robin. "New Foundations for Biblical Education with Children: A Challenge to Goldman." Ph.D. diss., Catholic University of America, 1985.

MacIntyre, Alasdair. *After Virtue.* Notre Dame, Ind.: University of Notre Dame Press, 1981.

Maguire, Daniel. *The Moral Choice.* Minneapolis: Winston Press, 1978.

Manson, T. W. *Ethics and the Gospel.* New York: Charles Scribner's Sons, 1960.

May, William F. *The Physician's Covenant: Images of the Healer in Medical Ethics.* Philadelphia: Westminster, 1983.

McFague, Sallie. *Models of God: Theology for an Ecological Nuclear Age.* Philadelphia: Fortress, 1987.

Meeks, Wayne. *The Moral World of the First Christians.* Philadelphia: Westminster, 1986.

Merton, Thomas. "A Letter to Pablo Antonia Cuadra Concerning Giants." *Emblems of a Season of Fury.* New York: New Directions Books, 1961.

Minear, Paul S. *Command of Christ: Authority and Implications.* Nashville: Abingdon, 1972.

Muilenberg, James. *The Way of Israel: Biblical Faith and Ethics.* New York: Harper and Brothers, 1961.

National Conference of Catholic Bishops. *Economic Justice for All: Pastoral Letter on Catholic Social Teaching and the U.S. Economy.* Washington, D.C.: United States Catholic Conference, 1986.

National Conference of Catholic Bishops. *The Challenge of Peace: God's Promise and Our Response.* Washington, D.C.: U.S. Catholic Conference, 1983.

Nelson, C. Ellis, ed. *Conscience: Theological and Psychological Perspectives.* New York: Newman Press, 1973.

Nelson, James B. *Moral Nexus: Ethics of Christian Identity and Community.* Philadelphia: Westminster, 1973.

Nelson, Ruben F. W. *The Illusion of Urban Man.* Ottawa, Canada: Square One Management Ltd., 1979.

Niebuhr, H. Richard, et al. *The Purpose of the Church and its Ministry: Reflections on the Aims of Theological Education.* New York: Harper and Row, 1956.

Niebuhr, H. Richard. *The Responsible Self: An Essay in Christian Moral Philosophy.* New York: Harper and Row, 1963.

Niebuhr, Reinhold. *Moral Man and Immoral Society.* New York: Charles Scribner's Sons, 1932.

Niebuhr, Reinhold. 1941–1943. *The Nature and Destiny of Man.* 2 vols. New York: Charles Scribner's Sons.

Ogletree, Thomas. *The Use of the Bible in Christian Ethics.* Philadelphia: Fortress, 1983.

Outka, Gene. *Agapē: An Ethical Analysis.* New Haven and London: Yale University Press, 1972.

Pelikan, Jaroslav. *Jesus through the Centuries.* New York: Harper and Row, 1985.

Plato. *The Republic.* 2nd rev. ed. Baltimore: Penguin Books, 1955.

Ramsey, Paul. *Deeds and Rules in Christian Ethics.* Edinburgh: Oliver and Boyd, 1965.

Ramsey, Paul. *The Patient as Person.* New Haven, Conn.: Yale University Press, 1970.

Rasmussen, Larry. "The Persistence of World Hunger." *Currents in Theology and Mission* 14, no. 4 (August 1987):245-251.

Rauschenbusch, Walter. *Christianizing the Social Order.* New York: Macmillan, 1912.

Rawls, John. *A Theory of Justice.* Cambridge, Mass.: Harvard University Press, 1971.

Reich, Warren T., ed. *Encyclopedia of Bioethics.* New York: Free Press; London: Collier Macmillan, 1978.

Reumann, John and William Lazareth. *Righteousness and Society.* Philadelphia: Fortress, 1967.

Richesin, L. Dale, and Brian Mahan, eds. *The Challenge of Liberation Theology: A First World Response.* Maryknoll, NY: Orbis, 1981.

Rifkin, Jeremy. *Declaration of a Heretic.* Boston, London, Melbourne, and Henley: Routledge and Kegan Paul, 1985.

Ringe, Sharon H. "Positive Force for Justice or Benediction to Abuse?" *Engage/Social Action* 11 (July–August 1983):26-29

Ross, William David. *The Right and the Good.* London: Oxford University Press, 1930.

Rubenstein, Richard L. *The Cunning of History: Mass Death and the American Future.* New York: Harper and Row, 1975.

Russell, Letty M., ed. *Feminist Interpretation of the Bible.* Philadelphia: Westminster, 1985.

Sabini, John, and Maury Silver. *Moralities of Everyday Life.* Oxford, New York, Toronto, Melbourne: Oxford University Press, 1982.

Sanders, E. P. *Jesus and Judaism.* Philadelphia: Fortress Press, 1985.

Sanders, Jack T. *Ethics in the New Testament.* Philadelphia: Fortress, 1975.

Sanders, James A. "The Bible as Canon." *The Christian Century,* 2 Dec. 1981, 1250-1255.

Sanders, James A. *From Sacred Story to Sacred Text.* Philadelphia: Fortress, 1987.

Schell, Jonathan. *The Fate of the Earth.* New York: Avon Books, 1982.

Schmemann, Alexander. *For the Life of the World: Sacraments and Orthodoxy.* New York: St. Vladimir's Press, 1973.

Schnackenburg, Rudolf. *The Moral Teaching of the New Testament.* New York: Herder and Herder, 1965.

Segundo, Juan Luis. *The Liberation of Theology.* Maryknoll, N.Y.: Orbis, 1984.

Shinn, Roger. *Tangled World.* New York: Charles Scribner's Sons, 1965.

Sleeper, C. Freeman. *Black Power and Christian Responsibility.* Nashville: Abingdon, 1968.

Sleeper, C. Freeman. "Ethics as a Context for Biblical Interpretation." *Interpretation* 22 (October 1968):443-460.

Smart, James D. *The Strange Silence of the Bible in the Church.* Philadelphia: Westminster Press, 1970.

Soelle, Dorothee. *Suffering.* Philadelphia: Fortress, 1973.

Spohn, William C., s.j. *What Are They Saying about Scripture and Ethics?* New York: Paulist Press, 1983.

Stendahl, Krister. "Biblical Theology, Contemporary." In *Interpreter's Dictionary of the Bible*, vol. I, 418-432. Nashville: Abingdon, 1962.

Strain, Charles E. *Prophetic Visions and Economic Reality.* Grand Rapids, Mich.: Wm. B. Eerdmans, 1988.

Stringfellow, William. *An Ethic for Christians and Other Aliens in a Strange Land.* Waco, Tex.: Word, 1973.

Taylor, Paul W. *Principles of Ethics: An Introduction.* Encino, Calif.: Dickinson Publishing Company, Inc., 1975.

Thiemann, Ronald R. "The Scholarly Vocation: Its Future Challenges and Threats." *Theological Education* 24, no. 1 (Autumn 1987): 86-101.

Torres, Sergio and John Eagleson, eds. *The Challenge of Basic Christian Communities.* Maryknoll, N.Y.: Orbis, 1981.

Trible, Phyllis. *Texts of Terror: Literary Feminist Readings of Biblical Narratives.* Philadelphia: Fortress, 1984.

Troeltsch, Ernst. *The Social Teachings of the Christian Churches,* vols. I and II. Introduction by H. Richard Niebuhr. Translated by Olive Wyon. Chicago: The University of Chicago Press, Phoenix Edition, 1981.

The United Methodist Council of Bishops. *In Defense of Creation: The Nuclear Crisis and a Just Peace.* Nashville: Graded Press, 1986.

Verhey, Allen. *The Great Reversal: Ethics and the New Testament.* Grand Rapids, Mich.: Wm. B. Eerdmans, 1984.

West, Cornel. *Prophesy Deliverance! An Afro-American Revolutionary Christianity.* Philadelphia: Westminster, 1982.

Wharton, James A. "Theology and Ministry in the Hebrew Scriptures." In *A Biblical Basis for Ministry.* Edited by Earl E. Shelp and Ronald Sunderland, 17-71. Philadelphia: Westminster, 1985.

Wilder, Amos N. "The Basis of Christian Ethics in the New Testament." *Journal of Religious Thought* 15, no. 2 (Spring–Summer 1958): 137-146.

Wilder, Amos N. *Eschatology and Ethics in the Teaching of Jesus.* New York: Harper, 1939.

Wilder, Amos N. *Kerygma, Eschatology and Social Ethics.* Philadelphia: Fortress, 1966.

Wilken, Robert L. *The Christians as the Romans Saw Them.* New Haven, Conn.: Yale University Press, 1984.

Wilson, James Q. "The Rediscovery of Character: Private Virtue and Public Policy." *The Public Interest* 81 (Fall 1985): 3-18.

Wink, Walter. *Violence and Nonviolence in South Africa: Jesus' Third Way.* Philadelphia: New Society Publishers, 1987.

Womer, Jan L., ed. *Morality and Ethics in Early Christianity.* Philadelphia: Fortress, 1987.

Yoder, John Howard. *The Politics of Jesus.* Grand Rapids, Mich.: Wm. B. Eerdmans, 1972.

Yoder, John Howard. *The Priestly Kingdom: Social Ethics as Gospel.* Notre Dame, Ind.: University of Notre Dame Press, 1984.

INDEX OF BIBLICAL REFERENCES